Across America by Bicycle

Terrace Books, a trade imprint of the University of Wisconsin Press, takes its name from the Memorial Union Terrace, located at the University of Wisconsin–Madison. Since its inception in 1907, the Wisconsin Union has provided a venue for students, faculty, staff, and alumni to debate art, music, politics, and the issues of the day. It is a place where theater, music, drama, literature, dance, outdoor activities, and major speakers are made available to the campus and the community. To learn more about the Union, visit www.union.wisc.edu.

Across America by Bicycle

Alice and Bobbi's Summer on Wheels

Alice Honeywell

Bobbi Montgomery

Terrace Books
A trade imprint of the University of Wisconsin Press

Terrace Books
A trade imprint of the University of Wisconsin Press
1930 Monroe Street, 3rd Floor
Madison, Wisconsin 53711-2059
uwpress.wisc.edu

3 Henrietta Street
London WCE 8LU, England
eurospanbookstore.com

1 3 5 4 2

Printed in the United States of America

Library of Congress Cataloging-in-Publication Data
Honeywell, Alice.
Across America by bicycle: Alice and Bobbi's summer on wheels /
Alice Honeywell and Bobbi Montgomery.
p. cm.
ISBN 978-0-299-24884-0 (pbk.: alk. paper)
ISBN 978-0-299-24883-3 (e-book)
1. Bicycle touring—United States.
2. Cycling—United States.
3. United States—Description and travel.
I. Montgomery, Bobbi. II. Title.
GV1045.H66 2010
796.6′4—dc22
2010011532

to Curt,
Booth, and Bob,
without whom . . .

We do not take a trip; a trip takes us.

John Steinbeck

Contents

Preface

When we began pedaling across America we didn't anticipate recording our experiences anywhere but in our personal journals and on our website, but the farther we traveled the more stories we gathered, stories that sprang from the people we encountered as well as from sights we saw and the way of life we experienced. Those we met along the way asked us questions, and we often answered them with a story about something that had occurred earlier in our trip. In North Dakota someone said, "I want to read your book." That got us thinking. We had planned to present slide shows to our friends, but when our stories grew to the point that no half-hour presentation could do them justice, somewhere between Minot and Cleveland, we decided to collaborate on a book. We had kept detailed notes of every day's events, and even though we had written our diaries for ourselves, we realized we could formulate the accounts into something to be shared with others.

The process of transforming our individual notes into a book resembled the bike trip itself—we each brought different strengths to the effort and wrote in different styles, but we complemented each other and enjoyed working together. We live a day's drive apart, so we had to be satisfied with virtual proximity made possible by e-mail and cell phones as we compiled our story.

Most travel memoirs are written by a single author, even if more than one person made the trip. We had cycled the country together, however, so we tackled the job of writing our book together. In response to readers' suggestions and to keep the prose as smooth and clear as possible, we wrote in one person's voice. Alice's name appears first on the book, so in fairness we chose to tell the story in Bobbi's voice. We hope our readers will understand that "Bobbi" is "us" in that we wrote the story together. Only in the final chapter—"Reflections"—does Alice write in her own voice, necessarily, because her impressions of the trip differed from Bobbi's.

Throughout the story, we cite many products that made our kind of trip doable. When we especially liked a particular brand of product, we named it, even though we don't own stock in those companies and they did not underwrite our trip. Conversely, we used generic terms when either the brand name didn't matter or we were not fond of it and wished we had used something else. Our readers will just have to wonder which was the case.

•

Our first expression of thanks, though it may seem self-indulgent, is a public one to each other for honoring the other's tastes and eccentricities for the sake of the final product, and for being—like the bungee cords on our bikes—infinitely flexible. Writing the manuscript, like riding our bikes, was also a good trip.

Thanks are due many people for helping us, both on the trip and while publishing our account. Artist Susan Hunt deserves special thanks for coming out of retirement to draw our maps. The University of Wisconsin Press staff was a joy to work with at every stage—Director Sheila Leary, Raphael Kadushin and Katie Malchow in acquisitions, Sheila Moermond in editorial, Terry Emmrich, Carla Aspelmeier, and Scott Lenz in production, and Andrea Christofferson and her team in marketing. They and others behind the scenes were extremely professional, and we benefited greatly.

Andrew Peppard did a fabulous job of building and maintaining our Web site during the trip, and we appreciate all he did to keep us in touch with everyone. A soldier who has served in both Iraq and Afghanistan since we began writing, he deserves a lot more than the cookies we periodically mailed him during our trip. Our friend Shirley Smith built the Web site that we now use (www.aliceandbobbi.com) to supplement the book with color photos and other information. We owe her.

We want to thank all our family members—our children and grandchildren, and especially Booth and Bob—for encouraging and supporting and loving us in so many ways as we tackled the challenge of riding so far. We're also grateful to them and to our friends for their patience and help after the trip as we worked our story into a manuscript. We took their comments seriously as we revised—and revised and revised. Thanks also go to Carol "Orange" Schroeder, Charles Anderson, Katrin Wilde, Fred Gooding, Kate Blumenthal, Steve Fox, Sharon Van Sluijs, Dory Blobner, Deb Larson, Steve Levine, Dennis Dresang, Max Austin, Peg Wallace, Ron Wallace, Betty Steinberg, Jan Blakeslee, Margaret Peterson, Mel Miskimen, and Gillian Kendall. We're especially grateful to Diana Cook, our official copyeditor, who found yet more ways to improve the telling of our story. We also cherish the advice and unflagging enthusiasm of our friends in the Cincinnati walking group, the Madison Word Nerds, and all our friends and bicycling pals in Wisconsin and Ohio. Curt Miller, to whom we dedicate this book, introduced us. He encouraged us to take the big trip and continually inspired us with his support and friendship.

Our "road angels" and all the kind and generous people we met along the way—in restaurants, libraries, service stations, stores, town halls, campgrounds, motels, on Indian reservations, on farms, even at a lighthouse or right along the road—are too numerous to name. We have included many of their first names throughout the book (though some have been changed out of respect for their privacy) and hope that they don't mind being singled out. They and myriad others, whose names we never learned, profoundly enriched our trip and our lives. Without them we would have no story.

Alice Honeywell
Madison, Wisconsin

Bobbi Montgomery
Maineville, Ohio

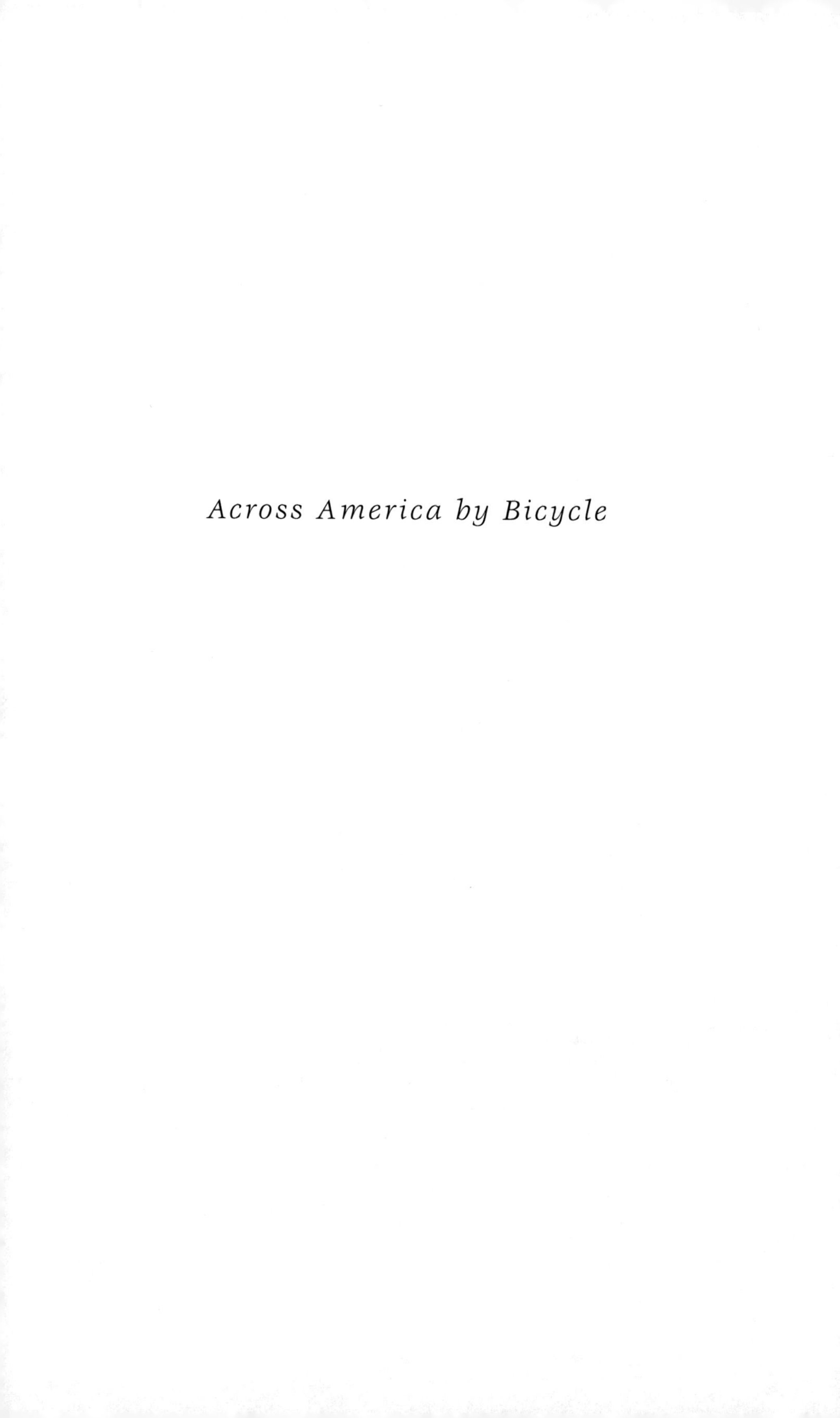

Across America by Bicycle

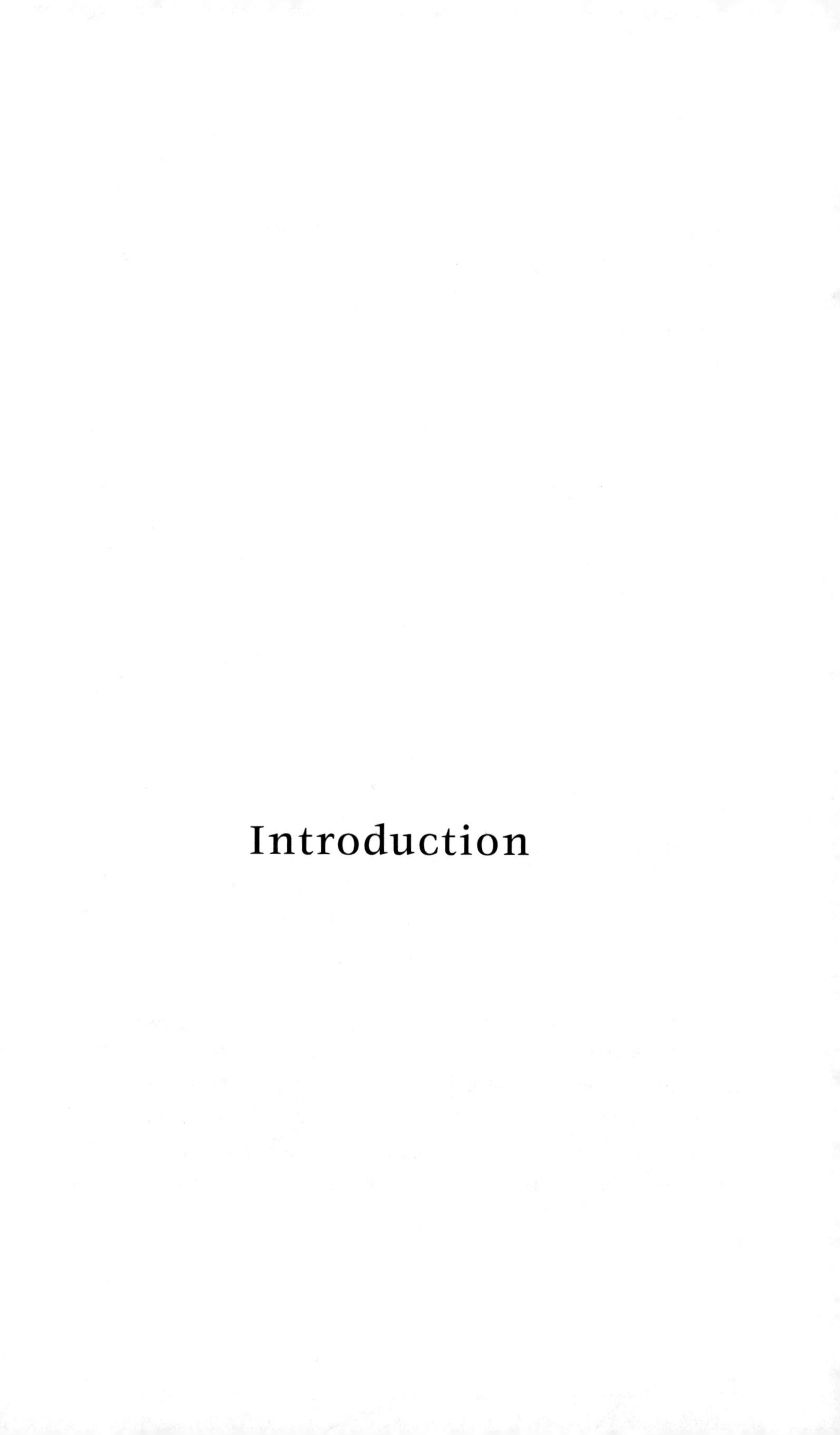

Introduction

When people fantasize about life after they retire, they tend to think of things they won't do anymore—get up early, fight rush hour traffic, deal with irksome coworkers or bosses. Perhaps they have something special they want to do—move to Arizona, cruise the Caribbean, build furniture. Our special retirement activity propelled each of us back into childhood. We dreamed of a long, long bicycle ride.

As a fourteen-year-old, Alice had been inspired by Anne Emery's *Vagabond Summer*, a teen romance novel about a high school graduate cycling across America with the American Youth Hostel program. Later, as adults, we both became fans of Dervla Murphy, the prolific Irish author of bicycle and trekking stories. Murphy's now-classic *Full Tilt* chronicled her ride from Ireland to India in 1963, through countries and across continents where it was unorthodox for a woman to travel solo, let alone by bicycle.

By the time we reached retirement age, we had enjoyed many week-long group trips, often with each other, sometimes not. In Oregon one summer we circled Crater Lake. In Glacier National Park another time we pedaled the Going-to-the-Sun Road. And in Colorado we scaled high passes. Each year we chose a different beautiful place: Wyoming's Bighorns, the mountains of southern Utah, the Finger Lakes region of New York, the Washington Cascades, and Virginia, as well as many areas of our beautiful home states of Wisconsin and Ohio. And on several occasions we pedaled in Canada.

One year we began to muse about the *big* trip.

"Why not?" we asked each other. The obstacles that had been present earlier in our lives—careers, family responsibilities, even health concerns—no longer loomed so large. My carpal tunnel problems had become manageable, and Alice's bothersome heart arrhythmia had been repaired with a catheter ablation. Our families were extremely supportive and encouraging, though our daughters—one a young mother, the other about to become one—were a bit more concerned about our safety than our sons appeared to be. Our sons' attitude was just "Go, Mom!"

For two years before we retired we planned, changing our minds numerous times about what to bring, how to carry it, where to stay, which roads to follow. How to pack would be a continual issue, and destination goals would come and go, but we eventually settled on a northern route going west to east, from Oregon to Maine. Following the Columbia River Gorge would enable us to avoid climbing the Cascades, and staying north meant that the highest passes over the western mountains—Lolo Pass in Idaho's Bitterroot Range and Rogers Pass in Montana—would be under 6,000 feet. It would be summertime, so we thought a northern route would be cooler, and we also hoped to take advantage of prevailing westerlies. Our assumptions about wind and weather would turn out to be quite wrong, but at least we had a plan.

To prepare ourselves and to try to foresee problems, we read numerous accounts of other cross-continental bicycle tours. We made up supply lists and collected our gear, choosing only what we thought was essential, knowing we would have to carry it ourselves. Many cyclists ride across the country in groups with a support van to carry their gear so they can ride light bikes. We had traveled with loaded bikes on many of our week-long tours in the past, and, even though we knew it would be harder, carrying our own gear would allow for more flexibility. Being self-sufficient would enable us to change our route or the day's destination on the run. We needed to be able to rendezvous with our families at various times during the summer, so working out the logistics for just two of us seemed simplest. All of this assumed that the substantial weight of our gear didn't overwhelm our bikes or our not-so-young bodies. It was a risk, we knew, and our choice to travel self-contained and without a group would not be without consequences.

Our final plan, set forth in a spreadsheet, called for us to be away from home for ninety days, pedaling most days but taking one or more rest days each week. We did not intend to race across America, but to absorb it—to listen to people, see how they lived, learn about the land, find out what it would be like to live so differently ourselves, and take time to smell (literally and figuratively) the roadside flowers. We couldn't anticipate what we might encounter, but pedaling such a long distance seemed like the right way to find out. We would simply have to quit talking and planning and just do it.

When we bought our airline tickets five months before leaving, we felt committed. Spring came, and we continued to put in long hours at our respective jobs until our long-awaited retirement dates actually arrived. During the spring prior to retirement, we rode our bikes as much as we could and went about our usual routines. Finally, late in June, after several practice packing sessions and rides with full loads, we packed our bags one last time, said our respective farewells, and left town. "Town" for Alice was Madison, Wisconsin, and for me, Maineville, Ohio, a village twenty miles north of Cincinnati.

UPS delivered our bikes a week ahead of time to a bike shop in Astoria, Oregon, and when we arrived there by rental car from the Portland airport, we found our trusty machines fully reassembled and ready to roll. We checked into the Rosebriar Inn, a convent-turned-B&B on a hill overlooking the harbor at the mouth of the Columbia River. Up two flights of stairs, we settled into the Lewis and Clark Room. Because our cycling route would not take us along the Pacific coast, we stashed our bikes for the afternoon and headed out by rental car to view the ocean scenery and visit Fort Clatsop, Lewis and Clark's winter camp of 1805–6.

At Fort Clatsop we modeled buffalo robes, watched a guide demonstrate his antique fire-starter, and heard a park ranger expound on what life was like for the Corps of Discovery almost two centuries earlier.

Because it was a warm day we had left the B&B in shorts and T-shirts, bringing along just bathing suits, towels, and our brand-new, white, long-sleeved "sunscreen" shirts. We drove to Cannon Beach and Seaside and joined the throngs of tourists walking the wide beaches, breathing salty air, and wading along the shore as the gentle waves filled the moats of children's sand castles. We felt far away from home.

Instead of swimming, though, we decided to flee the congestion and head north, across the Columbia River, to another state park—Cape Disappointment, Washington, the place Lewis and Clark and their Corps of Discovery struggled for two and a half years to reach. We wanted to watch the sunset from the promontory high above the crashing waves and look south toward Tillamook Head and beyond to the great gray "ocian" that Clark had joyously described in his journal. The bicentennial celebration of Lewis and Clark's exploration was beginning, so we planned to start our trip using some of the new Lewis and Clark trail maps produced by the Adventure Cycling Association in Missoula, Montana. The similarities between Lewis and Clark's pioneering adventure and ours were few, but we felt inspired by theirs anyway.

A lesson we learned that day was one that most travelers eventually learn: no matter how well prepared we thought we were, we could miss something. As sunset approached, wind off the ocean increased and temperatures plunged, and we had no warm clothes. Oh, we had packed our fleece jackets all right, but they were back at the inn, not in the car with us. Determined to wait for the promised Technicolor sunset, we huddled out of the worst of the wind in a small, partly sheltered indentation of the historic lighthouse while we ate our takeout salads. In our new, very short haircuts, our lightweight white shirts, and with our legs wrapped for warmth in white towels from the inn, we looked like shivering twin Krishnas. After snapping our obligatory sunset photos, we ran back down the trail to the car, cranked up the heater, and drove back across the mouth of the Columbia River to Astoria for the night. Lewis and Clark we weren't.

On Sunday we returned the rental car to the Portland airport and hopped a bus back to Astoria. Because a bridge was out on our route, our bus had to take a long detour, and the effort to get back to our bikes in Astoria took all day. It was the first of many lessons in patience.

We also got our first glimpse of how others might perceive our adventure. On the protracted bus trip we met a sophisticated-looking middle-aged couple. One precious gem or another decorated at least five of the woman's ten fingers. It turned out that the couple was bound for an Alaska cruise but had missed boarding in San Francisco because "someone" had not compensated for traffic as they drove past the Giants' baseball stadium at game time. As a result, they had missed the boat and had to race to Portland, catch the bus to Astoria, and find their ship in the harbor where it had docked its first night.

After briefly discussing our respective trips and commiserating about the hassles of luggage, the woman looked at us and paused, a perplexed look on her face.

"How do you carry enough dresses for restaurants on your trip?" she wondered.

We glanced at each other incredulously, trying not to burst into uncontrollable laughter. Dresses?

Unflinching, I began, "Well, we don't carry any dresses. We have two or three pairs of riding shorts and shirts, one pair of camp shorts, a T-shirt, and a fleece jacket. Oh, and a rain jacket. We also carry a small stove and pan for heating water, some tools, and our tents and sleeping bags."

Alice added, "Most of our gear is for camping and bad weather or for fixing our bikes. We have some pants, too, but dress clothes would make the bikes too heavy."

The bejeweled woman looked as if the bus was about to run off the road.

I hadn't mentioned the little black, wraparound skirt that I carried in a small pocket of my pannier to throw on over my bike shorts when I wanted to look presentable. That would have hurt our story and she wouldn't have understood how the thing worked anyway. It wasn't a real skirt, just a little covering with a Velcro fastener. Alice didn't have one so I wasn't about to bring it up.

This woman was the first of many who failed to understand our type of travel and its potential for discomfort and hardship, not to mention our extremely limited wardrobe. We had been embroiled in the planning for so long that we had forgotten that the idea had once seemed far-fetched even to us.

In many tourist towns the locals ask visitors where they are from and what they plan to see, and Astoria fit that model. In a restaurant on our last evening there, our server, Diane, asked about our travel plans. Her eyes grew big when she heard the answer.

"You are crazy!" she exclaimed. Alice and I both looked a little startled, so she changed that to "Well, I mean crazy in a good way."

We all laughed, somewhat uneasily, as Alice and I exchanged looks. Were we really going to do this?

As we paid our bills, she said, "I'll look for you tomorrow on my way to work. You'll probably be leaving about the time that I'm coming into town."

True to her promise, the next morning she honked and waved from her little yellow Beetle as we rolled east out of Astoria. Finally.

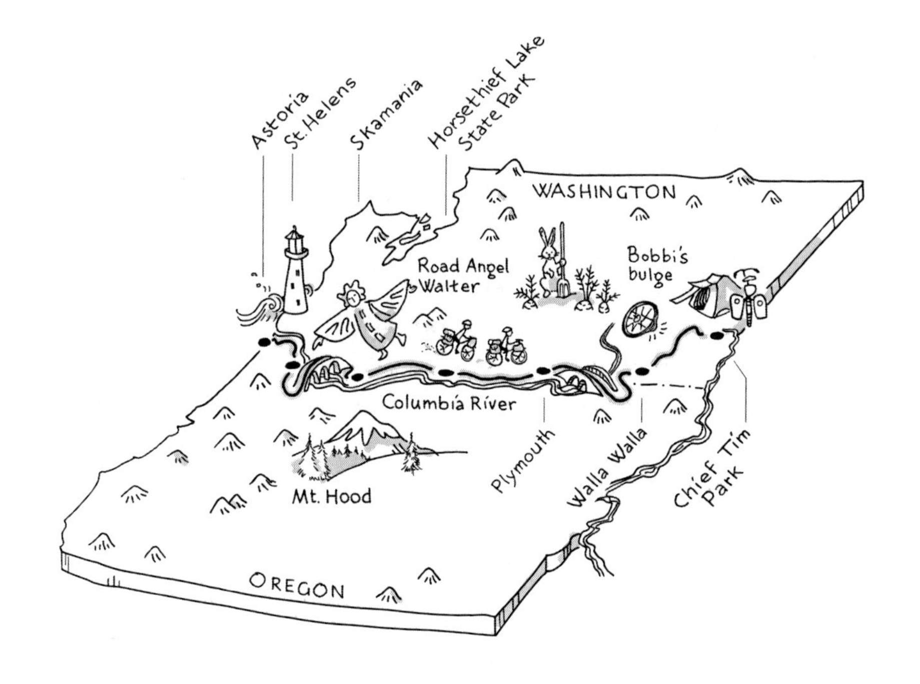

1

Through the Columbia River Gorge

Oregon and Washington

Where're you headed?" a rumpled old man shouted from the sidewalk. Unshaven and uninhibited, he was watching us slowly pedal our loads through the chilly drizzle in Astoria, Oregon, that first morning.

"Bar Harbor, Maine," I answered.

Without hesitating, he called after us, "God be with you."

I couldn't think of a better way to begin. It was not the only time we would be blessed or prayed for on our odyssey from Oregon to Maine, but that first benediction set a positive tone. All would not be sunshine and tailwinds, but the balance would tip in our direction more often than we could imagine.

We eventually grew used to people asking us where we were going and where we had come from—almost always their first questions—but neither of us took for granted their expressions of encouragement. The load on each of our bikes first drew their attention, but the fact that we were two fifty-something women traveling long distance without male companions contributed to their curiosity.

Day 1 — ***Monday, June 30***
Astoria to St. Helens
80 miles

Bikes with full panniers, otherwise known as saddlebags, handle far differently from empty bikes, and we hadn't toured "loaded" for several years. As we pulled uphill out of the heavy Olympic mist, past lush ferns and through the dense shade of dripping evergreens, we were just beginning to relearn the skill. Mishaps could occur.

After an hour or so, Alice needed to visit the woods for a "nature" break, so she called out, "I'm stopping." Unfortunately, she didn't stop at that exact moment because she was still peering into the woods scouting out just the right spot. But I stopped quickly. The result: Alice plowed into the back of my bike, and, bouncing off, she and her bike fell sideways onto the pavement. Luckily, the loaded panniers padded her fall and no cars were nearby, so she escaped with just a few bruises, a sore knee, and some chagrin.

Our first on-the-road policy discussion ensued. We agreed that whenever either of us wanted to stop we would call out, "Stopping," as before, but then neither of us would actually stop until the other person answered, "OK." Both of us would be looking straight ahead, aware of each other's position. The incident gave new meaning to the concept of rear-end collisions, and we wanted no more of them.

Despite that mishap, it didn't take us long to decide that I would continue to ride in front and Alice would follow—on roads where we had to ride single file. Once in a while we switched, but we both preferred the arrangement. On our previous trips, I had been the faster rider, so I didn't mind setting the pace. Alice, on the other hand, said she didn't want to lead—that she would feel pushed, thinking that I wanted to go faster. We had predicted that at times we would be far apart because of our different paces, but our assumptions on this subject, as on so many others, turned out to be wrong. My Softride Solo touring bike was heavier and more heavily loaded than Alice's Holdsworth Mistral, so we found that a usually faster rider with a larger amount of gear rode at the same speed as a slower rider with less. We would have no problem knowing where the other was because we would never be that far apart.

Our second mishap involved another "bathroom" break. At Knappa Junction, a convenience store clerk denied us a restroom—some "convenience"—but told us we would find one at Pacific Gas, a little farther up the road. Pacific Gas, we discovered, was for commercial vehicles, so it wasn't busy with regular traffic and it didn't have a store or an attendant attached to it. So where was the restroom? We finally spotted it—a portable toilet—at the far end of the gravel driveway. We leaned our bikes against a gas pump, one bike on each side, and walked through the dust and greasy gravel, taking turns using the facility. After remounting our bikes, which still felt cumbersome and slow, we continued the uphill climb.

A half hour later, Alice suddenly shrieked in panic, "Bobbi, I've lost my pannier! It's gone! It must have come off at the gas station!" Brought up a Baptist preacher's kid, she was not given to expletives, but she could work up a pretty loud scream.

Without hesitating except to check my rearview mirror, I mumbled, "Oh, shit," and made an immediate U-turn. Pedaling furiously, Alice powered into the lead. She raced downhill, finally rolling into the gas station's gravel driveway to see the pannier sitting in a puddle beside the pump. She later told me that Dionne Warwick's "I Say a Little Prayer" ran through her head the whole way.

Alice cried as she hugged the black bag. It contained her small PC, all her charging cords, our communal kitchen consisting of two pots and a stove, and her set of maps. Close examination revealed that the pannier had lost one of its clips, which explained why it had come loose. We wondered aloud what might have happened had we been any later. If a truck driver had come in for gas and found it, he wouldn't have known what to do with it even if he had wanted to return it. But we didn't wonder for long and were just grateful to have averted a second crisis.

I looked at Alice seriously. "We aren't going to tell anyone about this just yet," I said. "Our kids, especially, will think that we'll never be able to make it to Maine."

"OK, I think these are just some first-day wrinkles," she answered. "We have to give ourselves a break. We're just getting reacquainted with the road."

Such pep talks to each other were useful, and the lost pannier incident spawned another self-imposed rule: anytime we left a place, we would glance behind us to make sure we hadn't left anything. Good idea—when we remembered.

Back on the bikes again, we finally settled into a smooth cadence and churned out double-digit miles, wind at our backs. Despite the helpful tailwinds, however, much of Highway 30 was unpleasant—too much traffic and too little shoulder. We missed our quiet country roads in the Midwest. Caught in the draft of eighteen-wheelers, we fought to control our wobbling two-wheelers. Several times we winced, holding our handlebars in a death grip as semis thundered past. Once Alice called out, "Bobbi, that truck missed you by an inch!"

"I know it! I could feel it!" I was not enjoying this part of our first day.

We had assured our families and friends that this ride was not unreasonably dangerous, but we hadn't counted on heavy traffic speeding up and down such narrow roads with shoulders that were at best inconsistent, often nonexistent. We made frequent use of our rear-view mirrors, calling out warnings to each other periodically. The usual "Car back!" warning became "Big Mother back!" when logging trucks passed on their way from the forest to the mill. We were awestruck by the trucks with logs so immense that sometimes only one would fit on a truck. On most occasions drivers were courteous and gave us wide berth. The problem came when they approached each other from opposite directions and met at the point where we were pedaling. They were apparently unable to reduce their speed quickly when they came around a curve to find us hugging the white line, so they just blasted their horns and roared ahead letting us worry about the effects of their powerful draft. As the day went on we survived more than a few terrifying moments. Soon we realized we might sometimes need to alter our route. Cyclists learn quickly in situations like this, but this time we couldn't change our route—no other choices existed.

When we reached the road to the campground where we had planned to stop on our first night, I glanced at it and kept on rolling.

"That place looks pretty seedy—it might even be closed," I called back over the noisy traffic.

"Right," Alice shouted. "Let's just keep going. Stop when you find a place to pull over." As soon as it was safe we stopped at the side of the road and consulted our maps. We picked the Village Motel randomly from the three that were listed in St. Helens, and Alice used her cell phone to call for a reservation.

By the end of our first day, we were exhausted but still excited. Including the extra ten miles spent chasing down Alice's pannier, we had clocked eighty miles. Kristen, a friend of Alice's who had moved to Portland, drove out to eat dinner with us, and we enjoyed sharing the excitement of our first day's adventures with her.

Day 2 *Tuesday, July 1*
St. Helens to Skamania
76 miles

Getting ready to leave on our second day produced a flurry of activity and last-minute questions.

"Where did I put my sunscreen?"

"Do you think I need my sunglass lenses today or the yellow lenses for dark days?"

"How much Gatorade should we carry?"

"Don't forget your phone charger. It's still in the bathroom outlet."

And as we finally rolled out the door, "Oops, forgot to pump our tires."

It was a challenge to stop preparing and actually get on the bikes and go, especially when we hadn't slept well or settled into a routine. After myriad adjustments to our packing system, we were finally ready—at a disgraceful 11 a.m. Later we discovered that if we had left any earlier we would never have met our first "road angel" in Portland, the City of Roses.

Besides being draped with roses, petunias, and other brilliant flowers in their showiest stages at the peak of summer, Portland was crisscrossed with a maze of bridges, railroad tracks, and busy highways. People in St. Helens had warned us that the St. Johns Bridge over the Willamette River was closed for construction. Traffic grew intense as we neared the city, and we worried aloud about how we would get across first the Willamette and then the Columbia and onto our route in Washington.

Adventure Cycling, the bicycle touring organization based in Missoula, Montana, was our primary source for maps. Originally called Bikecentennial, it had first mapped a transcontinental bicycle route across the middle of the United States in 1976 to celebrate the country's bicentennial. In 2003 it released the Lewis and Clark route, parts of which we intended to follow.

We would frequently deviate from Adventure Cycling's recommendations, but the maps turned out to be good sources of information. Symbols show restaurants, motels, campgrounds, bike shops, and post offices. Phone numbers are listed for many establishments, as well as for local law enforcement agencies and emergency services.

We grew increasingly concerned about the St. Johns Bridge as we neared Portland, and we stopped at a gas station to buy a more detailed map of the city so that we could find an alternate bridge. After studying the map, we decided to wend our way to the Broadway or Burnside Bridge, whichever looked more negotiable when we got there. We were aware that this convoluted and uncertain route could cause major delay, but we thought we had no choice.

On our way, we had to pass the St. Johns Bridge, and, when we approached it, we saw that cars seemed to be crossing, one direction at a time in small groups. When a racer-type bicyclist whizzed by us heading toward the construction area, Alice decided to flag him down. With muscles bulging through his purple Lycra racing suit, he was pedaling a fast machine that we could only drool over. We were lumbering pack animals by comparison.

"Can we ride the bridge?" Alice called to him as she huffed and puffed up the incline toward where he had stopped by the other vehicles waiting their turn to cross. "Sure, follow me," he answered, brown eyes crinkling in a friendly smile. She waved for me to come on up to the bridge.

Perhaps realizing that he would have been over the bridge and out of sight if he had ridden his normal pace, he politely waved us ahead.

"I'll bring up the rear," he said.

It must have been hard for him to go as slowly as we did, but he held the traffic back and stayed behind us all the way across. Because the sidewalk was closed, we rode two abreast and took up the entire lane. The drivers following us seemed patient enough, but one oncoming pickup truck driver waiting to cross just as we were coming off the bridge favored us with an obscene gesture. It was one of only a few such insults we would receive on our entire trip. I thought it was pretty funny and would have returned the favor, but we were riding slowly and I needed both hands on the handlebars.

At the end of the bridge and out of traffic, we stopped to chat with our guide, who introduced himself as Walter. He asked us where we were headed and then how we planned to get into Washington.

When we showed him our maps, he said, "Oh, no. You can't take the I-205 bridge. It's way too high. The winds are much too strong. It's really dangerous. No one rides that bridge. I can show you a better way." So he proceeded to guide us through Portland over a network of back streets, bike lanes, sidewalks, and even a few parking lots. Walter had us island-hopping via bridges with panache. He saved us half a day of wrong turns and false starts, not to mention a

We love you Walter, oh yes we do.

bridge that would have been even scarier than the one we did ride over the Columbia River.

On the way through the city, he even took us to REI, where Alice got a new clip for her pannier and I had a gearing adjustment. We just loved REI. The clerks there were generous and friendly in every way and enthusiastic about our adventure. And Walter, our affable host, waited patiently, got his photo taken with us at the store, and then led us over the I-5 bridge. Even though the I-5 bridge was preferable to the I-205, I look back on it as one of the most harrowing parts of the entire trip.

The long view from the middle of the bridge was stunning. The river there is broad, and its winding shoreline includes varied cityscapes backed by rising hills and distant mountains. Alice exclaimed, "Oh, look! Can you believe we're really crossing the Columbia

River? Too bad Lewis and Clark couldn't have seen it from up this high!"

But as Alice chattered away behind me, I was having a terrible ride. Fighting to keep my bike upright on the narrow sidewalk that seemed to be swaying from side to side, I yelled back, "I can't look anywhere! Something's wrong! I'm having trouble! I can't hold it steady!" My bike seemed to have a mind of its own. It was wobbling fiercely and I thought the bridge was swaying. Thoughts of earthquake disaster movies with whiplashing bridges crossed my mind, but Alice seemed to be having a great time, so I knew it was just me. I wished I could enjoy the view of a city I'd never been to before, but I had to keep my eyes on the sidewalk so I wouldn't fall.

Alice then noticed that my entire load was listing to the left. Thinking that my tent and sleeping bag had merely shifted, I didn't look closer at the time, but instead pushed on to the end of the bridge. We stopped long enough to reposition the load by pushing all of it until it was back over the middle of my rear wheel. It wasn't until we unpacked at the end of the day that I noticed that one of the metal braces on the rear rack had snapped completely. The whole rack was supported on only one side. Like a car out of alignment, the bike pulled to the left as the wind buffeted it. If only I had known this when we had visited REI, I could have had it fixed there or gotten a new rack.

On the other side of the Columbia River we found ourselves in Vancouver, Washington. Our maps offered the choice of cycling on the Washington side or the Oregon side of the Columbia River, but we chose Washington because it was reported to have less traffic. The Oregon side had several stretches of off-road bikeways, but they involved stairways in some spots. Schlepping bikes and heavy gear up and down stairs held no appeal, so we opted for the Washington route. Walter led us through Vancouver all the way to the Evergreen

Highway, which would eventually become Washington Highway 14, running along the river through the Columbia Gorge.

It was there that we parted. Walter had spent three hours with us and made our feared passage through Portland manageable. Portland, we knew, is a bicycle-friendly city, but we hadn't done enough research ahead of time to understand all its amenities, so Walter was our savior. He told us that when we came upon him at the St. Johns Bridge he had just finished a day of training for the Seattle-to-Portland race that was coming up in a few weeks. He hadn't had anything else planned for the rest of that day except soaking in his hot tub, so he was glad to help us. We were grateful and thought of him often in the following weeks. We hope he had a good race.

The Evergreen Highway begins in a wealthy neighborhood on the northern bank of the broad Columbia, lined with lovely homes and riverside estates. By the time we started riding it, we felt relieved to be out of heavy traffic. We needed a rest break and a snack, so when I spotted a cool, grassy spot by a wrought-iron fence surrounding an estate, I signaled Alice that I was stopping. We dismounted, laid our bikes down, and spread out crackers and cheese on bandanna tablecloths. As we rested cross-legged in the sunshine, a gray-haired woman drove by in a minivan headed the opposite way. Noticing us, she made an abrupt U-turn, parked, walked back to where we sat, and plopped herself down on the grass beside us.

"So, what's up?" she inquired with no other introduction. "From the looks of your bikes, you are on a big trip. Where are you going?"

Then, "Where did you start?"

"How long do you think the trip will take?"

"What tools are you carrying?"

"What maps do you use?"

"How many miles a day are you going?"

"Where are you staying?"

She was asking all the right questions, and we took turns enthusiastically answering each one. She left no space between our answers and her next question, and we could tell immediately that she was a cyclist with some experience. She told us that she and her husband were retired and had done a lot of cycling themselves, though nothing as big as what we were attempting.

"I just like to meet people like you," she said. "It reminds me of all the trips I've been on."

We never learned her name, but she boosted our morale in the middle of a hard day of fighting potholes, bridges, and city congestion, the wonderful Walter notwithstanding. Neither she nor Walter would ever know how fondly we would remember them.

By nine o'clock we made it to camp, a private operation deep in towering pines near Beacon Rock and Skamania, seventy-six miles from St. Helens. We had intended to sleep at Beacon Rock State Park, site of an ancient rock sentinel rising several hundred feet above the water. The state park in which Beacon Rock stood, however, was several miles farther and up a long hill, and we were too tired to go on when an acceptable spot was closer. Our spreadsheet itinerary was not a rigid schedule to be adhered to for its own sake, but a budget, a goal, a guide.

Just before dark that night we set up our brand-new tents for the first time and made our first freeze-dried meal of vegetarian lasagna on Alice's miniature stove. All that was required for that type of meal were a few ounces of boiling water and a ten-minute wait while everything congealed. The quick one-dish meal, illuminated only by our headlamps, satisfied us. Too tired to bother showering or even changing clothes, we said our good-nights, and dived into our little one-person tents, where we inflated mattresses, unrolled sleeping bags, and crawled in. Taking a few minutes to record the events of the day, which would become part of the regular routine for both of us, I stowed my PC in its protective plastic bag and quickly drifted off in the damp, cool air of the maritime Northwest.

Day 3 Wednesday, July 2
Skamania to Horsethief Lake State Park
56 miles

Seven hours later I woke up. I had slept so soundly that I don't think I moved at all during the night, prompting me to exclaim, "Big Agnes, you are my new best friend!" Next door, I heard Alice giggle in her tent. Big Agnes is the brand name of our air mattresses, and she was a hit with both of us. Granted, she required twenty-eight breaths to inflate, but she was far more comfortable than our old self-inflating camp mattresses. Plus she weighed less and folded up into a smaller roll. Inflated, she was about two and a half inches thick and firm enough so that neither our shoulders nor our hips ever hit the ground—perfect for people our age who tend to be stiff after sleeping on hard, damp ground.

While chatting with our camping neighbors who had wandered over to inquire about us, we heated water for our first breakfast of the day—instant oatmeal and cocoa. We managed to get packed up and on the road by ten o'clock—still pretty late but better than the day before.

It was an easy ten miles to Stevenson for our planned second breakfast. As time went on, my standard restaurant breakfast became a poached egg or two and pancakes, which I never allowed myself in normal life, while Alice tended to sample something of everything, a departure from her usual bowl of oatmeal. Already, we were both eating more than we thought possible.

After breakfast, we located an auto body shop where we met Cody, who saw my broken rack as an engineering challenge. Cody gestured toward a car in the bay beside him. "That can wait," he said with an engaging grin. "This here is a serious bicycle problem that needs fixin'." Because the rack was aluminum, Cody said, it couldn't be welded, but he quickly went to work fabricating some metal clips. He then drilled a few holes in various places and, using the new clips, formed several braces. I watched the resolute, fair-haired man as he silently puzzled his way through the process.

In about an hour, the rack was good to go, stronger than ever. When I asked Cody if I could take his photo, he looked at the floor, smiled shyly, and said slowly, "Oh, no, the wife wouldn't like that." He also refused payment, so I hid a twenty-dollar bill under his desk blotter for him to find later.

While I was waiting for my rack to be repaired, Alice searched for a pay phone to call home. Her husband had been sick when she left Wisconsin, and thinking it was just a case of nerves about her leaving, she hadn't been too worried at first. But the last time she had phoned him, she learned that he was getting worse and had had to visit his doctor. Alice was concerned about him and was checking in as often as she could. To conserve the daytime minutes on her cell phone plan, she wanted to use her prepaid calling card at a pay phone. The only problem was that pay phones were disappearing.

Alice later told me about meeting Ole. He had seen the loaded bikes parked at the restaurant, and when Alice was walking down the street looking for a phone, he stopped her to inquire about the trip. She had to crane her neck to look up at the tall, blond man when she answered his questions. After she had satisfied his curiosity, she asked him where she might find a pay phone. He explained that there weren't any in the area, even in the county building, and then invited her to his County Extension office down the street. He showed her to his desk, handed her his phone, and stepped out of the office, closing the door behind him. Grateful for the privacy as well as the phone, she punched in her calling card numbers, reached

Booth at home, and learned that he was not any better. His doctor had scheduled some tests.

"So have you been able to do anything?" Alice asked.

"Nope."

"What are you eating?"

"Nothing."

The conversation's tone had troubled her. She filled him in on the events of our day and signed off, sad and concerned.

"I'm really worried about him," she told me, "but I'll call him tonight. I can't do anything to help him right now."

Pushing on from Stevenson, we exclaimed over the panoramic views of the river and the smooth road with broad shoulders, even though the hills seemed long as we worked our way up through the Gorge. The exception to the good road was a series of five narrow tunnels just after Cook. About sixty yards before each tunnel, we found a four-foot-tall post, painted with a symbol of a bicycle. A push button would allegedly produce flashing lights above the tunnel entrance, warning motorists that a bicyclist was in the tunnel. We didn't want to wait around after pushing the button to see whether the lights really flashed, so we just took off. Before the third one, we decided to check the system, so Alice pushed the button and I rode through while Alice watched for the lights. They did flash, but we still weren't completely reassured that they would be all that visible on such a bright, sunny day. Because only Alice had a rear blinking light, she rode behind as usual, hoping that it was bright enough to be seen. In the longest, dark tunnel, a car did approach from behind. The pavement had no shoulder and the lanes were narrow. To add to the terror, a train came roaring through its own tunnel right beside us, about twenty feet away. We had nowhere to go but straight ahead—at our breakneck speed of about fourteen miles per hour. As the motorist braked behind us, my muscles relaxed momentarily and I exhaled in relief, knowing that he or she

Casing the first of the terrifying tunnels

had seen either us or the flashing light at the entrance. Whew. When the fifth tunnel was behind us, we stopped to celebrate with long drinks of lukewarm water and an energy bar each.

"That was something. I pictured myself splattered all over the sides of that tunnel."

"Yeah," Alice laughed, "but I had another vision—me as flattened roadkill." We grinned and raised our plastic water bottles, tapping them together in a toast to our survival.

Near Lyle, Washington, we pulled over to watch the wind-surfing kite boarders. Strong breezes coming up the Gorge from the ocean and the river's current as it flows toward the sea create ideal conditions for this pastime. The boarders maneuvered their brightly colored kites skyward, somersaulting and twirling through the air before plummeting to the water. There they rode the current with their boards until they jumped into the next gust and sailed upward once again. Their vivid sails and the extent and variety of their twists and turns made for a breathtaking spectator sport. Because of the rising heat, we wished aloud that we, too, could flash along the waves and fly into the sky, but we were committed to bicycles and would have to relegate kite-boarding to our repertoire of fantasies.

After chatting with a few kite boarders who were taking breaks, we rode on until we reached a roadside diner where we stopped for fresh strawberry shakes. Finding food was quickly becoming a focus of our trip, as important as deciding where to stay and when to take rest breaks. We were already beginning to think of our bodies as machines, which if properly fueled would propel us efficiently to each day's destination, but we were hungry most of the time. We searched every town for a restaurant or ice-cream stand where we could get the carbs and protein that our bodies demanded. Some might not think of ice cream as the ideal recovery food, but it provided cool sweetness that refreshed our hot bodies and sometimes-fatigued psyches. Besides, eating everything we wanted without guilt or concern soon became one of our greatest pleasures.

Just before reaching Lyle we stopped at an overlook that marked the point in the Columbia Gorge where the Cascade Range met the river, separating "maritime west" from "arid east." This seemed an odd distinction because we midwesterners thought of the West as being arid and the East humid. Traveling on, our lungs noticed the change immediately as we stopped breathing humid air and began to feel parched. Heat became an issue as the temperature quickly rose above ninety, and we began drinking large quantities of water, at least a gallon every three or four hours. Our hydration packs, which could hold seventy ounces, became our main water supply, and we added bottles of sports drink to the cages mounted on the bike frames. If we thought the next services were more than twenty miles away, we would carry extra water bottles in our panniers.

Saying good-bye to Mount Hood

The landscape east of the Cascades also changed dramatically. Instead of the damp, green forests close to the road and all around us, the views widened to include vast irrigated farms greening the riverbanks and continuing up the hillsides in the otherwise desertlike terrain. Snow-crested Mount Hood, which we had watched from a distance for several days, receded into the background in our rearview mirrors as dry buttes began to appear before us in the distance.

The wind that allowed the kite boarders their sport affected us, too. A fine tailwind helped us roll up the sizable hills along the Gorge. We had deliberately chosen to go from west to east because popular opinion holds that westerly wind prevails across the continent. Bicycling literature promised us tailwinds only in the Columbia Gorge. We would eventually learn firsthand what bicycling literature states—that, except in the Gorge, cross-country cyclists usually experience equal amounts of headwind and tailwind no matter which direction they go. We did meet several cross-country cyclists heading west as we pedaled through the Gorge. They were struggling against what must have been about thirty-miles-per-hour winds, but they were nearing the conclusion of their trip, so they were strong enough to handle it.

Lying two miles off Highway 14 down a long, steep hill, our campground at Horsethief Lake State Park was tranquil and lovely, although it lacked showers and phone service of any kind. Alice sighed heavily when she noted the missing phone, and I knew she was worried about Booth and disappointed that she couldn't reach him. She walked to her bike and began unloading.

We expressed concern to each other about climbing back up the hill the next morning but agreed not to think about it until later. Alice didn't know that I planned to make friends with some camper in a pickup truck who might let us hitch a ride back up the hill. I didn't consider such an assist to be cheating because the camp road was, after all, off the planned route. Neither of us had a clear conception of what constituted cheating, but this wasn't it. Purists might disagree with this definition, but we valued flexibility. We both always had, which may have been part of the key to our friendship, but in this new, scaled-down lifestyle, it became an all-important trait.

The warm wind strengthened as the day ended and blew so hard we had to help each other set up tents. The fresh, mild scent of pine needles and waving grasses wafted over us, making me feel as if I were being washed clean by the breeze. We struggled to hang our laundry on our lines as the wind tried to snatch our clean clothes from their clips. As the evening sky darkened, trees became silhouettes against the sunset. A slice of moon rose over a distant ridge, pale gold in a cobalt sky.

Sponge baths, laundry, dinner, and journal-writing completed, we went to bed celebrating our third day. We had to shout our good-nights over the whistling wind, but it was so constant and we were so spent that it soon lulled each of us to sleep.

Day 4 Thursday, July 3
Horsethief Lake State Park to Plymouth
78 miles

When July 3 dawned, Alice emerged from her tent fussing.

"Bobbi, I don't want to ride up that steep hill with my heavy bike. It's two miles!"

"I agree. It's no way to start a long biking day. But I have a plan."

I shared my "adoption" idea with Alice and she liked it, so as we separately came and went from the bathroom, we each cheerfully greeted a different neighboring camper. One was a teacher, who was headed with his son to a family reunion; another was a professional photographer, traveling around the West. Each man had a pickup truck, and before we knew it, each of them had offered us a lift. Alice hitched a ride with the teacher, whose name she didn't learn, and I rode up with Wayne, the nature photographer. This "bump," the term we would apply to a four-wheeled assist, made it possible to start the day with refreshed legs instead of leaden ones, and we were grateful to these generous men.

It didn't take long for us to realize we were riding in a microclimate far different from what we were used to. The air was hot and dry, the land was hot and dry, our skin was hot and dry. Everything seemed downright desiccated. We climbed for part of the morning, but the hills were interspersed with flat areas so we made decent time, which for us was about twelve miles per hour. We came upon very few services and the temperature rose steadily.

Finally we made it to West Roosevelt, where a thermometer in the shade of the roof at the ramshackle store registered 107 degrees. We rehydrated ourselves and our containers and devoured some plastic-wrapped, ready-made sandwiches. They were stale and bland, but our intense need for fuel made them edible.

We were an unusual sight, with large bandannas tucked under the elastic of the legs of our shorts and tied around our ankles to protect us from the fiery sun. Along with liberal applications of sunscreen, we were able to prevent burning, but we looked like two circus clowns with the mismatched red, blue, yellow, and purple squares of cloth flapping as we pedaled. On top we wore white long-sleeved shirts, which proved essential. We took to pouring precious water from our water bottles onto the front and back of our shirts, enjoying a few minutes of cooling each time. Appearances be damned. The heat demanded flexibility and ingenuity. Besides, as long as we kept our helmets on, no one could tell what we really looked like, so we felt safe from any fashion police who might be traveling Highway 14.

While we rested at the store, a scraggly local character approached us. His beard reached to his waist, and he was dressed in too many layers for the blasting heat. He asked the usual questions—where had we come from, where were we going, were we traveling alone. For security purposes, we had planned to say that our husbands were ahead of us and we would be meeting them soon, but we didn't feel the need to spout that lie. We were always careful not to say where we would be camping at night, but in West Roosevelt, Washington, as in most other places, we did not feel threatened.

As we parted, our overdressed acquaintance warned us, "You girls be very careful out there. Traffic is real heavy." He was quite familiar with it, having walked that stretch of highway often. He also cautioned us that "there's lots of mean people out there." We were told this a number of times by people whom we might not ordinarily have crossed paths with. They were rural street people, and they wanted to advise us of dangers they knew about. Had we stepped out of an air-conditioned SUV, we might not have engaged them—and vice versa. Dressed as we were, however, carrying all our belongings on our bikes, we shared a nomadic lifestyle and caught glimpses of another world.

After lunch, we pedaled for miles along the river as we marveled at the complicated framework and the sophistication of the irrigation systems reaching up the brown, dry slopes to the vineyards, orchards, and vegetable farms on the ridges. We would never again take Washington apples, wine, or carrots for granted. As we made the final push of the day to Crow Butte State Park, we were looking forward to a break from the heat. We could never feel the perspiration on our skin, of course, just the salty residue left after the moisture instantly evaporated. We arrived at the park dusty, thirsty, and worn out, only to find a big green sign slapped crookedly on top of the original entry sign: CLOSED. Uh-oh.

"We're in trouble," Alice said. "The next campground is in Plymouth, which looks to be twenty-eight more miles." My heart fell as I contemplated those hot, dusty, hard miles. I didn't think my legs could handle 106 miles on my loaded bike. Alice didn't seem too happy, either, but she was kind of quiet.

As we pedaled through the deserted park, we could see that it was being cared for, but no one was using it. We exchanged speculative glances. We were tired enough, but were we gutsy enough to camp there even though the park was officially closed? Thinking we might be able to pitch our tents in an out-of-the-way place, I asked a man mowing the lawn if we could. He began his answer by shaking his head and then went on to explain something about the politics involved. It seemed that Native American groups, the U.S. Army Corps of Engineers, and a nonprofit organization that wanted to buy the park were arguing over various issues. The Corps of Engineers had jurisdiction, the state had recently given up its lease, artifacts needed to be preserved during any sort of development, and the place was in limbo until everything could be resolved. In the meantime, a Corps of Engineers manager was living in a house on the edge of the park—up a steep hill, of course—and we would have to talk to her.

"If you camp without her permission," he said, "they'll prosecute. They've already done it to another bicycle group."

"But seventy-eight miles is all we can handle in this heat," Alice responded. "We'll have to figure something out. We don't want to get arrested, but we also don't want to camp just anywhere along the road if we can help it."

He looked at our loaded bikes and then at us. "My wife and I live in the next town," he said, "so if the Corps woman doesn't budge, you could probably camp behind the school, where my wife teaches. The only problem is that there's no restroom."

We could deal with that but we would check with the manager up the hill anyway.

"She's a real hard-ass," he warned. "Good luck. I'll be here for another half hour or so if you need me."

We pedaled our loads up the hill to the modest ranch house, where the yard was cluttered with toys, dogs, and all sorts of well-worn gear used by a family that clearly lived a long way from the nearest town. I removed my helmet to cool off while Alice knocked on the door.

The woman who answered was the Corps of Engineers park manager, Renee. After Alice explained our predicament, she said firmly, "Oh, no, you can't camp here." I stepped closer and politely but earnestly appealed her ruling and Alice chimed in. After further discussion, we either wore Renee down or she took pity on us, we weren't sure which. At first she offered to let us camp in her yard, but we worried aloud that this wasn't such a good idea because we didn't want to traipse through her house to use the bathroom. Then she came up with another idea.

"OK, I'll drive you to the campground in Plymouth," she said.

"What a wonderful offer!" I exclaimed, relieved not to have to pedal another foot. As Renee retreated into the house to get her truck keys, we high-fived, celebrating the prospect of having a real campground to stay in, one with bathrooms and showers. We didn't much care that we wouldn't be riding twenty-eight miles of the "official" route. After all, it wasn't really a choice. We weren't being allowed to camp where we had wanted to. It wasn't cheating.

Renee called ahead, made sure they had room for us at the campground, and then summoned her husband, Tom, who had just arrived home from work. We removed all the panniers, and he helped us heft our bikes into the open bed of the pickup. We padded the bikes with the packs, and he motioned for us to get into the cab. He climbed into the back of the truck and squeezed between the bikes, lodging himself in facing backward, his head close to the cab's window. Renee instructed their adolescent children to watch after each other, then climbed into the cab and proceeded to drive us all the way to Plymouth. Tom chatted most of the way, sometimes having to shout through the window over the sound of the rushing wind. He explained his job as foreman of the nearby baby carrot farm and answered all our questions, including the one about the huge electronic signs we had seen suspended over the highway. He said they were there to warn drivers about dust storms. Since we hadn't known their purpose earlier, we had not felt any sense of foreboding as we rode under them. Now we felt lucky that we hadn't run into a stinging dust storm. That would have hurt more than the hot sun, and we probably wouldn't have been able to ride through it.

By the time they dropped us at Plymouth, we were more informed about the area and felt as though we had made some new friends. Before they introduced us to Harold, the campground manager, they gave us names and urged us to contact any of a number of their relatives in eastern Washington if we needed anything, and Tom gave us his business card. We were amazed that these good people would make a fifty-six-mile round trip in order to take a couple of strangers to a campground, but once again we were grateful. It was our second experience with road angels in only four days of riding, yet we had no inkling how many times such helpers would appear throughout our journey.

Harold, a neatly attired octogenarian, seemed to spend much of his time chatting with campers and putt-putting around the Plymouth Park Campground in his golf cart. As soon as Renee and Tom said their good-byes, he directed us to follow him. He led us to a level, grassy spot, pointed us to the showers, and didn't charge us a cent for our stay. His reason: no picnic table. As if we cared. Our tents went up quickly and we headed to the showers and the phone, where Alice tried to reach Booth. No answer, so she just left a message.

A valuable lesson came from the day's adventure—not to trust local gossip but to rely on people's basic goodness when we needed to solve a problem. We wished we hadn't needed to beg, but we figured it didn't hurt that we were two older women traveling without a motor vehicle. And, as Alice said to me, "Your gray hair probably helped. Good thing you took off your helmet when you talked to Renee."

Day 5 *Friday, July 4*
Plymouth to Walla Walla
59 miles

It was a red, white, and blue Fourth of July, and we were far from home, practicing a different kind of independence than that envisioned by the likes of Thomas Jefferson. Over a quick cup of instant oatmeal and some hot cocoa, we asked each other how we imagined this day would compare to other July Fourths—what we might see and what our kids and my grandkids were doing back home. After packing up, we headed toward the river, which we needed to cross to get back into Oregon, where we would ride for a few more miles before recrossing once again to Washington. Our maps showed an off-road bike path below the bridge and across the Columbia River, but when we came to where it was supposed to be, we saw it heavily barricaded.

The only option was to ride with traffic into Umatilla, Oregon, via the I-82 bridge. The bridge was a mile long, had a view-blocking hill at midpoint, and no shoulder. As midwesterners, we were not used to riding on limited-access interstate highways, but we knew that in the West, we were allowed to use them if no other route existed to get where we needed to go. Still, it was hard to go against our ingrained caution. I envisioned a car behind us barreling over the crest of the bridge at eighty miles per hour and sideswiping us. We psyched ourselves up for this death-defying crossing, but to our surprise and relief, traffic was gratifyingly light. Most people must have been sleeping in on the holiday. We took the first exit after the bridge and immediately found a breakfast spot where we gorged ourselves once again. When people say that breakfast is the most important meal of the day, they don't get any argument from us.

After breakfast, Alice finally caught up with Booth on the phone and learned that he had a doctor's appointment for the following week. He maintained that it wasn't an emergency even though his digestive system was not working well at all. While Alice talked to Booth I checked my own phone and found a distressing voice mail asking me to call home. I returned the call immediately and learned from my son-in-law that my daughter and he were having serious marital difficulties and that she had left him. This was a shock that seemed to come from nowhere as I had no idea there was any problem in the marriage. I tried to calm my distraught son-in-law and then called my daughter's cell phone. No answer, so I left a message. Throughout that day my mind returned again and again to the conversation. How could I not know my daughter was so unhappy that she felt she had to leave her husband? I couldn't imagine what was wrong, and I spent a lot of time that day wondering about what she was doing and feeling. And what about her three small children? How fast could I get home so I could try to fix things? I trusted my daughter's judgment, but I knew something was seriously amiss. Just what? As I rode, I pondered and fretted.

Problems at home would weigh on both of us often as we pedaled eastward. We were not undertaking this trip in a vacuum. Unlike some adventurers who flee home in a midlife crisis, we each had ties to family that we had no desire to sever. We knew we had to loosen the ties for a few weeks, but our commitments to loved ones were strong.

Back on the road, we watched the last bit of Oregon go by. We reentered Washington about eighteen miles past Hat Rock State Park, so named by Captain Clark for its distinctive geological formation. At last we said good-bye to the Columbia River and began moving toward Walla Walla along the Walla Walla River. The guidebooks' predictions of strong tailwinds every day so far had been accurate, and we expected to lose them when we turned away from the Columbia River, but they inexplicably continued in our favor. The tailwinds had not made our riding easy—but they had made it possible. We thought we had trained pretty well by riding 100 to 300 miles each week through the spring, but we felt more tired from the high-mileage days than we wanted to. Our training had been mostly on empty bikes and in seasonable springtime temperatures in Wisconsin and Ohio.

The heat was intense in eastern Washington and Oregon, and one effect was that the black electrical tape I used to keep my faulty sunglass lenses in their frame became slippery and useless. The lenses kept falling out and we kept stopping to retrieve them, relieved each time not to have run over them—or each other. Our "stopping" system was working, anyway. Alice offered some duct tape from the

All the comforts of home

small supply she kept rolled on a short pencil in her handlebar bag, and that took care of the lens problem.

Back on our bikes, we soon came across one of the more unusual of many "found" items that litter America's roadways. A decrepit old chaise, cheap, with narrow plastic tubes woven across the frame, was set up between some gigantic rocks about twenty feet off the road. No houses were in sight. No one was around. No evidence of any owner appeared. Perhaps it was an attempt to be hospitable in this arid land, although we wondered who would want to stop in the vicious sun and relax so near the sizzling blacktop. We, however, had no compunction about stopping because we wanted to digitize the discovery. So we posed on the chair and snapped "bathing beauty" shots. It was a good thing only one or two cars passed so we didn't have to disguise what we were doing for very long. Giggling, we remounted our bikes, ready for the final push to Walla Walla. We decided that being able to appreciate the ridiculous was one of the requirements of successful long-distance cycling. It perked us up and diverted our attention from the rising heat as we speculated on who put the chair there and why.

As we neared Walla Walla, the irrigated vineyards, orchards, and vegetable farms we had been passing gave way to huge onion fields. The road was dotted with produce stands, all selling Walla Walla onions. I love these onions and was so tickled to come upon whole fields of them that I made Alice stand by one of the fields so I could snap a picture. The scene was reminiscent of fourth grade social studies lessons when we had had to memorize the crops and products of various states. Here we saw it firsthand. Too bad that school kids couldn't cycle across the country as a regular part of the curriculum to make their lessons come alive. As a longtime teacher, I entertained thoughts of a rolling curriculum—twenty-five middle-school kids, a few parents, and a teacher, all experiencing America from the saddle of a bike. Perhaps I had tumbled onto my next profession. Then again, perhaps not.

In Walla Walla, we opted for the inexpensive Center City Motel, which was located a bit farther from the center of town than we thought appropriate, but because Walla Walla is not huge we didn't complain. Once we found the motel we unloaded our bikes and showered, then headed off on foot to dinner and the fireworks. Along the way, we saw a cab and Alice memorized the phone number painted on the side so that we could call it after the show for a ride back to our motel. At one point as we were walking through a neighborhood of rundown buildings, I noticed some rough-looking young men loitering in front of a 7-Eleven, scrutinizing us a bit too closely. I told myself I was probably wrong to be concerned, but I also believed in listening to that inner voice, based on my experience from years of high school teaching. I could tell when students were about to do something questionable, so I said to Alice, "I don't like the way that guy is looking at us. He is paying entirely too much attention. I've seen that look before, and it usually comes before trouble."

"OK," said Alice immediately, "let's call a cab. We still have a long way to walk."

The cab's phone number still fresh in her mind, Alice recalled it and punched in the numbers. She told the dispatcher the name of the intersection where we were, and although we kept walking, we made sure we returned to that same intersection when the cab appeared a few minutes later. From there he took us straight to the fireworks, where we felt more comfortable. It was the only time on the entire trip we felt the slightest bit threatened. The fact that it happened when we were not on the bikes and could not be identified as cyclists was something to think about.

Spending the Fourth of July far from home without family or friends felt odd. As we watched the colorful explosions and ooohed and aaahed with all the strangers around us, we tried to capture the sparkly displays with our cameras. We clapped at the grand finale just as we imagined people back home had been doing a couple of hours earlier. On our way back to the motel on foot, we saw kids shooting off fireworks at virtually every house. When we asked someone about this practice, we learned that this was the last year for private fireworks. Too many fires started accidentally each year, so home displays would be prohibited in the future.

Day 6 — *Saturday, July 5* — *Rest day*

And on the sixth day we rested. Sort of. After a huge breakfast, we were off to the post office, where we each mailed stuff home—three pounds, seven ounces for me. Only one pound, eight ounces for minimalist-minded Alice. Did I really need that extra shirt? Could we live without the radio? A small digital camera was enough—no need for the big SLR. Then we checked out the bike shop, where we each bought a few things, including new, better blinky taillights. We wanted to cut back on our gear, but these lights were necessary in case we encountered more tunnels or were caught pedaling in the dark trying to reach our day's destination.

The best part of the Walla Walla rest day was the therapeutic massage for each of us. Liz and Sheryl, therapists we met via the Yellow Pages, agreed to treat us at the Renewal Center, which occupied the first floor of a multiuse redwood-stained office building in a residential area of Walla Walla. They didn't usually work on Saturdays but when I explained over the phone how much we needed massages, they agreed to come in. I drew Liz—tall, blonde, and athletic-looking—while Alice got Sheryl, a rotund brunette in a bright, tie-dyed T-shirt right out of the 1960s. They gave us each a deep massage and sent us off with a souvenir tin of Tiger Balm, ready for a second week of pedaling. On the spot we decided that massages were a necessity, not a luxury. Even though we hadn't budgeted for them, we agreed that they could make the difference in how we performed. The painful truth was that we were no longer so young that we could punish our bodies with impunity. We determined to schedule more massages.

For dinner Liz and Sheryl recommended the Backstreet Bistro, where the restaurant's owner, Bob, greeted us with questions. He had seen our loaded bikes parked outside and figured out quite easily that we were the ones who went with the bikes. He disappeared, we ordered, and we enjoyed each course of our unusual and tasty dinner, especially the pasta entrees. While we were eating, he reported in at our table several times to express his enthusiasm for our trip and ask more questions.

"I've signed your Web site guest book, ladies, and I really enjoyed reading your entries. I read the whole thing," he said. "You know, I'm a cyclist too, but I've never done anything near what you are doing. I envy you for being able to strike out on this grand adventure."

Alice replied, "Maybe you can do it someday."

He smiled and said, "Well, I'm pretty busy with the restaurant, but you've given me something to think about." As we were leaving, Bob presented us with some fancy imported candies to take along.

•

Two nights and a rest day in Walla Walla meant we had to repack everything completely because when we arrived we had emptied our panniers and spread out. Considering ourselves generally well organized, we each would choose an area of the room for our own belongings.

"I'll take the nightstand, you can have the desk," Alice had said, and we piled up some of the contents of our panniers in our designated spaces. Frequently, however, despite our efforts to be careful, we found ourselves gasping with panic when we couldn't find some item or other.

Cries of "Oh, no, I lost my credit card!" or "I can't find my cell phone!" were so pitiful that the other person felt compelled to drop everything and join the frantic search. Inevitably the owner, wearing a sheepish grin, would apologize: "Oops, sorry, here it is. I had moved it to a new place."

After a few of these incidents, to avoid wasted effort and sinking hearts, we instituted a new policy—the fifteen-minute rule. No matter what was "lost," the loser had to look for fifteen minutes silently before panicking aloud.

"Have you looked for fifteen minutes?" one of us would ask when the other relapsed.

"Uh, no. Sorry. Oh, here it is."

As the days progressed, so did our ability to work the rule. Conversations went like this:

"Oh, no! . . . Uh, never mind. It's nothing. Just ignore me."

"Have you lost something?"

"No, not yet. It hasn't been fifteen minutes."

Then, "See? Here it is."

And finally, when the technique had been mastered, the "oh, no!" was internal, heard only inside the head of the loser as she scoured the area for her prized possession. Outwardly, all was as it should be.

Later in the trip, if one of us slipped and yelped, "Oh, no!" all the other one had to do was point her finger and say, "Fifteen minutes." Some people have no need of the fifteen-minute rule, but neither of us could claim membership in that elite society.

Leaving Walla Walla meant that not only was Oregon behind us, but we were almost through Washington and ready to tackle Idaho and the Bitterroot Range, that extreme challenge faced by Lewis and Clark's Corps of Discovery in the fall of 1805. We knew that paved roads made our travel incomparably easier, but we discussed those early adventurers as we pedaled parts of their route. We even dubbed ourselves the Mini-Corps of Discovery as we explored territory new to us. I'm sure that such blasphemy trivialized their extreme endeavors, but levity helped us pass the time as we watched our legs go up and down. We were, after all, on a great adventure of our own, out on the open road, exposed to the elements, making do with little, not knowing what the journey would bring to us, how it would challenge us, and how we would respond.

Being on the road for one week was not an unusual length of time for us. We had pedaled for a whole week in many previous summers, but at this point we were facing new territory—another full week of riding to be followed by eleven more if all went well. We weren't taking anything for granted, but we knew that we had done some tough riding already and felt stronger for it. We expressed optimism as we set out from Walla Walla.

Day 7 *Sunday, July 6*
Walla Walla to Chief Tim Park
90 miles

It would be quite possible to follow the Adventure Cycling bike maps slavishly, eating at the map-designated restaurants and patronizing other listed businesses as we traveled across the country. Being social animals, though, we inquired about other local eateries. We asked people on the street, at convenience stores, the library, or the post office where the best place was to eat—whether we wanted a full meal or an ice cream break. Invariably, we ended up off the planned route at establishments with excellent fare, where we met more colorful people and learned about the local culture. In Walla Walla, for example, we had been told not to miss the pumpkin pancakes at Clarette's. The pancakes lived up to their reputation.

Determined to be more efficient in the mornings, we managed to be on the road by nine o'clock, even after indulging in a big breakfast. We had to make it at least to Pomeroy (seventy-two miles), but we wanted to go even farther—to Chief Tim Park—because the next day was going to require two big climbs, taking us from 500 feet of elevation to about 3,800 feet.

Middle Waitsburg Road from Walla Walla to Waitsburg was the first low-traffic highway we had been on, and we pedaled it with relief. For the first time we could ride side by side, which was a welcome change and a less lonely way to pass the hours. Our rear-view mirrors still saw some use, but cars and trucks coming in either direction were rare on a Sunday morning. We rolled over series after series of pleasantly undulating hills, sun-ripened crops of grain rippling along both sides of the road.

The ready-to-harvest fields against the bluest of skies made us want to get off our bikes, don berets, and take up oil paints and brushes. Instead, we took photos, hoping to capture an indelible

Surfing the amber waves of grain

image of the bright golden hills. We recognized only the wheat, so we asked someone later that day what else we had been seeing. We learned that some of the grain was barley and some oats, but it was not rye as we had thought. Rye is an unwelcome grain. Sometimes young people are hired to pluck unwanted rye from the fields where it shows up. This was news to us and we agreed that we had a lot to learn about western agriculture. It would be a good idea to chat with more farmers and ranchers along our way.

After the great massages and meals on our rest day in Walla Walla, we both felt strong enough to push beyond Pomeroy even though, except for one three-mile downhill early in the morning, most of the day consisted of climbing. Sometimes we rolled along at between twelve and fifteen miles per hour while going uphill ever so slightly, but other times we crept along at five to six miles per hour.

As we were climbing one short, steep grade, I shifted and my chain suddenly jammed, the pedals stopping abruptly. My bike came to an instant stop. I couldn't get my shoe cleat unfastened from the pedal fast enough, so I fell over on my side. The full panniers padded my fall, and I popped back up, reseated the chain, and kept going. My hip hurt only a little, but the fall would have painful ramifications later.

The other problem that day, which affected us more immediately, was that my rear tire developed a bulge—making it thump at regular intervals. When we reached the top of the mountain, I called Bob at home in Ohio to ask his advice.

An engineer by training and a bicycle expert besides, he said, "Let some air out of the tire and don't let your speed build up much beyond twenty miles per hour as you descend."

"Do you think it will blow with all the weight on it?" I asked anxiously.

"As long as you don't go too fast, it shouldn't, but if it does, you'll be able to control the bike. You'll be fine—just take it slow."

Darn. After all that climbing I felt robbed not to be able to sail down at the forty-five to fifty miles per hour I had looked forward to. Safety was preferable to a premature end to the trip, though, so I followed his advice and kept my speed below twenty for the twelve-mile descent. This required braking alternately with front and back brakes, then stopping every few minutes to let the rims cool. We each carried a spare tire in addition to several tubes, but by the time we were ready to go down the mountain neither of us had the physical or mental energy to unload all my gear, change the tire, and reload. It seemed more sensible just to take it easy going down. In the morning I could put on the spare.

It was at that point that our true bonding began. I knew that Alice could have gone on ahead and flown down the hill as she likes to do, but she must have realized that this would be demoralizing to me and less fun for her than if we were both letting go. There would be other descents. This one she rode with me. Even going slowly, tightly alternating my grip on the brakes with my sore hands, which were vulnerable to carpal tunnel syndrome, I was quite tense, bracing for a blowout as we descended the long grade.

Neither of us talked about this at the time. It was much later that we realized what a defining moment it had been—for our friendship as well as for a successful trip. We were forming a true partnership. For the best trip, both of us had to enjoy it. We were a team but with no captain, no subordinate. We shared decision-making, consideration, and respect.

The day had involved long stretches of dryness and heat between the last couple of towns—thirty-seven miles from Dayton to Pomeroy and then twenty-two miles from Pomeroy up over the mountain and down to our camping spot at Chief Tim, which our maps showed as a state park. The State of Washington had been leasing the parkland from the Corps of Engineers (just like Crow Butte), but had let the lease go, apparently because of a serious budget shortfall. By the time we arrived, it was open with a private group running it. Yay!

We wished that the people involved with Crow Butte could have resolved their differences, too, by the time we had landed there, but we were pleased to receive an e-mail several weeks later from Renee and Tom telling us that things had eventually worked out and they were able to reopen Crow Butte.

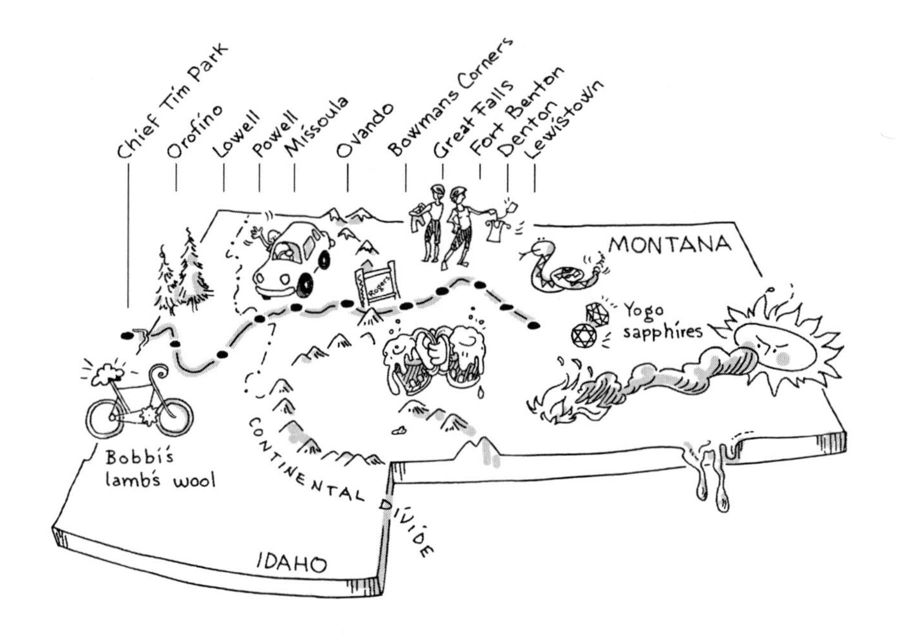

2

Over the Western Mountains

Idaho and Western Montana

Record heat, rushing rivers, forest wilderness, serious mountains, more heat, killer hills, wildfires: Mother Nature handed all this to us in Idaho and Montana. But striking scenery, new ways to enjoy life, and sociable people were also plentiful. On we rolled, eager for more outdoor entertainment.

Day 8 Monday, July 7
Chief Tim Park to Pink House Campground (near Orofino)
57 miles

In the valley at the confluence of the Snake and Clearwater rivers sit the twin cities of Clarkston, Washington, and Lewiston, Idaho. Named for their visitors from 200 years earlier, the twin cities were still welcoming adventure types. Clarkston advertises itself as an outdoor playground and the entrance to Hells Canyon. Lewiston, across the river, was our immediate destination because the temperature was already beginning to soar as we dropped into the valley, and we wanted to waste no time finding a new tire. We wished we could have explored the Hells Canyon area, but that would have to wait. A bike shop and an air-conditioned breakfast place were higher priorities.

Our maps promised three bike shops in Lewiston, so as we crossed into Idaho we began looking. Let someone else change my tire, I thought, while we enjoy breakfast in a cool diner. The first bike shop we targeted was closed on Mondays. The second shop, which apparently specialized in off-road cycling, did not have a tire in a size even close to what I needed. When the twenty-something mechanic asked us where we were riding, and we responded with our usual answer, "Oregon to Maine," he smirked and with a patronizing air said, "Oh, well, we'll see."

Alice glowered at him. I just said, "Yup, we'll see," cheerily as we headed to the door. Neither of us was so cocky as to give him a piece of our mind on the spot because we knew we had a long way to go, but we certainly had more confidence in ourselves than he did. Outside, we agreed that we almost wished he had stocked the tire I needed so I could have refused to buy it from him.

Actually, Alice and I differed somewhat in our confidence levels—or maybe it was just our expressions of confidence. Though of course I knew that anything could happen, I was always sure of my cycling ability—and hers—and was sure that our travel experience and other life skills would enable us to handle challenges that would come our way. She—whether because of superstition or her religious upbringing—was never willing to say with certainty that we would finish this adventure. Instead, she always said she was planning to make it to Bar Harbor, and then would quote her late mother, who always had reminded her to say, "Lord willing . . ." The truth is that neither of us would have undertaken this trek if we didn't believe that we could do it—barring some sort of freak event.

The last of the three shops listed on our map was Follett's Mountain Sports, and it had good bike repair facilities as well as friendly and encouraging mechanics. Follett's carried the exact heavy-duty touring tires that Alice used, so I bought one and arranged to have it put on my back wheel. The air-conditioned diner we had fantasized about materialized just a short walk away, so we mingled with the Monday morning business crowd. Back at the bike shop an hour later, we thanked the mechanic and wheeled our machines out the door and into the heat. With 120 pounds of pressure in each of our four tires as we left town, we began to enjoy some mighty smooth pedaling. Thermometers in the shade in Lewiston registered 107 degrees, just as they had in Roosevelt, Washington, but at least our tires rolled well on the hot pavement.

The employees at Follett's advised us to take U.S. 12 and avoid the longer route that our maps recommended, which had a long climb to Winchester State Park. When we told them that our maps warned us away from U.S. 12, they said that the maps were wrong, that going east was not a problem. The bike shop guys were correct. Traffic was quite heavy and logging trucks passed us frequently, but the shoulder was acceptable nearly the whole way. Going west would have been another story. We had heard from one cyclist who had seen in his rearview mirror a huge logging truck rapidly bearing down on him; with nowhere else to go, he clambered onto the concrete barrier pressing his bike against the barrier. He told us he thought he was dead but the truck whisked past him, sparing both him and his bike.

Following U.S. 12 along the Clearwater River, we climbed less than we had the previous few days, and the terrain became less arid as irrigated farmland gave way to pine forests of dark green needles atop towering, straight, brown trunks. Eventually we reached the campground at the U.S. Bureau of Land Management's Pink House Recreation Site, five miles west of Orofino. We pitched our tents on a little gravel patch bordered by railroad ties and raised off the ground to make a perfectly level pad. The gravel pad was impervious to our tent stakes, so when a neighboring camper saw us struggling, he brought us gallon jugs filled with water to use as weights. We were touched that someone was watching out for us yet again.

A short walk from our campsite took us to a small beach on a curve of the river. It was bordered by dark and wild forest towering over the banks on every side, which made a perfect bathtub surround. I enjoyed a cleansing swim in the frigid Clearwater, but the sun had set and the air had cooled so I didn't linger. Alice couldn't bear to go in above her waist, but we both managed to shed a day's worth of sweat and road grime, even without soap.

Now, where exactly are we?

It was time for a small celebration. We had completed the first map in our pack of fifteen, a distance of over 500 miles. Yehaa! Printed on heavy-duty Tyvek, the map had held up well and done its job. We had used its many helpful details and appreciated the information about the area's history and terrain.

A further comment on the Adventure Cycling maps: The Lewis and Clark bicycle route is quite new, so the map's information is mostly up-to-date, but because small businesses appear and disappear regularly, we relied on other sources in addition to the maps. Talking to the locals was usually the best way to learn what was up the road ahead, although people who drive cars often don't notice details that interest cyclists. They couldn't tell us, for example, about the condition of a road's shoulder or whether it even had one. Their concept of hills also differed from ours. Many times they said, "It's pretty flat. You'll love it." Ha. Flat in a car and flat on a bike are not the same.

Another difference was how we perceived distances. The standard type of reply to our query of "How far is it?" was "Oh, about twenty minutes." When we chuckled, they would admit that they didn't even know how many miles it was—just how long it took them to get there in their truck. If the information we were gathering was essential to our safety or even just to our well-being, we learned to ask several people and then compare their answers. The difference in answers often amused us, and on more than one occasion people argued with each other about how best to advise us. For the most part the information we gleaned from people we met along the way was helpful, and we enjoyed the conversations immensely.

Day 9 *Tuesday, July 8*
Pink House Campground to Lowell
60 miles

The air was still dry, so I was surprised to hear raindrops on my tent in the night. No thunder or lightning came near, though, and by morning skies had cleared, our tents had dried, and it looked as though it would be hot once again—in the low hundreds by late afternoon.

Orofino was only five miles away, so we headed there for breakfast and found the Krystal Cafe on Johnson Avenue. Our waitress was decidedly unfriendly, catering to the local patrons and ignoring us far longer than we thought appropriate. We tried hard to be pleasant when she finally presented herself, but her tone was sour. Alice asked her—politely, I thought—for a couple of pitchers of water, which was standard procedure after we ordered.

"Well, I'll bring you *one* pitcher," she responded.

She did and I quickly helped Alice pour it into her CamelBak. Without another word from either of us, she then brought us another. She offered no comment and no smile. We figured something must be wrong in her life and began whispering quietly about all the possibilities.

"Maybe her kids are in trouble in school," I ventured.

"Yeah, or maybe her husband had a logging accident and he can't work and they don't have insurance," suggested Alice.

"I know what it is. She just wants to wear snappy Lycra biking shorts."

Our imaginations were becoming overactive. We couldn't guess what her problem was, but, not following our usual policy, we left a generous tip anyway and wished that something good would happen to her.

In Orofino, unlike other places, most people just stared at us without smiling. By taking U.S. 12, we were off the Lewis and Clark bike route and we supposed that the residents weren't used to seeing the likes of us, dressed as we were and pushing the loads we had on our bikes. We must have looked pretty weird to them. By the time we reached Kamiah (inexplicably pronounced KAM-ee-eye locally), it was well past lunchtime. Spotting a loaded tandem bicycle on the sidewalk, we parked near it and met a couple coming out of the Laundromat. We joined them for a gourmet lunch at the Hearthstone Bakery and Tea House and discovered that they were middle school teachers from Connecticut. Ray and Christy were using part of their summer vacation to add the Portland-to-Missoula segment of the Lewis and Clark route to their repertoire of bike trips. After lunch, we took a closer look at their tandem and learned that it broke into three parts and packed into two regular suitcases, avoiding the usual extra handling charges for bikes on airlines. Nifty.

I was suffering from a very tender spot on my derrière that had troubled me increasingly since my fall in Washington—not a skin sore, but something deeper inside—right in the area of my "sit bone" and reaching into my hip. A day or two after the fall, I could pedal for only a few rotations before resting because the stabbing pain would subside only when I wasn't pedaling. Alice had noticed my constant shifting on the saddle and had thought that my bike shorts or saddle were irritating because of the heat. I didn't want to complain and alarm Alice, but I was beginning to be quite concerned that this pain could curtail my riding.

Before leaving Kamiah, we split up for a couple of errands. Alice went to the grocery to find provisions for the next day and a half because we would be without stores until we reached Montana. I went to the pharmacy to find a piece of lamb's wool. Something would have to change, so for the time being I would try applying the lamb's wool to my saddle as a cushion.

With the soft cushion taped to my saddle and both of us fed and watered, we left Kamiah in overwhelming heat. Despite the temperature, we loved the exquisite forest scenery as we followed the Clearwater River winding along the edge of the Nez Perce Reservation. The water looked so pristine we could see every submerged rock as we glanced down from the road. The occasional small, sandy beach looked inviting, and the bristling firs marched up the steep hillsides into seemingly unending wilderness.

A strange sight lay ahead as we rolled alongside the rushing river. In the midst of this display of nature, a middle-aged woman loaded with a bulging backpack pulled a large blue suitcase on wheels. She trudged determinedly along, staring fixedly ahead. Her stringy blonde hair was pressed down by a baseball cap. She didn't seem to notice us or her surroundings as we overtook her. In my rearview mirror, I thought I saw her mouth moving as if she were talking to herself. I wondered where she had come from and where she was going—the same things people wondered about us. But her mode of travel and her demeanor seemed out of place for the Idaho wilderness—she looked more as if she belonged in an airport terminal. Because my rear end still bothered me and because Alice needed to find a phone to call home before her husband went to sleep, we swept on, intent on getting to our evening's destination. The woman receded quickly in our rearview mirrors, but not in my mind. Later, I wished we had stopped to hear her story. But we hadn't, and the suitcase lady remains forever a mystery.

After passing through Kooskia (pronounced KOO-skee by the locals), we headed to our camping spot at Lowell. On our way to the campground office to sign in, we met a couple of other cross-country cyclists, two retired men whose wives were taking turns driving their support van. Unlike us, they were raising money for a cause—their community college in California. We were a teensy bit jealous of them for being able to ride empty bikes, but we lapped up their praise for our toughness.

Dinner that night was quite poor. We had arrived after the small resort dining room had closed and we were out of freeze-dried meals, so we cooked up the macaroni and cheese we had bought in Kamiah. The only problem: the mac and cheese box dinner called for milk and butter. We wouldn't mind the noodles sticking together without the butter, but milk would have been nice. The camp store, such as it was, was out of milk, so we took the last three tiny coffee creamers, each with about a teaspoonful of cream. That would have to do. We added a package of foil-packed tuna for protein—not our best meal, but we were hungry enough not to care.

Day 10 **Wednesday, July 9**
Lowell to Powell
50 miles

It rained briefly in the night again, so we packed up damp tents in the morning before we headed up the gentle grade. We felt the weight of our heavy loads, especially as temperatures rose. I was still extremely uncomfortable on my saddle despite the lamb's wool, which had flattened out and become less than cushy. From Lowell we began following the Lochsa River through the Clearwater National Forest, parallel to the Lolo Trail that Lewis and Clark rode on horseback. The Lolo Trail remains rugged, and on the map it looked virtually impossible to us with its many steep ascents and descents. Mountain bikers apparently enjoy it but we were committed roadies.

The Lochsa River was even lovelier than the Clearwater. The constant sound of rippling, sometimes rushing, dark water alongside us, a variety of darting birds that we had never seen before and could not identify, and the bluest sky over a hundred shades of green in the upper and lower forest canopies created a moving art show. The road surface was excellent, too, so we thought this was about the most perfect cycling anywhere. We learned that the highway we were on had not been built until 1969, much more recently than we had imagined. The terrain beyond the highway was part of the Selway-Bitterroot Wilderness, the third-largest designated wilderness area in the lower forty-eight.

At one point we took a break at a quiet little beach where we spread out our tents and sleeping bags on bushes to air-dry. We waded in the river while the sun and breeze did their jobs. Knowing we had a long ride that day, it was hard to take the time, but neither of us wanted to pitch a wet tent and climb into a damp sleeping bag. It was good to be out of the saddle in the middle of the day—to feel the cool water against our legs instead of just looking at it from the road, smell evergreens up close, and let warm sand sift through our toes. Time seemed to stand still. A lazy half hour later everything was dry and we were on the road again. Going uphill all day would be slow, but we decided not to worry right then about getting in before dark.

A bit later we stopped for a potty break, glad to be riding in a forested area that made privacy easy to come by. When we emerged from the woods, we noticed a cyclist riding toward us from the direction we were headed. He stopped and told us that he was doing part of the Lewis and Clark route from east to west, so we traded information about what each of us would find ahead. We had met only a few long-distance tourists so far, and it was always fun to talk with them. Exchanging information was usually a valuable exercise, and helped us realize that we had joined a special fraternity. Yes, not a sorority. Most of those we met were men, but occasionally we would see women, either with a man or in a group of riders supported by a van.

As we stood chatting on the road's shoulder, a car came hurtling up the road—so dangerously fast that we were all glad we weren't on the road at the time. We wondered who would be driving so carelessly on such a curvy road. We said our good-byes and headed on our separate ways.

About ten minutes later, we heard a siren from behind us. We quickly got off the road and watched as a police car screamed by. We figured it was chasing the driver we had seen shortly before, and then our imaginations went off again as we speculated about what crime had been committed and whether the perpetrator would crash into a tree while trying to elude the police. We half expected to come upon twisted wreckage a few miles farther, but we never found out what had prompted the apparent chase.

This mini-event was yet another story without an ending. We always wished we could know the outcome of an event or that we could learn more about the people we met along the way, but we had to be satisfied to be part of one little episode of some larger tale.

Often it was frustrating to have to move on before we had learned more about a place or a particular person, but it was typical of our strange existence. We moved in and out of scenes, in and out of narratives, in and out of other people's lives.

At lunchtime we stopped for a break at the Lochsa Historical Ranger Station, a site maintained by the U.S. Forest Service, where an older couple, both former forest rangers, shared stories of being at such outposts in a bygone era—a remote existence as they described it. Now, retired people volunteer for a week at a time to educate visitors about the way of life long ago. The volunteers there that day had brought along their niece and nephew, Sue and Bill, from Washington, and we enjoyed chatting with them all. Between sentences we applied our squeeze-tube peanut butter onto crackers and washed them down with Gatorade. The afternoon heat was building, we had a long trek uphill before our day would be finished, and Alice needed to get to a phone to find out about Booth's doctor's appointment, so we reluctantly parted with these friendly people and pedaled off into the heat.

Several hours up the road at a scenic overlook, as Alice rested her legs and I gave my rear a break before the last challenging eighteen miles, we were surprised to see Bill and Sue pull up in their white four-by-four truck.

"We got to thinking about how hot it was," said Bill, "so we decided to come and check up on you."

Sue asked, "Would it be cheating if we gave you a ride to your campground? We'd really like to do that."

"It's your call, Alice," I said. I did not really want to accept a ride, but I knew Alice needed to find a phone, and Sue and Bill seemed to think that we would lose daylight before reaching our destination. Alice had no qualms about accepting their offer, and I quickly agreed. My irritating seat problem helped me agree to the "bump," and I also wanted to talk to my daughter, so that was that.

We carefully laid the bikes on top of a pile of gear in the truck bed, stuffed our packs into the backseat of the cab, and squeezed in ourselves. Sue and Bill became the most recent additions to our list of road angels.

Eighteen miles farther up the road—and it was indeed up—we thanked them and said good-bye as they helped us unload our gear at the U.S. Forest Service campground at Powell. I set up the tents while Alice walked across the road and placed her call.

Returning, she filled me in. Her husband began the call with, "I'm sorry, dear, but I just don't think I can come see you. I'm too sick." He went on to name the dreaded diseases his symptoms could signify, according to his doctor—kidney failure, gall bladder disease, hepatitis, or liver cancer. None of them sounded good and he clearly wasn't up for the rendezvous he had planned with Alice in Missoula. He would have to continue to wait for more test results.

"Well, then, I'll come home instead," Alice said.

"That's up to you," he said. He didn't pressure, but he also didn't reject the idea. Another call—to her son, Ted—assured her that he would share his frequent flyer miles and make her airline reservations to Madison from Missoula. Such a good son.

A few minutes later from the same phone, I reached my daughter and asked whether I should fly home to help with the kids. She said, "No, Mom. There's nothing you can do. I don't want you to stop your trip for this. I can handle it."

"Are you sure you don't need me?" I asked.

"Really, Mom, there's nothing you can do."

Saddened, I chatted a bit more and then hung up, feeling too far away from my family. I wondered again if I should just fly back to Ohio anyway.

Dispirited by our family concerns and worn down from the unrelenting heat of the day, not to mention the continued climbing and my rump pain, we trudged back across the road and up a short hill to the Lochsa Lodge, a commercial operation with cabins, restaurant, and showers. We gladly purchased showers for three dollars apiece, towel included. On a quest for energy, we ate huge dinners at the lodge—fresh fish from the Lochsa River, vegetables, rice, and mountainous helpings of warm blackberry cobbler topped with ice cream.

In the lobby of the lodge after dinner, we met a man who told us he had just come off the Lolo Trail pulling a trailer with his mountain bike. He had found it more rugged than he expected and had decided to leave his trailer in camp for a few days and "spin" over the paved roads instead. He, too, was planning to ride over Lolo Pass the next day, continue on to Missoula, and then come back with a car to retrieve his trailer. "Maybe you'll see me tomorrow," he said airily, but I inferred from his tone that we wouldn't see much of him because he figured he would burn past us going up the pass. We both took a mild dislike to him. Was he implying that we wouldn't be able to keep up with him? It seemed so.

Maybe his talk about spinning over the roads on an empty bike affected us more than we liked, or maybe it was our tummy-aches from the rich cobbler that made us grumpy. Back at our campsite, we confessed to each other that the trip, as great as it was, wasn't quite as leisurely as we had hoped.

"Why aren't we taking naps by the river or lounging in camp for a couple of hours a day, writing in our journals?" asked Alice. "And why can't we ever stop at a nice spot and read the novels we brought along?"

"Yeah," I agreed. "Why are we always setting up our tents so late that we don't eat until after 9 p.m.? It's a good thing the days are so long that it doesn't get dark until 10, or we'd be in trouble."

"And we're so tired that we sleep late and don't get an early start in the morning," Alice pointed out.

"At this rate," I said, "I'll never get to use the nail polish I brought for a manicure and pedicure, and those three bottles add weight. We just don't have enough time to savor the experience. What are we doing wrong?"

Then we realized that we had made the mistake we had been warned about: attempting too many miles with our heavy loads. We were averaging nearly seventy miles a day in extreme heat, and Dave, an experienced cross-country cyclist we had met on the Internet before our trip began, had told us fifty miles a day was probably the maximum if we were carrying our own gear and wanted to enjoy ourselves. Of course, being macho bikies, we had thought fifty miles was wimpy. But we were beginning to face reality. If we wanted to truly enjoy the rest of this trip, we had to cut back on our daily mileage or stop less and talk to fewer people. Meeting people was a priority, so we knew what we had to do—we would rework our itinerary. Lowering the daily mileage meant sometimes taking main roads that were more direct (and with more traffic) than the ones we had planned, but we could also try to be more efficient—especially in our camping routine and packing. We could still make Bar Harbor in our planned thirteen weeks.

Day 11 — *Thursday, July 10*
Powell to Missoula
60 miles

Reaching the top of Lolo Pass involved thirteen miles of climbing, the last five of which were a 7 percent grade—not bad, but work for sure. Just as we reached the steepest part of the climb, we looked ahead to see Mister Arrogant, whom we had met the night before, resting by the side of the road. When we reached him Alice decided to stop for a quick snack before tackling the last four miles. I preferred climbing on an emptier stomach and I had a point to make, so with a grin on my face and malice in my heart, I rode by with a friendly "Hi, how ya' doin'?" as I continued up the incline. Minutes later I was working harder and making good progress when I looked in my rearview mirror to see a dark speck gaining on me.

"Shoot," I breathed aloud to myself, "here he comes. I'll be damned if he catches me before the top."

I dug harder into my pedals, lowered my head, and picked up the pace. The speck receded. "Aha!" I thought, tasting victory and wondering why I was feeling competitive. I reached the summit before I expected to and turned into the parking lot of the visitor's center, staying near the road to wait for my unaware nemesis to catch up. I wanted to greet him with a friendly smile. Alice would come along, too, I knew. To my surprise, though, it was Alice who appeared next.

"Yehaa!" I yelled. "Oh, Alice, I'm so sorry. I thought you were that guy we didn't like. I thought he was catching me so I sped up. There was no way I was going to let him pass me."

"I wondered what was going on," Alice laughed. "It seemed like you were going faster and I couldn't figure out why. He was still resting when I took off." Alice had stopped twice to catch her breath and take in some fuel but still rode the pass without much trouble. I felt a bit guilty about running away from Alice, but we girls had won the contest. He, of course, did not even know there had been one.

It was 11 a.m. Pacific time when we reached the attractive log-hewn visitor's center at the top of Lolo Pass. My partner, Bob, had planned to arrive in Missoula from Cincinnati the previous evening, rent a bike, and ride to meet us at the top of Lolo Pass. He was to meet us at noon, but I wondered whether he would be thinking in Pacific or mountain time. Because Lolo Pass is the dividing line between time zones as well as between Idaho and Montana, it was a reasonable question, one I had not considered in advance.

We waited an hour. I found a phone and called the motel where I had reserved a room for Bob the night before, only to learn that he had not checked in. Oh, dear. Airline troubles, no doubt. Cell phone service was nonexistent, so we started down the pass toward

Missoula, forty-six miles away. Soon after we started our descent, we saw a little red car speeding up the mountain. It swung into a pull-out on the opposite side of the road with a flourish and stopped.

"Alice," I yelled over my shoulder. "That's Bob! I can tell by the way he is driving that car!"

Sure enough, as we braked, Bob climbed out of the car, grinning widely. I greeted him with a big hug and kiss. He had arrived in Missoula only an hour before, he explained. One leg of his flight had been canceled and he had spent the night in Salt Lake City.

Being a helpful guy, he took all our packs, leaving us with just our spare tubes and a few basic tools. We would meet him for lunch in Lolo, a few miles down the road.

In the restaurant at Lolo, a man who apparently had passed us on the way down the mountain approached our table.

"You bikers shouldn't be allowed on the roads. Too dangerous," he harrumphed.

Alice looked up, smiled sweetly, and said slowly, "Yes, the roads can be quite dangerous. But cars are the problem, not bikes. We would prefer to outlaw cars."

We all laughed at the absurdity of such a statement. He returned to the ladies he was traveling with, and we went on to enjoy our lunches. As we prepared to leave, the man came back over to us and apologized, saying he had just been kidding and wanted us to know that. We weren't so sure, but we thanked him and chatted pleasantly about the scenery. Lunch over, we left Bob with his car, arranging to rendezvous at the Adventure Cycling headquarters in Missoula, and headed down the mountain.

It didn't take long to realize that we were riding into a pretty strong headwind—downhill. So much for the forty-six-mile coast after Lolo Pass that we had dreamed of. Even on empty bikes, we were working. And then, without either warning or provocation, *ping!* A spoke snapped on Alice's front wheel. We stopped. Still straddling her bike's frame, Alice located the broken spoke and twisted it around a neighboring one. She then hopped off and used a small wrench to loosen the front brakes so they wouldn't rub on the wobbling wheel. It was as if the bike were protesting the loss of all the gear it had become accustomed to.

On our endless, into-the-wind push to Missoula, an incident reminded me of how easy it was to become a victim of a motorist's idea of fun. Drivers almost always passed us politely, and the encounter with a hell-bent, game-playing driver would occur only one other time in our entire trip, but both occurrences were unforgettable. Immediately after passing us on that hot Montana road to Missoula, a pickup-truck driver swerved onto the dusty shoulder, accelerated, and looked back laughing as clouds of pebbly dust blasted us. We both sputtered, coughed, and turned our faces to the side, and I cussed him as he sped off into the distance.

We didn't reach the Adventure Cycling headquarters until after 6 p.m., but Julie, one of the staff, welcomed us warmly. She had stayed after hours because we had called ahead to say we were coming. We knew that scores of cyclists came through each summer, but she treated us as though we were special. At her invitation, we stored Alice's bike in the back room and headed off on foot to our motel, tired after two weeks of pedaling and ready for a four-day break. Bob retrieved Alice's bike the next day, replaced the broken spoke, and trued her wheel. Bless him and his invaluable mechanical abilities.

Days 12 to 15 ***Friday, July 11, to Monday, July 14***
Rest days

On Friday morning Bob and I went off to explore Montana, including Glacier National Park, while Alice flew home to Wisconsin.

Before driving to Glacier for some hiking, Bob and I cycled up Lolo Pass, this time from the Missoula side. Coming back down toward Missoula was the same story—wind in our faces and not much of a coast. Bob may have thought it a bit strange that I wanted to ride on one of my days off, but I wanted him to get a flavor of what I had been doing for the last two weeks. Because he always rode a light bike and carried minimal gear, he couldn't imagine maneuvering a loaded beast such as my mine. I knew that after this interlude I wouldn't be seeing him until September, so despite the pain in my hip and rear end, I accompanied him most of the way up the pass. He and I spent the rest of the day scouring Missoula's many bike shops for a more comfortable saddle and a stronger bike rack. We found both items, which Bob kindly installed for me.

On our way to Glacier, Bob and I discussed the family situation back home. We agreed that if I went home, there was really nothing I could do to change things. In all our phone calls, my daughter had insisted that I should continue the trip. Reluctantly, I accepted the fact that sometimes a mother has to let go.

Alice later reported that saying good-bye to Booth on Sunday evening in Madison was hard, but that he stoically assured her that he would be fine and that she needed to keep going.

When she returned to Missoula, Alice brought a set of clean clothes, a better flashlight, and a new supply of sunscreen and energy bars. On Monday we bought a fresh butane fuel canister for her little stove and explored downtown Missoula, which was baking in the continued heat wave. Local residents said the temperature was twenty degrees above normal, which meant it was usually in the eighties but was rocketing to over one hundred degrees each day. So much for choosing a northern route across the country to avoid summer heat.

After Bob left for home in the afternoon, we both enjoyed much-needed massages. Even with our break, all our muscles were tight, and my hip and back were still painful from my fall. Amy at the local massage school was young and enthusiastic, and she spent more than an hour and a half kneading and pressing, with the result that I felt better than I had in a long time—almost normal, in fact. Alice's massage at a health club on the outskirts of town was a different story. Her therapist practiced the Ashiatsu technique. This Eastern style of massage involved the therapist's walking on Alice's back while holding onto bars attached to the ceiling. Always open to new adventures, Alice seized the opportunity. She stretched out face down, while her therapist mounted steps to the table where she stood over Alice. For the next hour, she pummeled Alice's shoulders, back, and legs with her feet. Although the treatment did loosen Alice's tight muscles, she didn't care much for the full weight of the woman on her back or the feel of her bare, rough, scratchy heels. She needed regular pedicures if she were to hope for any more of Alice's business.

Our first two weeks had been more intense than we had expected—long days of too many miles, lots of figuring out where things were in our panniers, packing each morning and then repacking as we determined the best place for everything from candle lanterns to clotheslines. Concern over family members back home added to the intensity. The four days of rest had strengthened us, and we felt confident that we could get into a rhythm and become more efficient—in both our packing and our riding. Our families assured us they would survive, so on we went, eager to fine-tune our traveling techniques and discover the benefits of our new lifestyle, not just the complications.

Day 16 — ***Tuesday, July 15***
Missoula to Ovando
52 miles

We managed to leave Missoula by 9:15 on Tuesday morning—a new record for early departures. For some reason, Alice always seemed to be ready before I was and often cheerfully announced, "I'm ready!" while I still hadn't brushed my teeth, packed my charging cords, or put away my clean laundry. When this happened several days in a row, I decided to speak up because I felt pressured to be behind when she was always ready to go. No problem. She began slowing down or busying herself with other activities while I was finishing packing, and eventually we settled into comfortable morning routines.

We heard that we would continue to face serious heat across the rest of Montana, even at the upper elevations, so we were pleased to get in half of our miles before lunch in Potomac. We gave the cook's Special Cheeseburger Chowder five stars, maybe not because it was objectively so good but because we were famished.

Although we climbed for most of the day as we approached the Continental Divide, the road meandered up and down just enough to give both our legs and our psyches (though not my hip and rear) occasional relief. Pine forests gave way to open ranch land, and we began passing huge horse ranches and beef cattle operations. We were still following waterways, paralleling first the Blackfoot River and then Union Creek. Mountain foothills surrounded us all day and we could see the Rockies in the distance.

At Clearwater Junction we spotted a commercial truck scale. On a whim, we pulled in and asked the officials if they would weigh our bikes.

"Sure," said the one whose name badge read "John." When a big truck rolled in soon after we arrived, John waved it on as if to say, "Some other time. I'm busy here." Apparently the novelty of weighing two ladies' bicycles was more interesting than his usual duties. Through the plate-glass window, John's assistant informed us that my bike weighed one hundred pounds with all its gear, and Alice's weighed eighty pounds. No wonder we were working so hard.

"Well," John informed us, "the scale could be ten pounds off in either direction, but looking at you ladies and your bikes, it seems to

Black Beauty weighing in

be about right." We wondered what he meant by "looking at you ladies."

I was surprised that my bike was so heavy but was glad to have a general idea of how much I was pushing.

John seemed unhappy to learn that we were traveling by ourselves. He asked with a little frown, "How do you girls protect yourselves? There's a lot of crazies out there."

Immediately I replied, "Oh, we're highly trained in the martial arts." I smiled broadly as I wondered where that fib had sprung from.

"And we have this," Alice added, pulling a can of pepper spray off her handlebar mount. I drew out my can of pepper spray also.

He nodded, somewhat reassured.

Back on the road and safely out of earshot, we went into hysterics, laughing until we nearly toppled from our saddles. We had received the pepper spray from my police officer son-in-law, but neither of us knew a thing about martial arts. As the trip went on, we used the line on a few other occasions when people seemed concerned about our safety.

Fifty-two miles, we learned that day, was a good distance. What we had discussed in Idaho appeared to be right. We decided to stop in Ovando because we needed an early start the next day to climb Rogers Pass, so we called ahead and reserved a room at the Blackfoot Inn B&B. Consisting of a handful of buildings surrounded by mountains, Ovando is mostly a ghost town. The B&B, an apartment above an old saloon, was comfortable and our hosts were friendly. Skip, one of the locals, was a talkative cowboy who appeared to spend more of his time out of the saddle than in, just hanging around on the boardwalk that stretched the length of the building. He offered to get a key to show us the museum in a postage-stamp-sized, clapboard building across the way, but we were too tired and too hot, so we declined his offer.

The owner's niece was visiting Ovando with her boyfriend, whose name was Tiger's Eye. Brightly attired in a psychedelic, tie-dyed T-shirt and raggedy pants, he showed interest in our bikes, our gear, and everything else about our adventure. He told us about the bike he had made from scavenged parts and how he loved to ride it.

We answered a few more questions from Tiger's Eye after checking in and then excused ourselves. Without bothering to unpack, we just cleaned up and put on our only off-bike clothes—shorts and

T-shirts. We had one option for dinner—Trixi's Saloon and Fine Dining, a half mile up—literally up—the road. Rather than pedal another inch, we walked the sweaty half mile uphill and collapsed onto our chairs to swig cold sodas and await dinner. Alice had decided before the trip to avoid alcohol because it had been a culprit in setting off a heart arrhythmia on previous bike rides. After trying various medications, her cardiologist had repaired the problem, but she didn't want to take any chances of a recurrence. In solidarity, I joined her in sticking to nonalcoholic beverages.

Only one other table at Trixi's had customers—a group of men who had come to Monture Creek to fish. The restaurant deserved more visitors, we thought, because our steak dinners were great—fifteen dollars each, baked potato and salad included. We may have been trying to have low impact with our means of travel, but in this part of the world we were not about to become vegetarians.

Day 17 Wednesday, July 16
Ovando to Bowmans Corners
64 miles

After a full western-style breakfast at the Blackfoot Inn, we left to tackle Rogers Pass. It was the lowest spot we could find to cross the Rockies and one of the reasons we had chosen the route we had. Lolo Pass over Idaho's Bitterroot Mountains stretched behind us; the Continental Divide loomed ahead. After Rogers Pass we expected gentler terrain until reaching New York's Adirondacks.

In her hurry to pack up and with her penchant for being sidetracked, Alice failed to secure her newly washed clothes onto the back of her bike with bungee cords as she usually did. These indispensable stretchy cords also make fine laundry lines, fastening wet clothes on top of packs to allow drying during the day's ride. She later vaguely recalled setting her clothes down on the back of the bike and then rushing off to take care of another last-minute chore. The result: a favorite shirt and pair of shorts blew off the back of her bike, gone forever. We thought that Tiger's Eye, with his beautiful tie-dyed shirt, might appreciate Alice's T-shirt with the picture of "Bike-o-pelli" from New Mexico on the front. We hoped Alice's loss was his gain.

Moving away from ranch land, we headed once again into forests as we followed rivers upstream into the mountains. Along the Blackfoot River we spotted a kingfisher diving for breakfast. Our hosts at the Blackfoot Inn B&B had told us that Monture Creek, which we crossed a few miles into our ride that morning, was home to nine grizzly bear families. One of Alice's fears was coming upon a grizzly bear, so she hoped not to see one splashing through the brook. Farther on, as we pedaled along Union Creek, a bald eagle rose from the stream and flew directly over us, its underbelly so close we could see separate feathers and individual talons. We learned later that, according to Indian legend, a sighting such as this meant that good fortune would be with us. Good news. Even though we had already enjoyed such luck, more would come, we were sure.

At a small grocery in Lincoln, we stocked up on food—Gatorade, V8 juice, bananas, crackers, and cheese—for a celebration when we reached the top of Rogers Pass. As we checked out, the store's owner looked at us closely and said, "You know, this is the home of the Unabomber." She sounded almost proud of Lincoln's claim to notoriety for being the closest town to Ted Kaczynski's wilderness hideout.

While stopped at the store, we met a cyclist following the Great Divide, a mountain bike route on gravel roads mapped by the Adventure Cycling Association, which intersected our route at Lincoln. He was on a mountain bike with rear panniers and pulling a trailer. He appeared exhausted, and when we asked him what the route was like, he complained that it was much harder than he had anticipated.

We noticed several cans of food in his trailer, which surprised us. Cans? Had he ever heard of freeze-dried food for traveling lightly? Poor guy.

We climbed all day through landscape that became more and more desolate and desertlike. The temperature rose steadily. We saw no homes, only trees and brush along the road. By 1:45 we had put Rogers Pass behind us and hoped that the rest of the day would be pretty easy. Descending the eastern side of the pass at forty-two miles per hour was great fun, although with full loads we still tapped the brakes periodically. Never mind that Lance Armstrong likes to fly down mountains at sixty-five miles per hour and more. We have both become more cautious with age, and we know when fast becomes too fast.

For several miles we looked for a shady place to rest and eat lunch, as it had been too hot to snack at the summit. Finally we spotted a lone crab apple tree not far off the road. It seemed an anomaly because east of the pass the terrain was devoid of trees. The little bit of shade was extremely welcome, though, and once we determined that it was not an illusion, we spread out our bandanna tablecloths and devoured cheese and crackers, energy bars, and bananas. We celebrated our successful climb over Rogers Pass, noting that with the pass behind us and only about twenty miles to go, the rest of the day should be a huge piece of chocolate cake. We climbed back onto our bikes in high spirits.

The cake metaphor fell flat because to our great dismay, Rogers Pass was not the only major challenge of the day. In fact, it wasn't as bad as what was yet to come. The maps were inaccurate in their topographic details—not that they claimed to be perfect, but the elevation graphics usually bore some resemblance to reality. This time the pictures showed flat terrain, giving no warning of the long, hot hills, each one stretching for a mile or two in desert conditions. But we pushed on through the afternoon heat.

"Bobbi, it has to be at least 110 degrees," Alice said as we checked the status of our last water reserves—only one bottle left between us, half full. Soon we would need more. We scanned the horizon for a sign of human habitation. None. Nothing but scratchy-looking, desiccated scrub, sand, and fence line under an infinitely high, intensely blue dome. Big sky, no kidding. Ranches occasionally appeared above the heat shimmers along the highway, but their approach roads were gravel, at least two miles long, and not rideable on our narrow tires. We had been slogging up these insane mini-mountains for too long. Why hadn't our maps indicated how bad they were? Where were we going to get water? Just as we were about to run out, a building appeared in the distance. Was it a mirage? No, it was real, perhaps too real.

That morning, we had seen on our map that the only choice for overnight accommodations was a campground at the crossroads of Montana Highway 200 and U.S. 287. It was named Bowmans Corners, and Bowman's Saloon was the building we had seen from far away—a lonely, dilapidated wood structure, right out of *Gunsmoke* but without Miss Kitty or the rest of Dodge City. The campsite our maps had promised consisted of a bumpy patch of dirt outside the saloon along a fence. It sported a broken-down picnic table, a water spigot coming out of the ground, and an odiferous portable toilet long overdue to be emptied. A good number of dried-up cow patties dotted the area. We eyed the several Harleys parked in front, leaned our own wheels against a pole, and approached the no-frills building, wondering what kind of reception we would get.

It was dark and a little cooler inside, although the only air-conditioning consisted of two screenless windows. The Harley patrons turned out to be several friendly, middle-aged men who chuckled when I immediately stepped up to the bar and said, "Two root beers—both for me."

Well, they hadn't propelled their vehicles under their own power for the last twenty difficult miles, so perhaps they didn't understand my kind of thirst.

When Alice asked Mel, the proprietor of the saloon, how much he charged for a campsite, he said, "Aw, you girls don't cost me nothin' out there. Just come on in here and spend your money."

Which we did. For the second night in a row we ate steak for dinner. He was out of potatoes for baking, he said, but could fill in with lots of bread. He didn't have anything on the dessert menu except vanilla ice cream, so we ordered ice cream and more root beer and made ourselves floats. It was the best reward at the end of a hard day's ride. While we were eating, the saloon filled up with families from the neighboring ranches, one celebrating a birthday, others working out a business deal. We realized that Bowman's Saloon was the community gathering place, though the "community" was far-flung, stretching across desertlike ranch land for many miles.

After taking turns doing our laundry and sponge-bathing in the telephone-booth-of-a-bathroom, which felt like a sauna, we went out to tinker with our gear and get ready for the night. When I saw four cute little girls playing on the saloon's hitching post, I struck up a conversation with them. I hadn't realized until that moment just how much I missed my grandchildren.

"Girls," I asked, "may I take your picture?"

"Sure," replied the tallest. She marshaled her sisters, and they climbed astride the hitching rail as if on horseback. Their mom, Elaine, soon came outside, and Alice and I enjoyed talking with her. She and her husband were there, she told us, to negotiate a land deal. The men inside were talking about buying, selling, and leasing land. While the men talked business, she and the girls asked us about our adventure.

In the course of the conversation, Alice said, "Do you think it's OK for us to spend the night here? Aren't people apt to get rowdy when it gets late? No one else is camping here and it looks like we'll be alone when the bar closes."

Elaine laughed. "You'll be perfectly fine. It's a Wednesday night, not the weekend—and this is Montana!"

Exactly what did "and this is Montana" mean? We felt slightly relieved but still a little nervous. Everyone except us would be going home, and we wondered who else might wander by or what kind of night creatures might keep us awake.

When the men finished their business inside, one of them, in a crisp white shirt, the westerner's requisite blue jeans, and well-worn boots, strode over to our campsite. He had a guitar slung over one shoulder. The little girls followed close behind.

"Elaine here tells me you gals are worried about your safety," the cowboy drawled, a smile splitting his handsome, weathered face. "Well, let me just tell you—this is Montana."

There it was again. Without explaining further he picked up his guitar and began to sing. We don't recall the name of the first song in his serenade, but it was a medley that included strains of "Home on the Range." Alice snapped his photo as he sang one tune after another, while I wished just for a moment that I could trade in my bicycle for a horse and live the cowgirl life. He ended the impromptu concert with "Cowboy Jack," a tragic tale of love and loss on the frontier, allegedly the oldest cowboy song in the West. After singing, he shared some Montana lore with us and answered our questions about ranching. He talked about a rancher's "brand book" and drew pictures in our notebooks to show how brands are designed and how they are modified and passed down through the generations. He even showed us how our own initials might be used to design brands for our families. We learned his real name, but we will forever remember him as Cowboy Mike, the man who set our minds at ease about our safety in Montana.

The saloon emptied. Mel, the ranchers, and the Harley riders went home or moved on, and we went to bed, relaxed and tired enough not to lie awake worrying about anything. Trucks geared down at the four-way stop all night long, so it wasn't exactly tranquil. I used my trusty earplugs, but Alice didn't have any and would feel tired all the next day from waking up so many times.

Day 18 *Thursday, July 17*
Bowmans Corners to Great Falls
52 miles

We ate, packed up, and headed out around 6 a.m., hoping to make some miles before the heat became unbearable. The beginning of the day presented a few hills, but none like those four killers at the end of the previous day. Yes, our legs were fresher, but the steepness of the grades was also decreasing as we approached the northern plains. We had hoped to have a second breakfast at the restaurant in Simms, but it was out of business. The gas station would have to suffice. We bought V8 juice and a package of Fig Newtons to assuage our rumbling stomachs and headed for Sun River, the next town. There, at the thirty-mile mark for the day, we had a huge second—or would it count as third?—breakfast at Ginger's Cafe—a feast of omelets, pancakes, and french toast. It felt so good to have full stomachs and energetic legs.

At Ginger's we met Joseph, a ten-year-old who asked questions one after another about us and our bikes. Most children we met along the way would whisper to their parents, and then the parents would start asking questions. As the children listened, they would eventually overcome their shyness and speak themselves, especially after we began directing our answers and interest toward them. Joseph, however, wasn't like most kids. Sitting at the counter, eating breakfast with his uncle, he asked all the questions we were used to and a few that we hadn't heard.

"Do you have children?" he wondered.

"What's in your backpack?"

"Why is that tube coming out of it? Oh, it's for water! Wow!"

Joseph was into details. He was interested in all aspects of our trip, including our bikes, gear, and route. He came outside with us after breakfast to check everything out and say good-bye. Alice kept a few Sacajawea dollar coins in her handlebar bag for special occasions, and she presented Joseph with one just for fun. His eyes lit up, and his smile widened.

Then he noticed our pedals. "Do you have special shoes that stick on those pedals?" he wondered.

We showed him the recessed cleats that attached our shoes to the pedals so we could be efficient and pull up as well as push down. We clicked into our pedals, and as we wheeled away, Joseph called after us, "Someday I'm going to ride my bike around the world."

Way to go, Joseph. Hope you do.

We did pretty well for the next twenty miles or so—over flat terrain with little wind, averaging about fifteen miles per hour, a little faster than usual. Once "these beasts," as I called our heavy bicycles, got going, they gained momentum and could move right along. We found ourselves pedaling in high gear, an uncommon event.

Sometimes people asked us how many "speeds" we had, as if the more we had, the faster and easier we could go. My bike had twenty-seven gears and Alice's had eighteen, but we tried to explain that the "speeds" were really gears, which regulated how hard it was to get the wheels to revolve. No matter what gear we were in, high or low, we still had to pedal to move our bikes along. In a flat area with no headwind, once we got going, we could make more progress with fewer revolutions of the pedals, but momentum made a huge difference in the amount of effort it would take. Extremely low gears, as we had, made climbing mountains possible because one revolution of the pedals didn't propel the bike very far, so less effort was required. The result: on steep climbs we moved quite slowly while maintaining a fairly quick cadence. When it became so steep that our cadence slowed to the point that it was impossible to balance the bike, we would walk. This happened to Alice several times but I had to walk only once or twice. Alice's rule was that when her speedometer showed less than three miles per hour she would walk because she could walk at between two and three miles per hour, even on a steep incline.

The last ten miles of the day from Vaughn to Great Falls were on a frontage road along I-15 and were extremely difficult—but not because of the terrain. The temperature had risen to well over one hundred degrees, and we felt like Idaho potatoes baking in a Montana oven. Even the headwind was a hot, hot breeze, not at all cooling as a headwind can sometimes be. I was thinking about how to find a chiropractor to look at my backside once we reached Great Falls, and together we fantasized about which flavor of milkshake we would order at McDonald's or a local ice-cream joint, whichever came first.

As we entered Great Falls, I spotted what appeared to be a brand-new St. Vincent de Paul store, and the lure of air-conditioned shopping postponed all our other plans. We spent the next hour in cool comfort, purportedly to replace Alice's lost off-bike wardrobe but also just to add something "new" and different to our usual garb. The only rule was that it had to be lightweight and easy to wash and dry. It was a big store and no one seemed to mind how sweaty and icky we were as we moved in and out of the dressing rooms with item after item. We each left with new outfits: a black-and-white "skort" set for me for four dollars and some navy shorts and a red sleeveless top for two dollars for Alice. Not bad.

Great Falls had a hostel that advertised itself as a B&B. Alice said it should have been called just a *B*, however, because breakfast was not included. It also was not air-conditioned, but we were the only guests, and we had the whole second floor, including a bathroom with shower down the hall, all to ourselves. Our room with its multiple bunk beds was equipped with a large floor fan. Todd, the owner, an avid cyclist himself, charged us only nine dollars apiece, so we figured it was cheaper and a little more comfortable than camping.

After unloading, we took our bikes to the nearest bike shop, where we scheduled some gearing adjustments and drive train cleaning. We decided to take the next day off, explore Great Falls and some of the Lewis and Clark sites, and start riding by 5:30 Saturday morning.

Day 19 — *Friday, July 18*
Rest day

Somehow our rest day flew by. At 110 degrees, it was too hot to walk or pedal anywhere, so after checking our Web site and e-mail, we behaved like ordinary tourists and bought a ticket for a tour on the town trolley. Downtown Great Falls seemed to be surviving economically, but we did notice signs of decline. Some stores were empty, including a famous old Montana saloon, and we didn't see tourists swarming the Lewis and Clark sites, despite the fact that it was the beginning of the Corps of Discovery's bicentennial celebration. Probably it was the heat, in spite of which we managed to check out the famous site on the Missouri River where a grizzly bear had chased Lewis into the water. This year the river was much lower because of a five-year drought.

I succeeded in finding a chiropractor and was able to get my hip adjusted. Miraculously, the pain immediately receded, and I banished any further thought of suspending the trip. Only after my hip improved did I tell Alice how close I had come to giving up that day in Kamiah when I bought the lamb's wool.

We picked up our cleaned and adjusted bikes from the shop and started to ride them back to the B&B, but I couldn't pedal. With each stroke, my right pedal wouldn't circle correctly and I couldn't raise it up smoothly on the back part of the rotation. Neither of us could see anything wrong, so we returned to the shop, where a young mechanic took a look, saw the problem, and confessed, shame-faced, that he had not put the cranks on correctly. They were not set truly opposite each other, at 180 degrees. So that explained the imbalance. Relieved that my bike didn't need major repair, we returned to our stifling hot room in the *B*.

The western mountains lay behind us and the plains stretched ahead. The next day would bring more hot riding.

Day 20 — *Saturday, July 19*
Great Falls to Fort Benton
52 miles

Our alarm went off at 5 a.m. on Saturday, and we were ready to go by 6:15. We were actually becoming efficient—at least for today. Bikes loaded, water bottles and bags full, we were out the door and ready to mount when I noticed that my back tire was flat. Shoot.

By the time we unloaded the gear, changed the tube, and pumped up the new one—while our host watched silently from his porch chair—it was 7:30. Oh well, it was still the earliest we had ever left. After we had gone a block or so, I asked Alice why she thought our host couldn't have busied himself with something else instead of watching every move we made as we changed my tire.

"Were we that interesting?" I wondered.

"I think," said Alice, "anyone who advertises a B&B with no

air-conditioning and missing a *B* is impossible to understand. Let's just get out of here."

Once again we deviated from the Adventure Cycling maps because several people had advised us to take the newly paved Highwood Road rather than busy U.S. 87. It was a few miles longer and a bit hillier, but the hills were worth it because for the first time since Waitsburg Road in Oregon, we didn't have to ride single file.

The road meandered by wheat fields and vast ranches. No more than ten vehicles passed us the entire morning. Every driver waved, and one time, when we were stopped to apply more sunscreen, a man pulled over to make sure we were OK.

"Do you girls need any help?" he shouted out the window.

He didn't know how much we appreciated the gesture. We realized then that if we ran out of water—or needed any other sort of help—a passing motorist would undoubtedly help us. We discussed the idea that when people live in unforgiving climates or difficult terrain, they seem to look after one another, and they watch out for strangers, too.

We reached the tiny town of Highwood and stopped at its only public building—the post office. The postmistress herself filled our hydration packs from the water cooler. Ooooh—cold water! What a treat! She told us it was about seventeen miles to Fort Benton, so we were encouraged that we might be able to make it there by noon, before it reached one hundred degrees. Unlike the Midwest, the afternoon temperatures peak between 4 and 7 p.m. The earlier we could ride, the better off we would be.

The new experience of the day involved grasshoppers—huge, shiny grasshoppers several inches long, not the little ones we were used to in the Midwest. We thought they were dining on the wheat that lined both sides of the road, but millions of them had ventured onto the asphalt as if to examine us, strange interlopers into their territory.

"Ouch!"

"Eeeuw!"

"Ow!"

"Ping!"

They vaulted onto our bikes, hit our legs, zinged our faces, and ricocheted off spokes and rims. Several rode along for miles on our panniers, front and rear. We wondered how they would ever find their way home, if grasshoppers have homes. For the most part, they were nimble enough to avoid being smashed under our tires, but we did hear an occasional crunch. We finally figured out that the closer we rode to the centerline the fewer the hoppers, but that had its own set of problems. We had to watch our rearview mirrors carefully as well as scan ahead for fast-approaching vehicles from either direction.

We finally rolled into Fort Benton just as the temperature hit one hundred degrees, and we immediately found the information center on Main Street. A local volunteer proudly pointed out the fort and the signs along the river that explained the history of trading and navigation in the area. Although we love history as much as tourists who ride in cars, it was just too hot to stop to read any signs or make our way to any museum. We would have to catch up later on the golden days of steamboats and the role Fort Benton had played in the American fur trade, gambling, and the sale of illegal whiskey. Instead, we scouted the six blocks or so of the sleepy river village to find a motel.

The only two motels in town did not appear habitable. One was a flat-roofed building made of unpainted gray cinder blocks with no evidence of air-conditioning, the other a bombed-out-looking structure with several black mongrels snarling and drooling in the gravel parking lot. The old, recently restored hotel, on the other hand, was so fancy that we banished the thought of rolling our grungy bikes across the plush carpet of the lobby and hefting them up a flight or two of stairs. Besides, it was expensive, so we opted for a B&B listed

Have bicycle, will travel

on our map. To call it a B&B was once again a stretch. It turned out to be a basement room in a woman's home. It had no air-conditioning, but being below ground made it cooler than any of the alternatives, including camping. We paid fifty dollars for the night—a bit much, we thought—but it was clean and quiet, and we were glad not to be in the stifling outdoors.

Some riders we had met in western Montana had told us not to miss Fort Benton, so we expected a bustling town alive with tourists. A few tourists meandered along the quiet street facing the Upper Missouri River, but it was obvious the town was in need of an economic shot in the arm, despite the Lewis and Clark connection. We spent much of the afternoon in Bob's Riverfront Restaurant on Front Street and liked the lunch menu enough to return for supper. That was when we discovered that we were no longer eating as ravenously as we had at the beginning of the trip. Either the heat was sapping our appetites or our metabolisms were changing as our bodies became used to the level of activity we were demanding of them. Or maybe it was just that we were no longer scaling mountains.

Determined to get to bed by 8:30 p.m. in order to be on the road by 5:30 a.m., we returned early to our room and started packing our bikes. It was then that I found another flat tire on my rear wheel. I spent the next half hour, past bedtime, changing the tube. Both that tube and the one I used the day before were defective, or at least not made for the kinds of loads we were carrying, because they both seemed to have weak seams near the valve. I put in a different type of tube and hoped my flat tire problems were solved for a while. This tire changing was becoming annoying, not to mention time-consuming.

Day 21 ***Sunday, July 20***
Fort Benton to Denton
52 miles

The tire was still holding air in the morning, so we were up and out by 6:30. We needed to leave before the usual breakfast hour, so our hostess had promised that she would leave us some cold cereal and fruit. The milk was sour and the overripe fruit was swarming with fruit flies. Disappointed that our fifty dollars hadn't even bought a decent breakfast, we ate an energy bar apiece from our own supply and drank our own sports drink. On our way through town we met two loaded cyclists traveling in the other direction. We didn't want to take the time to stop because we knew temperatures would rise soon and the heat would be blistering, but trading information with other cyclists was useful, so we stopped to talk to them on the street outside Bob's restaurant.

We told them about Highwood Road, and they informed us about troublesome drinking water east of Fort Benton. They said that not only was water hard to find because the towns were so far apart, but when they did drink the local water, it upset their stomachs. We decided to buy bottled water for the next few days.

We climbed all morning, reaching Geraldine by lunchtime. The convenience store out on the main road was the scene of a bit of excitement, indicated by a squad car in the driveway and a flurry of activity inside. The store had been broken into overnight and we would have to buy our drinks with credit cards because the till was empty and they couldn't make change for even a five-dollar bill. As we rested on the front porch swing swigging our drinks, we heard someone inside say that the culprit had just been caught in the next town with the cash in his hand. We weren't surprised. There were so few escape routes here and so few people that any likely suspects must have been easily known to just about any local resident.

The town of Geraldine, a quarter of a mile or so off the main road, was typical of many of the struggling towns we pedaled through in Montana—and some we would see later in North Dakota. Named after Geraldine Rockefeller, niece of John D., the town may have been thriving in the early part of the twentieth century, but by the time we passed through, it was in a tailspin. The highway sign listed the population at 284, but we sensed that it was out of date. A museum established in the railroad depot was listed on the National Register of Historic Places, but it was open by appointment only. The one grocery store in town was not open on Sunday, so we were glad we had enough provisions to get by. Our squirt tube of peanut butter and box of Wheat Thins that we always carried would come in handy once again.

A bar was open for business but it looked dilapidated, dark, hot, and so unappealing that we didn't even peek inside. Instead we sat gingerly, for fear of splinters, on a wooden bench beside the wide, part-asphalt, part-gravel main street and ate our meager lunch. Flies buzzed aggressively around us and dogs ambled by, their tongues hanging in the heat. We read later in a *New York Times* feature story on Montana's declining population that Geraldine had a school, but the football team had only seven players, a common situation in rural Montana. In fact, we were told of the severe population drain by more than one native, and judging by the last few towns we had seen, they and the *New York Times* were right on the money.

It was getting hot again fast, so we hurried on toward Denton, still climbing. "Hurried" was a relative term. We were averaging about ten miles per hour and were pleased with that speed, considering the heat and hills. Eight miles east of Geraldine we came to the next town on our bike maps, Square Butte. It looked even sorrier than Geraldine, so we kept pedaling, and in twenty more miles we reached Coffee Creek. We needed a rest and some shelter from the sun for a few minutes, but the only shade we could find was under the smallest of tin roofs—at the mini-post office. That and a few small, shabby homes were all that was left of Coffee Creek.

We rolled into Denton, population 301, at about 2:30, spied the cafe—apparently the only establishment open on Sunday—and stopped to ask how late it would be open.

"Three o'clock," chirped the blonde, teenaged waitress.

It was a good thing we had asked this question rather than going first to set up camp in the town park at the far end of the street. Without hesitating, we plunked ourselves down in one of the cool, Formica-laminated booths. We hadn't eaten a restaurant meal all day and needed more than energy bars and water. Our young waitress was a high school senior whose family lived on a 10,000-acre wheat farm. Unlike so many waitresses we had met, she bustled about energetically, eager to satisfy our appetites. She asked about our adventure, and we asked her about her plans for after high school.

Rx for happy cycling: strawberry milkshake

"I want to go to college in Texas . . . or maybe Chicago," she said dreamily, and then paused, smiling. "Somewhere far away."

She was the president of her high school Future Farmers group, but she expressed no interest in following that profession. We suspected that she would excel no matter what vocation she chose.

She whipped up fresh strawberry milkshakes with real ice cream. None of that soft-serve stuff for us. "Hard" ice cream was what I had been craving, and I was excited about getting some. It was one of those moments when, after I had lifted the spoon to my lips, I closed my eyes, feeling deep satisfaction. There we were—relaxing in air-conditioned comfort, waited on by a cheerful, devoted waitress, with smooth, high-calorie coldness soothing our dry throats. Life was good.

After the strawberry shakes, we downed a hearty lunch. Our waitress gave us some apples for the next day and finally rang up the bill. The clock said 4:00, but she had not rushed us, which we appreciated. Completely stuffed at last, we waddled out, mounted our bikes, which by that time had acquired names—Big Bertha (mine) and Black Beauty (Alice's)—and pedaled down to the park, where we were told we could camp for free. The swimming pool was open, so after we pitched our tents we joined the fun in the water for two dollars apiece.

Later, in the locker room, we asked a woman about the quality of the drinking water in the area. She smiled brightly and replied encouragingly, "Oh, it has a lot of nitrates in it, but we drink it all the time. It won't hurt you. Only pregnant and nursing women aren't supposed to drink it." Alice and I shot alarmed looks at each other.

We had filled one water bottle apiece at the cafe, because it was the only water available, but we decided to drink as little of it as possible. The vending machine on the corner got our business several times that evening, and we had more than our fill of orange soda.

One little girl at the pool recognized us as the women on bikes they had passed in their truck many miles west of Denton as they headed to the pool an hour earlier. We had waved to them and they had waved back. They fired questions rapidly, and we had fun asking them what bugs they studied in school, what books they read, what they did in summer. We learned that they were cousins—one from Bend, Oregon, and the other from Seattle. They were in Denton to stay with their grandma for a week. Such lucky children.

Another family, having seen our loaded bikes from the swimming pool, came over to talk to us where we had set up our tents. They warned us of rattlesnakes, especially in the road and especially at night. The dad rolled up his pants to show us where he had been bitten on the leg the summer before. We learned several things about rattlesnakes in that exchange: (1) rattlesnakes come out on the roads at night to enjoy the warmth of the asphalt; (2) baby rattlesnakes can look much like worms, because their rattles often aren't developed; and (3) baby rattlers have the most toxic bite even without visible rattles because they don't regulate the dose of venom they inject into their victim.

This rattlesnake information verified a story we had been told back in Washington. As the story went, a medical student was pedaling across the country by himself, and because it was so hot he decided to try cycling at night instead of during the day. He had a decent lighting system on his bike and set off happily his first night. He enjoyed the cooler temperatures, but as the sky turned dark he realized that he would not be able to stop—for a food break or for any other reason. There with him on the night road were rattlesnakes that had come out to warm themselves. We had thought this story far-fetched, but we became believers. Now Alice had something new to watch for. No more concerns about grizzly bears. From that point on it would be rattlesnakes.

Day 22 ***Monday, July 21***
Denton to Lewistown
42 miles

We were up at 4:30—our earliest start yet—and on the road by 6:30 with no rattlesnakes in sight. We checked. A vivid pink and Creamsicle-orange sunrise above the Montana landscape was a breathtaking backdrop to an endless expanse of giant rolls of harvested wheat dotting the fields. The early morning air was a cool seventy-five degrees—perfect for cycling. After pedaling uphill for about eight miles, we spent the rest of the morning crossing gently rolling terrain past immense ranches where wheat was being harvested and horses were roaming in their pastures. A gentle tailwind eased the way. We saw a couple of antelope, and at one point seven powerful young bucks, one after the other, bounding single file along a trail parallel to ours fifty or so yards away. They traveled silently alongside us for nearly a mile until their route disappeared into a coulee. "Coulee," we had learned, is westernspeak for a dry gulch.

As we rode on toward Lewistown, we began to make out hazy buttes in the distance. Being a midwesterner, my first thought was that the haze was humidity, but I knew that wasn't possible. It was terribly dry here. Then we began to smell the reason—smoke from wildfires. We had overheard talk of volunteers going "up on the butte" to fight the fires and realized that we were looking at that butte. We didn't sense any danger, though, so we had no idea what part the fires would soon play in our journey.

By noon we arrived in Lewistown and chose the Mountain View Motel as our home for the next couple of days. Lewis and Clark may have stayed cool on the rivers, but that was then. This was the hottest summer in twenty years, or so we had been told. We needed to find out more about the fires, so we bought a newspaper and turned on the TV. We also talked to local residents. Our research convinced us that it would be unsafe and maybe even impossible to ride east from Lewistown because the wildfires around the Missouri Breaks area were too close to our intended route. The fires had already burned 30,000 acres near Jordan and were still out of control. If we rode up to them we might not be able to find a way around them, or we could be turned back by the authorities. The smoke, combined with the extreme heat, would make our planned ride too tough to handle. It was still over 100 degrees every day with temperatures in the fire region reaching 112, and there was too much territory between Lewistown and the North Dakota border without services. It was the most remote section of our route, a section that we suspected would be unrideable in a few years without a support vehicle, even without fires.

So we went to the only rental car facility in Lewistown—the Oldsmobile car dealership—and reserved the only car available, which was due back on the lot from somewhere else the next day. We learned we could drive it to Glasgow, which was north of the fires on U.S. 2, about twenty miles west of where we planned to be in a few days. We would miss about 180 miles of pedaling, but we would join U.S. 2, which the locals call the Highline, some miles before we would have reached it had we gone east first and then north as our maps suggested. Although we didn't want to wimp out, we felt that prudence was the wiser choice.

Day 23 — *Tuesday, July 22*
Rest day

Our day and a half in Lewistown turned out to be fun, hot as it was. Settled in 1879, the town first boomed when western lands opened to settlers and homesteaders besieged it. We found the county seat of Fergus County to be quite alive, with businesses lining the main street and friendly people everywhere. We started our rest day taking turns for a massage apiece from Lynnette, whom we found in the Yellow Pages, and who was good at softening neck and shoulder muscles. While she worked on us we learned about Lewistown culture and got several recommendations for places to eat and visit.

One excellent recommendation of Lynnette's was the computer store, Lewistown On Line, where we could download photos from our cameras to CDs. We followed her advice and met John and his son, Robert, who made the process easy. John also offered us additional server space in case we ran out on our current site. He did a local radio tech show, he told us, and would feature our adventure and how we used technology, and would set up links from his site to ours. We loved witnessing his enthusiasm for his work, his son's obvious interest in the business, and their warm relationship. From his store we moved on to the post office, where we mailed the CDs so the photos could be posted to our Web site.

Down the hall from Lynnette's massage studio, we also met Mary and John, who were working in the office set up for the Upper Missouri Breaks National Monument, a federal site established in 2001 to preserve the natural area on the Upper Missouri River north of Lewistown. They described to us the exotic beauty of the glacier- and river-carved stone of the Missouri Breaks. We discussed at some length the fires in the area and how we would try to circumvent them. They were eager to help us, they said, in any way they could, and Mary even gave us souvenir T-shirts. Here again were two friendly people, truly dedicated to their work and eager to help a couple of strangers.

At the other end of Main Street we found the Mountain Men Antler Art Gallery, a one-of-a-kind shop filled from its wood-plank floor to the rafters with everything from bead-studded boots to antler chandeliers. Behind the counter, Frank looked like a true mountain man with his tousled long hair and untrimmed beard. Well-worn jeans and a faded blue plaid shirt completed what was almost a caricature. From Frank we learned about the locally mined Yogo sapphires. The British-owned mine in the nearby Little Belt Mountains produces the only sapphires in the world that are naturally blue, he told us. Others, he said, are heat-treated to get their blue color. According to Frank, Princess Diana had worn Yogo sapphires. Others in town suggested that Frank's claims regarding Princess Di were nothing short of mythical, but no one disagreed about the Yogo sapphires' beauty. The gems are undeniably spectacular and the demand for them apparently outweighs supply, so they are expensive. I treated myself to a pair of earrings set with tiny stones.

"I'll give them to my granddaughter someday," I explained to Alice. In the meantime, I would wear them proudly for the rest of the trip.

Twice in two days we stopped by the Bon Ton, the local soda fountain, where we chatted with Jan, the owner, and Sarah, her adopted daughter. Their root beer floats, turtle sundaes, and raspberry "creamies," which were Jan's own semifrozen creations, were just what we needed. Jan and Sarah offered us their inner tubes for an evening float down Spring Creek, a pastime that everyone in the area seemed to indulge in on hot summer evenings. Pleading weariness, we opted out, but we appreciated how easy it was to make friends in Lewistown.

A gourmet meal both nights at the Mint Bar and Grill made our visit to Lewistown complete. It demonstrated again the importance of asking local people where to eat. In a weary old warehouse-type building on a back street, the Mint Bar provided a fabulous dining experience we would never have found on our own.

Lewistown is the biggest town for miles around (population 5,800), and yet it is a small town. Everyone seems to know everyone, and after we spent a day and a half there they all seemed to know us. Because our motel was at the top of the hill at the edge of town and it was too hot to pedal, we walked everywhere. By the end of our time there we were recognizing people we had met the day before and were beginning to feel at home.

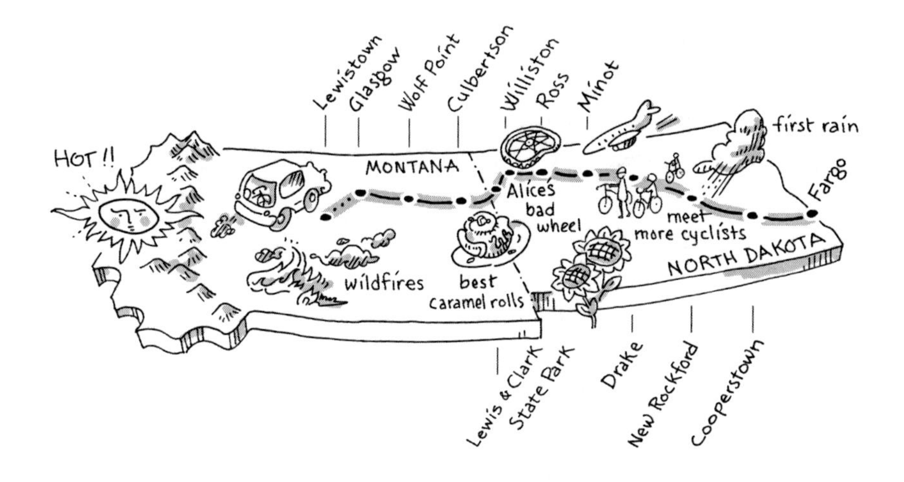

3

Across the Northern Plains

Eastern Montana and North Dakota

Despite the intense heat and scarcity of people, Montana and North Dakota would place high on our list of favorite states. Much of the population has left for more prosperous regions, but many of those who remain befriended us in extraordinary ways. The people of the plains would inhabit a special place in our memories. They live the ideal of the good neighbor.

Day 24 ***Wednesday, July 23***
Lewistown to Glasgow
Fire detour

Alice packed up in the motel room while I walked to the Oldsmobile dealership where we had reserved the car for getting around the wildfires. As I approached the desk, I was feeling a little guilty because I hadn't told them we were planning to transport two bikes and a lot of gear in addition to the two of us. They would not want greasy bikes in their vehicle, but I knew that we could figure out how to do it without soiling the car even if we had to pad the roof and strap the bikes on with duct tape. Desperate times called for desperate measures.

As I sat down at the desk the gray-haired man looked at me sympathetically. "I've got bad news," he said. "The rental car didn't come back."

With a sinking feeling, I wondered how long we would have to stay in Lewistown. To my surprise, he then smiled and said, "But I have a van on the lot you could use. I'd charge you the same as the car. Would that be OK?"

"Well . . . I guess so."

Then, deadpan, he said, "Shall I remove the third seat for you?"

I felt like jumping up and down and hugging him, but instead could only mumble, "We do have a lot of stuff to put in it." It was too late to tell the whole truth. Someone had obviously done it for us. We would never know who effected this minor miracle but would always be grateful—and a bit embarrassed.

"This van is for sale," he explained, "and you can just drop it off at my brother's in Glasgow."

"Your brother's?" I was confused.

"Yep, he has a car lot up there. It'll get back here soon enough."

I couldn't help thinking: This is Montana—what a fine place!

The countryside in northeastern Montana, even the part that wasn't in flames, was extremely dry and desolate. On our drive north toward U.S. 2 we stopped for lunch at the James Kipp Recreation Area near the Upper Missouri River Breaks National Monument, hoping to see up close some of the rock formations and wildlife that we had heard about. We found a patch of shade for picnicking, but again it was over one hundred degrees, too hot even in the shade to spend much time outside. Back in the van, we realized how difficult it would have been to ride this section because there was no water anywhere—and no home or business anywhere along the route to get it from. It would have been close to impossible to add several eight-pound jugs of water to the rest of our load.

When we reached Glasgow we stopped by the car dealership to ask how to return the van after hours. We had planned, as long as we had the van, to drive down to Fort Peck and see the technological wonder there, the Fort Peck Dam.

Julie, the dealership manager, said, "Just park it here and leave it unlocked."

I couldn't believe it. "You mean with the keys in it? Aren't you worried someone might steal it?"

"I've lived here all my life," Julie said, "and nothing crazy like that has ever happened. This is Montana! If someone gets into your car, it's to check and make sure you turned everything off."

Once again reassured about the trustworthiness of Montanans, we traveled on. We booked the only motel room left in town and then went to see what the guidebooks say is "the largest earth-filled hydraulic dam in the world." It was built as a WPA project in the 1930s and '40s and still generates electrical power for much of Montana and even some parts of California. Led by a perky college student working as a Corps of Engineers guide, we toured the power generator, saw the massive, three-story-tall turbines, and learned a little bit about how electricity was generated on the site.

Back in Glasgow, we left the unlocked van at the dealership as instructed and then rode our bikes back to the motel, stopping along the way for some fantastic pizza at Eugene's, which deserved its high praise from the locals who recommended it. When we pulled out our maps to peruse our next day's route, people at the next table offered unsolicited but welcome route advice. More evidence of the helpfulness of strangers.

Day 25 — *Thursday, July 24*
Glasgow to Wolf Point
52 miles

It felt good to be on our way again. Alice was sad, however, because her husband had undergone laparoscopic gall bladder surgery while we were getting around the fires. It had been a relief to learn from the test results that neither his kidneys nor his liver were failing, but removing his gall bladder had to occur at the surgeon's convenience rather than Alice's. Suffering a full-blown case of "the guilties," she wished she could have figured out how to get home to be with him, but if all went as planned, they would see each other when he came to Minot, North Dakota, the following week.

Back on our bikes, we pedaled over gently rolling terrain east of Glasgow where much of our route paralleled U.S. 2 on a Bureau of Indian Affairs road through the Fort Peck Indian Reservation. We saw almost no traffic, with only about five cars passing us in a thirty-five-mile stretch. We stopped to rest as the road rejoined U.S. 2 and met a couple of other cyclists—the first we had seen in several days. They were a brother and sister in their early twenties, cycling from New York City to their hometown of Anacortes, Washington. They had left New York on June 22 and had been on the road a month, averaging about a hundred miles a day. We traded information, wished them luck, and moved on—at our slower, more "mature" pace.

In the cool hours of early morning we saw wildlife that usually eluded us—fox, coyote, and pronghorn. The majestic pronghorn, sometimes called pronghorn antelope, are not true antelope, but they have horns that curve backward and branch out like the antlers of deer or antelope. These were standing still, but on a previous bike trip, in Wyoming, I had been riding alongside one that was running—until it decided to take off. It left me choking on its dust. From all reports they are the fastest mammal in North America and can reach a top speed of fifty-three miles per hour. They seemed content to munch on their breakfast as we passed by in the cool of the morning.

After we left the reservation the terrain changed and we began seeing the "prairie potholes" that are common to eastern Montana and western North Dakota. These are depressions that hold water in an otherwise dry landscape but are surrounded by cattails and other pond vegetation. Terns, seagulls, and other water birds flock to these oases that dot the rolling northern plains. It seemed strange in such arid land to find water birds, but according to the information printed on our maps, the area is considered one of the country's primary "duck factories."

By afternoon the temperature was projected to rise above one hundred degrees again, so we were glad to reach Wolf Point by noon. At a gas station and convenience store on the edge of town, we were eating sandwiches when we noticed two Native American adolescents staring at our bikes parked on the other side of the window from where we sat. Leaving the air-conditioning, we struck up a conversation with the boys.

"Hi, guys. How ya' doin'?" I asked.

"OK," one said as he stared at the ground.

"We noticed you looking at these crazy bikes. Did you have any questions?"

"Naw," he answered, again avoiding eye contact.

"Those are pretty neat bikes you have," Alice indicated, pointing to their BMXs. "What are those extra long axles for on the back wheels?"

That started the conversation. They told us about the pegs they stand on to carry another rider, and then their questions began.

"How do your pedals work?" one boy wondered, and we showed them how our shoes had special cleats for clipping in.

After several more rounds, one of them asked, "So, how much money do you carry?"

"We don't really carry any cash," I said, "just plastic."

"Yeah, but you must have to have some. How much?"

He wouldn't give up and I became cagey.

"Oh, just a few bucks," I answered, hoping he would drop the line of questioning.

"Like maybe fifty bucks or so?" he said.

"Yeah, maybe."

That answer seemed to satisfy him, and we parted ways and pedaled on into Wolf Point. There we found an air-conditioned motel, unloaded our gear, and headed out to search for the post office and library. Such activities had become part of our routine whenever we came to a large enough town.

Wolf Point struck us as a depressed place but different from the shrinking towns we had seen previously and would continue to see. The town itself seemed to be run by white people—the store owners, mayor, even clerks and waiters—but we were on the Fort Peck Indian Reservation, which appeared to be populated mostly by less-than-prosperous Native Americans. We wondered about the area's economics and politics but had no way, without staying longer, to check on relations between the residents of the reservation and the town's ruling elite.

With the rest of the afternoon to kill, we roamed up and down the hot, deserted streets, into and out of the drugstore, a variety store, and the saddlery, just to see what they carried. The saddles in the saddlery certainly looked more comfortable than the ones we perched on day after day, but we loved our own "horses," even with their minimal seats. My new, cushier bike saddle, purchased in Missoula, had proven to be a smart choice. I was back to normal riding form and secure enough to mail my old saddle home rather than carry it any farther.

Our most important destination in Wolf Point was the library, a short walk from the town center. As our trip progressed, we frequently looked for libraries when we had the time because they had easy Internet access and we could take care of e-mail and read our Web guest book. By the time we reached Wolf Point, messages were pouring in. Besides the supportive "Go, girls!" or "You ladies ROCK," we received more humorous notes: "You girls will be an inspiration to me . . . in my next life." The guest book supplemented our weekly reports informing friends new and old of our progress.

Policies on Internet access vary from library to library. Sometimes we were allowed unlimited use. More often we had limited time, anything from fifteen minutes to two hours. Sometimes a fee was involved—a dollar or two or five. Occasionally we became library patrons for a few months even though we wanted only an hour or so of access. The Roosevelt County Library in Wolf Point had a unique policy: users—us included—could be on a computer for a half hour but local residents had bumping rights. This policy may have worked well most of the time in Roosevelt County, but it didn't work for us.

We had just settled ourselves in front of two of the three computers when the librarian informed us that we would have to give up our spaces. It seemed that instead of going to a swimming pool on a suffocatingly hot night in Wolf Point, area adolescents gravitated to the library. They were not there to explore the world of books but to play video games on the Internet. So we got up and stood around while the kids sat down to play. Their half hour went by and we were able to get on again.

After five minutes of our second attempt to read our messages, we were bumped again.

"C'mon, Alice. Let's get out of here," I said.

"No," she answered, stubbornly, and then whispered, "If we stick around it will help them realize what a stupid policy this is. Besides, where else do we have to go?"

We too liked the air-conditioning, so we went through three aborted rounds—five minutes on, twenty-five minutes off. At one point we tried persuading the librarian to make a temporary exception to the bumping policy—for just one of the three computers. We explained what we were doing in Wolf Point, that we had very little ability to communicate with people other than through our e-mail and the guest book on the Internet, and that we wouldn't have another opportunity for some time.

"No," she said sharply. "Policy is policy. I can show it to you in writing."

We did not express interest in seeing the written policy, but she brought it out to show us anyway. We both just shook our heads and walked away, disappointed. In retrospect I wish we had offered the kids a few bucks apiece for their time in front of a screen.

By the time we gave up and set out for our motel room we were looking forward to the next library on our route, maybe in Williston, but we doubted it would be open on a Sunday.

Day 26 ***Friday, July 25***
Wolf Point to Culbertson
57 miles

When Friday, July 25, dawned we slept on. We had heard that relief from the heat was coming, and the forecast was for a high in the eighties, so we allowed ourselves a later start. We dilly-dallied over breakfast in the motel's restaurant, where Alice enjoyed the unusual addition of fat-free rather than whole milk. A resident of the Dairy State, Alice always asked whether it was possible to order skim milk but the answer usually was no. The waitress in the motel's restaurant seemed surprised by Alice's excitement. We explained that it was unusual for a restaurant to have it. Wolf Point was just not like other places.

We left town at 8 a.m. and on our way met Jeff, a lone, fit, sun-weathered cyclist in his thirties riding from Virginia to Oregon. He was hauling all his gear in a trailer. He told us that before the trip he had once "maybe" ridden fifty miles in a day. It just proved that anyone could do this if he or she wanted to badly enough.

U.S. 2 wasn't very busy although we still rode single file. It rained lightly—not hard enough to make us put on raingear but just enough to keep us cool. The clouds and drizzle offered welcome relief after the heat of the previous several weeks.

By 10 a.m. we had arrived in Poplar, an even more depressed-looking town than Wolf Point, still on the Fort Peck Indian Reservation. We stopped for Gatorade, a few snack items, and a restroom at the town's only store. As we arranged our purchases in our packs, several carloads of people came and went. Everyone smiled, greeted us, and stopped to chat, voicing interest in our trip and urging us to be cautious. We enjoyed and appreciated their friendliness but we became a bit nervous when, as we were preparing to leave, two tough-looking young men approached us on foot.

One, whose deeply creased, mottled complexion showed evidence of more than one fight, stood back a few feet while the more outgoing man addressed us in slurred speech.

"This is a real nice town." With eyes glazed over, he drew out his words and offered the next thought with even longer separations between words. "I don't know why that New York journal said this was the deadliest town in the West. I just don't know why. This is a real nice place." He paused, as he struggled for what to say next. "Well, you ladies have a good time."

"Thanks," Alice answered, and he ambled off with his silent buddy.

We continued through the reservation for thirty more uneventful miles on a Bureau of Indian Affairs road that had even less traffic than U.S. 2. It was great to be able to ride two abreast and share stories to pass the time. We talked about our generally happy childhoods, earliest memories, struggles of adolescence, and first boyfriends. The miles flew by, partly because of the conversation, partly because the terrain was quite flat, skies were cloudy, and the temperature didn't rise above eighty.

About five miles past the end of the reservation we came to Culbertson. The heat had definitely broken and no rain was scheduled, but the mosquitoes! Oh, my. We both hated the thought of battling them all night, so we decided that at forty-two dollars per night, the King's Inn was suitable for us commoners, too.

When Alice called home that night to check on Booth, he seemed in good spirits and didn't want to talk about himself. Instead he asked about our day, and after she told him about the motel we had for the night, he asked, "Do you think you will ever camp again?"

"I think so," Alice had told him, "but we don't really care."

Our resolve to camp for most of the trip was weakening. Bears, rattlesnakes, rain, heat, mosquitoes—what other excuses would we find to have air-conditioning and indoor plumbing? We weren't sticking to our budget very well but our bodies appreciated not camping. We told ourselves that we had paid our dues with many years of sleeping in tents. Now we were opting for "luxury." Simple living wasn't necessarily defined as camping. Our scaled-down lifestyle had many other facets.

When we checked in, the motel's owner suggested we visit the local museum, so after we laundered our bike clothes, showered, and dropped our latest postcards and trip literature at the post office to add to our scrapbooks back home, we walked the equivalent of a few blocks down the road to see the museum's collection of Montana farm memorabilia. Room after room was filled with items of great nostalgic value to the two ladies who showed us around. The memorabilia seemed to be organized in no particular order and by no particular time period. It felt as though we were visiting a bursting antique mall where nothing was for sale. We were charmed, however, by the obvious pride our guides felt in the history of their area. While at the museum, we were treated to our first "uff da"—a Norwegian utterance that I had never heard before—when the guides heard about our adventure. I was amused by what seemed to be the elderly woman's version of "Wow!"

On our walk back to the motel we noticed a group of cyclists at a convenience store. They were from Dartmouth College, riding coast to coast from east to west. Drivers of their support van planned the route, carried their gear, and maintained the bikes. They were raising funds for Habitat for Humanity and were staying mostly in churches along the way. They gave slide shows about their trip and their work, and members of the local congregation prepared their dinner and breakfast. They invited us to stop by for the show, which we did after we had our own dinner at a nearby restaurant.

Day 27 Saturday, July 26
Culbertson to Williston, North Dakota
72 miles

We began the next day with breakfast at the Wild West Diner. The sticky buns there were the best we had ever had and would have probably been breakfast enough all on their own, but of course we added the other usual items. Ah, the benefits of riding all day every day for many weeks—we could eat anything we wanted with impunity.

We pedaled off in the coolest temperatures so far, waving goodbye to the Habitat cyclists going the other way, some trailing colorful streamers from their handlebars, one in a pink tutu tied around the waist of her bike shorts.

We still felt full when we reached Bainville, the last town in Montana, fourteen miles east. The diner looked appealing but what really motivated us to stop was the stunning, wrought-iron Welcome to Montana sign. It was a perfect snapshot, even though we were leaving rather than entering the state. While we were stopped, three other cyclists rode up: Kent, Joe, and Joe's father, who were pedaling east to west accompanied by Joe's mom driving a van. The usual exchange of information ensued.

"You are going to love North Dakota," said Kent. "The world's friendliest people live there. It's our favorite state so far."

I asked, "What's your least favorite?"

"Michigan," came Joe's emphatic reply. "Watch out for those drivers. We thought we were going to die several times in that state."

We would recall that conversation later on.

On that day we enjoyed cycling at its best. Bright clear skies overhead and waving wheat soothed our eyes, and the eighty-degree temperatures bathed us in pleasant warmth rather than excruciating heat for a change. Relief. We were feeling so good and enjoying the weather so much that rather than ride just forty-three miles into Williston on U.S. 2, we decided to take a side trip to see Fort Union Trading Post, a National Historic Site depicting what the American Fur Company was like in the mid-nineteenth century. The fifteen-mile route down to the fort, located on the Upper Missouri River, was hilly—some long ups but mostly long downs—and free of traffic. We should have thought about the fact that it was mostly down, but we were loving the easy pedaling. Several times we flew along at thirty miles per hour or more and realized we were coasting downhill at the speed that Lance Armstrong averaged on his last few days of the Tour de France. Go Lance!

At the fort, guides in period costumes reenacted a typical transaction as they sat on buffalo hides in the trading post. We learned that wampum consisted of beads imported from Italy and England and that the Crow, Assiniboine, and Sioux, among others, had traded at Fort Union. We inspected other wares that were popular at the time—tin cups, buttons, and woven scarves.

We lunched on peanut butter and crackers sitting on the porch of the Bourgeois House at the center of the fort, conversing with a middle-aged couple vacationing on their Harley. The woman was a fourth-grade schoolteacher and her husband was a United Airlines pilot. They too had adventurous spirits, even though their mode of transportation was quite a bit louder and a whole lot faster than ours. They told us that each of their four grown children also rode Hogs.

On our way back to U.S. 2 we paid for the morning's enjoyable downhills. We had to pedal a series of fairly steep uphills, each reaching farther and farther up, and each revealing three more long hills to climb. It seemed as though the sets of three would never end. We both felt strong, though, and it was not too hot, so we took our time, and by 5 p.m. we had made it to Williston, where we found a motel. A coin laundry right across the street made me think we were living right. Our odometers showed we had pedaled close to 1,200 miles since leaving the Oregon coast. We had left the hot, dry terrain behind and were already seeing green fields, even on the far western end of North Dakota. We had entered the central time zone, which made us feel closer to our homes in the Midwest.

Day 28 — *Sunday, July 27* — *Rest day*

We must have been more tired than we thought because we set sleep records on the first of our two nights in Williston. I clocked nine hours and Alice snoozed on for a total of ten before we rose and moseyed into the coffee shop for a leisurely Sunday morning brunch. Then I headed for the free Internet service in the lobby, a perk that moved that motel way up in our accommodations ratings. The unbelievable price of forty-two dollars added to El Rancho's charms, and our room was one of the roomiest yet—which meant that we didn't have to rearrange all the furniture to get the bikes inside. The motel earned our five-spoke, two-wheels-up rating.

It was Sunday and, being a practicing Presbyterian, Alice decided to attend church while I busied myself with laundry, writing in my journal, and other odds and ends. By the time she had pedaled to the downtown area where most of the churches were, she told me later, it was 11 a.m. and the Presbyterian service had been going for a half hour. She moved on to the Methodist church, where she would be only fifteen minutes late. After locking her bike to a pole on the church's back lawn, she went around to the front, up the steps, and into an empty pew toward the back. She was dressed in her Sunday best—the navy cotton shorts and red tank top she had purchased at the thrift store in Great Falls. She set her handlebar bag and helmet next to her on the maroon velvet cushion, found her place in the hymnal, and joined the singing.

After the service the people in the pew behind her smiled but said nothing. On her way out she joined the line to exchange greetings with the minister. No one spoke to her as she stood in line. When her turn came, the minister shook her hand, smiled, and wished her good morning. Outside, at the back of the church near her bike, she saw a group of parishioners gathered around a table on which sat numerous boxes of Bing cherries that appeared to be for sale. Thinking she might buy a quart to surprise me, she asked how much they were. Everyone just stared at her, then looked at each other.

"Oh, you must have had to order them in advance," Alice guessed.

"Well, yes," a man answered hesitatingly.

"I see."

Alice turned and walked back to her bike. After she unlocked it she walked it across the lawn toward the street and was about to mount when the same man came running after her.

"Here, Miss," he said. "Would you like some cherries?" He offered her a handful.

"Well, sure, thank you," Alice responded. She found a plastic bag in her handlebar pack and dumped them in, wondering if the man had suddenly recalled the story from the Gospel of Matthew where Jesus urges his followers to "offer a cup of cold water." She went away perplexed at how reticent the parishioners had been—compared with other strangers—to engage her. It must have been the funny clothes, she suspected, probably a Sunday service no-no.

Day 29 Monday, July 28
Williston to Lewis and Clark State Park
25 miles

On Monday most of the rest of the world went back to work and so did we—although biking each day was more fun than work most of the time. Another good night's sleep and a second hearty breakfast at El Rancho Cafe put us in good shape.

It was a good thing we hadn't looked too closely at the topographical map of the day's ride because it was almost all uphill. Anyone who thinks North Dakota is flat is wrong. The western half definitely is not. We went up and down, up and down, over consecutive rolling hills, gaining altitude as we went—from about 1,800 feet to almost 2,500 by the end of the day. Alice's back and hip gave her some trouble in the morning but by afternoon her joints had loosened up. She thought she had probably become addicted to bicycling and that rest days were doing her more harm than good. I thought she probably just needed to stretch more.

Because Alice rode more slowly that day while I pedaled my usual pace, I felt free to stop at one of the many homemade roadside memorials to accident victims that appeared periodically. Before I could take a picture of one unusually constructed shrine, I just had to fix it. The metal angels mounted on the top wire of the fence were askew, so I refastened them securely and rearranged the plastic flowers that had fallen from their container in the center of the memorial. When I was satisfied, I snapped a couple of shots and returned down the hill to my bike. I hoped the owners would be pleasantly surprised when they came to visit the site commemorating their lost loved one. I became fascinated by these spontaneous expressions of love and loss and photographed many of them along our way.

The vast Lewis and Clark State Park lies on the north shore of Lake Sakakawea, which is formed by a dam in the Missouri River.

Waiting for friends and family

Yes, North Dakotans spell "Sacajawea" that way and pronounce it with the hard *k*. North Dakotans maintain that although she was born Shoshone, by the time Lewis and Clark engaged her husband's services as guide, Sakakawea had been adopted into the Hidatsa tribe. Their spelling reflects the theory that her name was probably a Hidatsa term meaning "bird woman"—from *sakaka* (bird) and *wea* (woman). Although most of us grew up pronouncing her name as Sack-a-juh-WEE-a, many modern anthropologists now believe that such pronunciation was incorrect, because the journals of Lewis and Clark most often spelled her name with the *g* rather than the *j*. No versions with the *k* spelling can be found in their journals. Nationally, the new standard pronunciation seems to be Sah-KAH-guh-WAY-ah (with a hard *c* and hard *g*). Not wanting to insult any North Dakotans, we adopted the Sah-ka-ka-WEE-a pronunciation when we were in their state.

Finding peace, living simply

Hardly anyone was at the park on a Monday, and we found it peaceful and pleasant. It was in the midnineties by the time we set up our tents near the lake, so we opted for a swim. The clean, sandy beach attracted us and the warm water soothed tight muscles. As we ventured farther out and found the deep channel of the Missouri, the temperature dropped and our swim suddenly became "refreshing."

I struck up a conversation with a photographer adjusting his tripod as he shot landscape photos from a camera with a huge lens. He was from Canada and was creating a picture book of prairie scenes and already had an editor, a publisher, and an advance. It wasn't until much later that I would recall the encounter and wonder whether our book would ever appear in print.

The only bad news of the day was that Alice's rear wheel developed a problem. One time when I happened to be behind her, I had noticed that it wobbled some and suggested she get her spokes tightened and have the wheel trued when she next visited a bike shop. That would be in Minot in a couple of days. After Alice unloaded her packs, however, she discovered that it was more than a simple truing issue. A piece of the flange of her rear hub had broken completely off, liberating two spokes in the process. No wonder the wheel was wobbling. A Campagnolo hub was supposedly the strongest available but she had had it for many years and had even reused it when she had new wheels built. She didn't know that hubs can fatigue.

Alice called the 800 number for Budget Bicycle Center in Madison, and the mechanic there sounded sympathetic.

"What should I do?" she asked him after explaining her dilemma.

"Just ride it until you can't ride it anymore."

Great. She wondered if he had any idea how remote an area she was in. But the mechanic went on to tell her that if she could make it to Minot, someone in the bike shop there could probably replace the wheel or build a new one. She should call ahead to find out. If they couldn't do it, he said, he would build one and overnight it to Minot. She went to bed wondering whether she would be able to ride the injured wheel all the way to Minot—110 more miles. If no more pieces of the flange broke off, maybe she could. In the meantime she would avoid big bumps, release the rear brakes so that the wobbling wheel wouldn't rub, and be careful going downhill because she knew that braking on only the front wheel could send her over the handlebars. We hoped that the roads between the state park and Minot would be smooth, the grades gentle, and that braking wouldn't be much called for. She figured she could always walk down a hill if necessary.

That night I wrote in my journal:

> This is such a beautiful spot and we had time to enjoy it because the ride was short today. The trip is much more pleasant now, and I am enjoying the simplicity of it. That seems a little silly to say because we are enjoying our electronic devices inordinately and we are always rushing to a bigger computer with Internet service if we are in a town with a library. But life is distilled into pretty simple events: We cook or order our food, eat, ride. We study maps, set up

camp, wash our clothes, write postcards, record the day in our journals, and go to bed. I love it. I'm going to make a real effort to simplify my life at home.

But things were to become a bit more complicated in the bicycle repair department.

Day 30 Tuesday, July 29
Lewis and Clark State Park to Ross
52 miles

Two thunderstorms passed over in the night but we stayed dry in our snug tents. As soon as it was time for stores to open, Alice called Minot, but the bike shop there did not have an already-built wheel in stock that would fit her bike—nor did they have the right parts to build one. Her bike and its wheels were old technology and the rear wheel required a freewheel for its gearing, not the more modern cassette, which most shops carried. So she called Madison.

Zack, her trusty mechanic, came to the phone. "Did you release the brakes?" he asked.

"Yup," she answered, "and I'm trying not to hit any bumps."

"Good. While you're riding that wheel as far as you can, I'll find out whether we have all the parts here to build you a new one. Call me later and I'll have the answer for you." He hadn't mentioned the day before that he might not have the right parts. Maybe he knew she had needed to sleep.

So off we went. We altered our route once again and headed up to U.S. 2 rather than taking Highway 1804 to New Town. It might be easier to get assistance if the wheel gave out on U.S. 2 than if we were on the smaller road. We also heard that the route we had planned to ride had just been oiled and graveled and that the smaller road would stretch for fifty miles with no services. This decision seemed a no-brainer. In situations like this we talked about the options and always arrived at a satisfying conclusion. If Alice felt strongly about which route to take, where to stay, or when to stop for lunch, for example, she let me know, and vice versa. We didn't ever seem to hold strong views on the opposite sides of issues, so the one who didn't care as much gave in. Sometimes we had to describe on a scale of one to ten just how strongly we felt, and that worked. It might have seemed too rational an approach for some people, but it worked for us, sometimes to our surprise.

The only problem on the ride to New Town was a strong headwind from the north—at twenty-five to thirty miles per hour. Before we turned into the worst of the wind we stopped at Lund's Landing Lodge for lunch. From there Alice called Zack again to get the verdict. Zack told her he thought he had the right parts but she would have to measure the distance between the rear dropouts, the slots in each side of the bike frame where the hub of the rear wheel attaches. This meant taking off all the gear and removing the wheel to allow the dropouts to spread naturally and then using a ruler to measure the empty space that was left. The answer had to be in millimeters, so we felt lucky that the owner of Lund's Landing Lodge had a metric ruler. We got the answer—130 millimeters—and reported the number to Zack.

"OK, I'll build the wheel and overnight it to Minot," Zack promised. We were to be in Minot for a few days, so that seemed like a good plan. After all, we had seen a UPS truck on the road every day so far.

Finally packed up again, we were able to ride ten miles paralleling Lake Sakakawea before turning due north, straight into the wind—and uphill. We soon learned that our "no-brainer" was a cruel misnomer. The hills seemed to stretch interminably, again in several series of three. We would grind up one huge hill with two more in view. When we finally reached the top of the third one, three more appeared in ever-ascending steps up and up and up. It reminded us of the ride out of Fort Union times five. Continuing to see killer hills was disconcerting, but if we had been able to see all the steps in this ladder of pain at one time, we might have been even more demoralized. The ten-mile stretch uphill and into the wind took more than two hours. At least it was a clear, sunny day, so we tried to concentrate on appreciating the colors—deep-green fields of corn underneath a canopy of brilliant blue sky dotted with Georgia O'Keeffe clouds. Our pep talks to each other about the light traffic and the absence of big bumps seemed to help.

Even though the rest of the fifty-two miles presented several long hills, it wasn't so bad because the headwind became a crosswind when we turned east. U.S. 2 was a fairly busy road for North Dakota and several miles had no shoulder, but everyone who passed us or came toward us waved in greeting.

So much time had gone into packing, phoning, unpacking, measuring, and repacking that we didn't reach our campground at Ross until 6 p.m. The greasy menu and smoky atmosphere at a nearby bar didn't strike either of us as appetizing, so we returned to our campsite and boiled water for another freeze-dried meal. We were in bed by 9:30.

Our campground was between the highway and a railroad track, and I feared we would be awakened by trucks and train whistles. Alice hoped she wouldn't lose sleep with wheel worries. Instead, neither of us heard a thing or suffered from any wheel nightmares and woke up nine hours later. Thank you, killer hills.

Day 31 — *Wednesday, July 30*
Ross to Minot
64 miles

In contrast to the day before, the ride from Ross to Minot went about as well as it could. A tailwind of twenty-five to thirty miles per

Sunflower fields forever

hour pushed us all day. What fun. Scenery was peacefully pastoral—green and blue fields of grain, frisky quarter horses running alongside us, temperatures in the seventies. Alice's wheel continued to wobble badly, but she seemed to be getting used to it and I didn't hear her complain.

We learned that the striking blue-colored grain covering rolling acres of land was flax. We also began to see huge sunflower fields with rows of brown-and-yellow smiling faces, and we couldn't resist stopping to take photos. We picked up some broken flowers to mount on the backs of our bikes for decoration. Life had become much scaled-down, and we found happiness in a silly thing like decorating our bikes.

For our second breakfast we visited Joyce's Cafe in Stanley. No wonder we weren't losing more weight. Rather than worry about

Berthold's allure

weight we ordered our usual favorites and turned our attention to the local customers. The people in the cafe were among the friendliest we had met anywhere. They explained how we could avoid a busy section of U.S. 2 by taking "Old 2," and they asked us all the usual questions, which we were happy to answer.

The miles flew by again, made easy by even more helpful tailwinds, and soon we were approaching the tiny dot on our map called Berthold. We were looking for a gas station where we could replenish our water supply when we saw a large, shabby billboard: Berthold—Next Three Exits.

"Look, Bobbi," Alice said, laughing. "Someone in that town has a sense of humor."

Not the usual roadside marker, the dilapidated sign showed nineteen different symbols—white in squares of blue—for available services, some of which were tricky to decipher. There were the usual icons for gas station, restaurant, and campground, but in one blue square we saw a weight lifter complete with upraised barbells and in another, a hammer and saw.

When we came to the knife symbol that looked like a machete, we were both stumped. "What does that stand for?" I wondered aloud. "Let's go check out this town. It's only a quarter of a mile off our route."

It turned out to be one of our best side trips ever.

A few cars graced the front of what appeared to be the most thriving establishment in town—the Tumbleweed Café, complete with boardwalk and hitching rail. We felt like Old West cowgirls as we hitched our mounts to posts and sauntered toward the entrance. Several men leaving the restaurant greeted us and stopped to chat. They were natives who had moved away and were returning to look into a business venture—something about turning tires into oil. When I told them that the sign had enticed us to come into town, one man laughed.

"My brother the mayor got a lot of flak for that sign," he said.

"Well," I responded, "tell him it worked on us."

Off they went, and we entered the Tumbleweed. Jean, the owner, a forty-something woman with very short dark hair and sporting a colorful vegetable print bib apron, welcomed us and directed us to the lunch buffet. The food was set out in charmingly mismatched bowls and plates resting on ice, plastic wrap partially covering each one. We could build our own sandwiches and have several fabulous salads—spinach with strawberries, broccoli with nuts and berries, and red coleslaw. It was as delicious as some church potlucks and better than most. The price was right at five dollars, beverage included.

I admired Jean's ultrashort haircut and, knowing that Alice wanted one soon, asked her where she got it. Jean said she went "all the way to Minot," twenty-two miles east. Alice explained that we would be resting in Minot for a few days because her husband was scheduled to visit. Without hesitating, Jean picked up the phone and dialed her hairdresser, who apparently told Jean she was pretty tightly booked because we heard Jean pleading with her to make room for Alice.

"Here, talk to Alice," she said into the phone as she handed it to Alice. Before Alice knew it she had a haircut appointment for 7:15 the next morning.

The next two hours passed quickly as Jean and her business partner, Cher, who was also her baker, told us their stories and asked to hear ours. Jean's parents, who lived in Minot, had come for lunch, as had her boyfriend and a number of other local patrons. Everyone in the cafe was immediately friendly and the atmosphere became party-like. Jokes flew across the room in several directions between patrons. Leo and Charlotte, Jean's parents, had much wisdom to share also—about Minot, about North Dakota, about how to get around in that part of the country, and what to see. Leo and everyone else in the Tumbleweed Café said that we mustn't miss the Scandinavian Heritage Center in Minot. Judging by the number of times we had heard "uff da" in the last couple of days, we were beginning to appreciate the pride people took in their ethnic heritage.

Before they left, Leo and Charlotte gave us their number and told us to call them if we needed anything anywhere in North Dakota. After they were gone, I remarked to Jean on how much fun they were. Jean said, "Well, Dad likes a good joke. He gets it from his father. I remember an off-color story Grandpa liked to tell. He really hated one of his neighbors and didn't stop with his usual blustering. To indicate the level of animosity he felt for this particular man, he used to say, 'I wouldn't piss up his asshole if his heart was on fire!'"

Well, we had never heard that one and as we burst into laughter we realized that we would not forget it any time soon. On our way out, as we went to pay, Jean said, "Oh, no, lunch is on us."

"So, what's your favorite charity?" I asked her.

"Oh, I don't know. Prob'ly me," she said, laughing. We each left a few bills under our plates for her to find later. By the time we finally parted—with packages of Cher's peach pie wrapped to go—we had heard more than a few North Dakota jokes and also some lurid stories about Berthold as the Peyton Place of the northern plains. They included reports of who had wrecked whose marriages and what a problem a certain woman was in the community. We even saw a photo of her. We were sure that she would never dare set foot in the Tumbleweed Café. We hoped that we, however, would be back someday to visit with the two spirited, hardworking women.

As we rode toward Minot we agreed with the cyclists we had met as we were leaving Montana: North Dakotans were warm-hearted, friendly people. They had fed us, amused us with good-natured ribbing and jokes, found us a hairdresser, and arranged our next night's accommodations, all in the space of a few hours. Alice was even sure that if her wheel gave out completely she would be able to get help if she needed it.

The twenty miles into Minot seemed quick. By the time we settled into our room at the Comfort Inn, where Jean's boyfriend had reserved a room for us by phone, we realized that the hills and mountains of the West were behind us and we were one-third of the way through our adventure. We really were making progress, even with a bum wheel.

Days 32 to 34 — *Thursday, July 31, to Saturday, August 2* — *Rest days*

"Why not Minot?" people asked whenever we mentioned the city of 35,000 in the middle of North Dakota. The well-used slogan had apparently begun as a way to prompt visitors to pronounce the name the way the locals wanted it pronounced. We would later meet some French Canadians who—predictably—said they had been through "Minn-OH," so perhaps the corny slogan was a useful pronunciation guide.

Minot began as a railroad town beside the Souris River in the late nineteenth century and had sprung up so quickly someone had labeled it Magic City, and the nickname stuck. Railroad tracks still crisscrossed the city, and because over- and underpasses occurred willy-nilly, navigating by bicycle was not easy. Streets and avenues were numbered, streets going north and south, avenues east and west, but none of them went very far in any direction without being interrupted by the river or a railroad track—or two or three—some of them at dangerous angles that could easily catch a tire and cause a spill. Several times, after false starts, I wished we could beam ourselves magically to our destination.

After Alice's ten-minute razor haircut early in the morning, we pedaled to the library to read our e-mail and Web site guest book. From there we separated—a rare event—to check in to our respective homes away from home—the Best Western for me and the Dakotah Rose B&B for Alice and Booth, who had recovered just enough to get on a plane. Alice pedaled on to pick up a rental car and meet Booth at the Minot International Airport, where he eventually emerged from its one and only passenger gate. She told me later that as she eagerly embraced him he pulled back quickly. Alas, his incisions had not healed. And she noticed that his shirt was hanging loosely—not tucked in as he usually wore it. Oh, dear.

While Alice was with Booth the rest of that day and the next, I became acquainted with Minot and some of its citizens. I enjoyed a massage, got a facial for the first time in my life, visited the library twice, and saw *Bruce Almighty* for free with a coupon I picked up at the Scandinavian Heritage Center. I spent only about ten minutes there and saw all the exhibits—primarily large wooden structures representing various aspects of Scandinavian life. Among the exhibits were a huge horse, a scaled-down church, and a few other icons. I wasn't in a touristy mood so I didn't linger.

I confessed to Alice later that during our time in Minot I watched a lot of cable TV and ate too many cookies and way too much chocolate. While I was visiting the chocolate shop, the owner of the music store next door saw my bike leaning against the window, noticed its unusual frame with the beam supporting my saddle, and went looking for me. He virtually accosted me as I was leaving the chocolate shop.

"He's a bit simple, but harmless," joked the chocolate lady, so I followed him into his shop, where he wanted to show me his ultra-high-tech mountain bike. Very light, suspension, silver—impressive. He wanted me to listen to his life-sized Alice Cooper doll and watch the video of Alice he had recorded at the state fair the previous week. I listened to the doll but passed on the tape. His buddy came by and insisted on showing me his high-tech mountain bike also. They chatted about cycling for a few more minutes before I finally escaped.

We gave UPS until the end of the day on Friday, but no bike wheel arrived for Alice. On Saturday morning Booth and Alice took her bike to the only shop in Minot, hoping they might be able to rig up something—anything. No luck. The mechanic took one look at her 1982 frame and said, "Nope, we don't carry wheels for antiques. You should just repaint that thing, hang it on the wall as an art object, and get yourself a new bike." Alice was livid.

"I can't believe he said that about my wonderful Black Beauty" became her mantra, which I heard at odd moments for weeks afterward.

In the afternoon we set the wheel dilemma aside and turned ourselves into more conventional tourists. With Booth we drove in the rental car south to Fort Mandan, where Lewis and Clark had spent the winter of 1804–5 and where a new interpretive center had just been built. We would soon be leaving the Lewis and Clark route and heading straight east, so we were glad to have the car for that day in order to take in Fort Mandan. From the car windows, we remarked on how fast the prairie scenery sped by. We weren't used to moving at seventy miles per hour.

After Booth and Alice retired to the B&B that evening, I attended an evening outdoor concert featuring five local middle-aged women harmonizing 1960s rock-and-roll songs. I enjoyed watching the hometown crowd playing and relaxing in the park almost as much as the music itself.

Day 35 — ***Sunday, August 3***
Minot to Drake
60 miles

Alice put her bike in the rental car for the drive to the airport. She was overjoyed that Booth had made it to Minot, especially considering that he had not healed as well as he should have. When he reached home he would have to seek some resolution to his continuing abdominal discomfort. Alice shared how she had reluctantly left him at the departure gate, kissed him, and gingerly hugged him good-bye without coming near his belly. As she pedaled back down the hill toward my motel she had to blink away tears in order to dodge the potholes.

Back at my motel, we turned to the job of trying to true her wobbly wheel. With two spokes gone from a thirty-six-spoke wheel, Alice figured she could manage as long as no more of the flange broke off. As we bent over the wheel another cyclist happened to see us and stopped to offer his expertise. With his help and with copious notes from my long telephone conversation with Bob the day before, we succeeded in straightening the wheel somewhat. It wasn't like new, but it might get her to Fargo. We couldn't wait in Minot for the new wheel to arrive, so she would have to arrange somehow for UPS to redirect the shipment to Fargo.

Having learned in Berthold that U.S. 2 was under construction east of Minot, we once again altered our route and headed southeast on U.S. 52. Even though this new route would have more traffic, we would get to Fargo a day ahead of schedule, and that would help us later on. We had realized back in Idaho that we had miscalculated the mileage when we originally made up the route across Wisconsin, so we needed to add days to our Wisconsin schedule rather than ride eighty or ninety miles each day. In North Dakota, however, we had different reasons for wanting to ride shorter days. In Idaho we had primarily been considering our physical capabilities. By the time we reached North Dakota our stamina was no longer an issue, but we had other reasons: (1) we didn't like to get up before 6:30; (2) we did like to linger in local cafes over leisurely breakfasts and lunches; and (3) we were moving east in the central time zone, so it was getting dark by 9. Days of more than seventy miles made it too hard to enjoy the ride and still have time to chat with people at our rest stops. That was not to say we wouldn't do long days again, but it wouldn't be our first choice. Simpler and simpler—that was how we wanted things most.

Drake was our destination that day—sixty miles—partly because we got a late start but also because we heard that participants in CANDISC, a local ride for 400 people, were going to stay there that night. CANDISC stands for Cycling around North Dakota in Sakakawea Country.

On our way to Drake, population 300, we stopped for lunch in Velva, a town of 1,000 that proudly proclaimed itself as the hometown of Eric Sevareid, the late CBS news commentator. We ate lunch at the Lariat Lounge, Velva's only restaurant, and met three lovely women: Helga, a patron who farmed nearby, and Glenda and

Lorraine, who worked at the restaurant. In response to our questions about sunflowers, Helga told us that the huge flowers always face east. Contrary to what we had thought, their "faces" do not follow the sun, except when they are very young and presumably more nimble. All three of the women took great interest in our trip, and we had a lively exchange.

Arriving in Drake via a route that was different from CANDISC's, we created a bit of a stir with our fully loaded bikes amid 400 riders on empty bikes. Unaware that we were not part of their group, some people asked why we were carrying all our own gear. One person shouted after us: "There's a truck for that stuff, you know!" So we explained.

A friendly cycling couple from northern North Dakota bought us root beers and invited us to camp near them on the lawn of Saint Margaret Mary Catholic Church. Others came to inspect our little bitty tents and showed interest in our other equipment as well. Because these riders already knew about long-distance riding, the conversation centered more on the technical and equipment aspects of touring: gear ratios, models of derailleurs, tire brands, and pump technology. Although we never tired of responding to the regular queries, we enjoyed fielding the more specialized questions that came from experienced cyclists.

It appeared that every single person in Drake and the surrounding community was volunteering in one capacity or another for the event. We were entertained during dinner in the school gymnasium by a high school clarinetist, some vocalists, and a few performers attempting standup comedy. The volunteers not on duty for that particular meal ate with the cyclists. We made friends immediately with Sarah, an off-duty volunteer, who offered us her home in case the showers in the school were too cold by the time we got to them. When she learned that Alice needed to call home to check on her husband, she offered her phone, too. More North Dakotan hospitality.

Day 36 *Monday, August 4*
Drake to New Rockford
67 miles

By the time we woke at 6:30, two-thirds of the 400 riders were already packed up and on the road. We were among the last to leave, but we took the opportunity to eat pancakes, eggs, and ham, courtesy of the local Knights of Columbus. Our friend Sarah from the night before was there again, having drawn breakfast duty. We enjoyed socializing with her and her husband and found ourselves staying longer than we had intended. It was 8:40 when we left town. Early departures were still not our forte.

Fairly strong winds were coming out of the southeast as we headed in exactly that direction, and they slowed us to eleven miles per hour. We didn't mind the cloud cover and cool temperatures. The CANDISC riders went off in another direction, and when they disappeared we reflected on their event. People had come from all around the United States to ride together in North Dakota, and we could understand why. Roads were smooth with good shoulders and little traffic, terrain was gentle but not boring, and the locals were big hearted.

As soon as we had good cell phone reception, Alice stopped to call UPS to figure out where her wheel had gone astray. After a number of complicated conversations in which Alice explained that she would no longer be in Minot when the package arrived, she was given a reason for the delay: someone at UPS in Madison had accidentally put the package in the barrel marked Ground rather than Air. This meant that when it was time for us to leave Minot, the truck carrying the wheel had been somewhere in Minnesota. Worse yet, the package was no longer just late—it needed to be redirected. The phone representative said she would take care of it, so Alice gave her an address for a bike shop in Fargo that she had looked up earlier, hoping it would get there by the time we did.

Twenty-five miles from Drake, in the gravel driveway of a Cenex gas station in Harvey, we met Kay and Frank, an older couple driving a shiny Model A Ford—Frank's hobby car. When we admired the car, they began asking us about our vehicles. Then they told us that we absolutely had to have a hamburger in the Cenex station's cafe.

"Best burger around and only ninety-nine cents," Frank exclaimed. "Why don't you sit with us?"

Frank farmed nearby with his sons, and he also owned the Artos Motel down the road, which his daughter ran. "Look at these hands," he said with pride. "Dirty from good hard work—and the tractor's steering wheel." He didn't see any need to wash them before lunch.

Frank and Kay took turns explaining to us that they were both widowed and had met in Yuma, Arizona, where they each happened to be on vacation. Kay, with her wavy white hair and looking trim in her red T-shirt and jeans, had retired as head housekeeper at a nursing home near Minneapolis.

"Frank called me up back home in Minnesota and asked me to help him clean up his motel. He knew that I just love to clean . . . so here I am," she said, giggling as she snuggled up to Frank.

She also shared her love of adventure and was highly approving of our having retired so that we could explore the country by bicycle. Although most people seemed to enjoy the stories we told them and the answers we provided to their many questions, they often expressed reservations about our trip and concern for our safety. Kay and Frank, on the other hand, were nothing but positive and encouraging.

Our next stop was Dakota Seasonings, just down the road from the Cenex station. A woman in Minot had told us we shouldn't miss it, but Frank had said it wasn't much. At first we agreed with Frank: located in a corrugated metal box of a warehouse with an unappealing facade, the place was not exactly welcoming. But we leaned our bikes against the building, walked in, and discovered a small world of gourmet foods. We saw several women putting together all sorts of mixes for scones, dips, and soups. It turns out that Dakota Seasonings is a thriving mail order business with a small retail shop. We bought several packets of soup and arranged to mail them home. That was our kind of shopping. The little gem of a business proved once again that we had to take what some people told us with a bit of skepticism. If we had listened to those who lived right down the road from Dakota Seasonings, we wouldn't have stopped there and would have missed out.

After fifteen more miles of fighting the wind, we arrived in Fessenden and made our last water, Gatorade, and ice-cream stop of the day at yet another Cenex station. More phone calls were needed to see how the wheel was faring on its trip, and Alice learned that it finally had been redirected to Fargo, where she could supposedly pick it up in a few days. The wobble continued, less troublesome since our effort to tighten and loosen a few other spokes. No more pieces of the flange had broken off, so we hoped it would hold up.

A group of local farmers was having afternoon coffee in one of the cafe booths at the Cenex station. Because they had kindly moved to allow Alice the only booth where there was a phone connection, they had eavesdropping rights. When Alice hung up they started asking questions.

"How far did you come today?"

"Where did you start this trip?"

"Where're you going?"

"How many miles a day do you do?"

It was about to rain, and we were eyeing the sky outside when one of them asked with a devilish grin on his face, "Suppose I was headin' to New Rockport? If I stopped and offered you a ride, would you take it?"

I smiled and said, "It would be tempting."

He grinned widely. One of the men who hadn't said much spoke up teasingly, "Better watch out for him. He's still got fire in the furnace."

This elicited guffaws all around, and as I picked up my things I said, winking to them, "C'mon, Alice, we had better get going!"

Alice looked at the grinning farmers. "You know, we're highly trained in the martial arts!" And we hightailed it out the door, amid general laughter, just as it began to rain.

The wind eased as we headed straight east, and the rain picked up. It wasn't pouring, but because the temperature had dropped, we were not exactly enjoying ourselves. We rode for twenty-seven more miles over flat terrain, the rain stopping and starting periodically. Fields of nearly ripened grain and pastures with horses lined the highway. In one field we saw our first herd of bison, which we stopped to photograph despite the animals' apparent uneasiness when we stood near their fence. The rain had let up just long enough to snap a picture, but darker clouds were moving in our direction.

The Bison Lodge on the edge of New Rockford seemed an appropriate name for the first motel we came to, and we were grateful to reach it. Just as we pulled our bikes under the eaves of the motel's roof, thunder roared, lightning flashed, black clouds burst, and a deluge ensued.

A man standing in the open door of the room next to ours watched us maneuvering our bikes into the room.

"What do you do if you blow a tire?" he shouted over the sound of the pouring rain.

"We fix it!" I replied cheerfully.

"You mean you got the stuff for fixin' things?" he continued.

"Yup," Alice chimed in. "We can also fix a broken chain or replace a cable."

He shook his head in disbelief, began to walk away, and then turned back to Alice, reaching into his pocket.

"Here," he said, holding out his keys, "why don't you take my truck and go find a restaurant in town? There's nothing decent around here." Wanting just to be dry and warm, Alice declined his kind offer, thanked him politely anyway, and disappeared into our room, where I was already shedding cold, wet clothes.

After cleaning up, we walked to the only place we could find nearby for supper—a place the locals referred to as the Dairy Queen but which was clearly a substandard eatery. The words "Dairy Queen" on the sign had been covered over and the sign repainted. Once we saw the menu and ordered a few items, we realized why it was probably the "former" Dairy Queen. The high school kids behind the counter and at the grill were sullen and lethargic and acted as though they would rather be doing just about anything than slinging gray burgers, throwing brown lettuce into paper bowls, or even ringing up sales. They needed a crash course in both cooking and customer relations.

Wishing Alice had taken up our motel neighbor's offer of his truck, I began an earnest discussion about when to assert our independence and when not to.

"Look, Alice," I said, "people want to help us. They enjoy it, maybe even more than we do. We like being independent and self-sufficient, but there's something to be said for accepting people's kindnesses."

"You're right, I know you are," Alice responded.

And with that, we agreed to try to take people up on their offers of assistance whenever possible. We had accepted a couple of rides earlier and had even sought one ourselves. There would be times when we would have to make tough choices, but one of the benefits of our cycling lifestyle had been meeting people and learning from them, and we knew that accepting their help was a good way to do that.

Alice and I never really argued, but occasionally we attempted to persuade each other of our point of view, and what we found was that we always came up with an agreement that satisfied us both. Some people wondered whether we would be able to get along since we didn't know each other well and hadn't spent a lot of time together before we began this adventure, but as the weeks went on, we came to respect each other's competence and judgment.

Day 37 Tuesday, August 5
New Rockford to Cooperstown
65 miles

Tired from fighting the wind and rain the day before, we overslept. Waking up at 7:40 to another rainy day was terrible. Heavy rain would slow us down. How would we ever get to Cooperstown before dark? By 9:00, in less than the two hours it usually took us to get back on our bikes, we were packed up with every item in every bag wrapped in at least two layers of plastic. We headed to the local cafe in the center of town in search of breakfast.

New Rockford is the county seat, so it was a bit more alive than other towns we had been passing through, but we wondered about its future and, indeed, the future of all of North Dakota. Population was declining statewide, and buildings of all sorts—in villages and on farms—were in various stages of decay. The land was clearly productive, but consolidation over the last several decades was obviously taking its toll. Wheat was ripening, corn was tasseled and tall, and field after field of perky sunflowers bent their bright yellow faces eastward. Productivity may have been up, but we saw firsthand that people were leaving and family farms were disappearing. Farmhouse after farmhouse was boarded up, windmills had fallen down, outbuildings had collapsed.

The cafe was crowded with farmers that morning, however, perhaps because they couldn't continue harvesting in the rain.

Dave, a farmer of our generation, sat on a stool next to Alice at the counter. "My son rode his bike across the South," he told us, "so I think I get why you are doing this, even when it rains." Such an insightful man.

Alice asked Dave a question we had mused on for some distance: "How big does a farm have to be to stay solvent?"

"It isn't the acreage," he told us, "but how much debt it is carrying. The farms handed to the next generation with the least debt are the ones that succeed."

His own children, he told us, had all decided not to farm. One son was learning Korean while working for the U.S. Army, another son worked for the Army Corps of Engineers, and his daughter was studying occupational therapy in college. They had no interest in inheriting the day-to-day operations of their family's farm.

Reluctantly we gathered ourselves and went out into the rain. It wasn't a driving rain, and no lightning or thunder could be seen or heard, so it could have been worse. The "waterproof" socks that Alice had bought before the trip were a big flop, so she planned to return them when the trip was over. Too bad they had to take up space in the meantime.

After almost twenty miles we reached Carrington and downed steaming bowls of beef dumpling soup and cups of hot chocolate. Across the street from the restaurant we bought more water and Gatorade, because the next forty miles or so would have no towns with services.

Nine miles before Cooperstown we came to Glenfield. We had no idea whether Glenfield would have a store, so we were overjoyed to find a small grocery on the main street. Denise at the cash register was shy at first when she saw us walk in looking like drowned rodents, but she soon warmed up. She didn't have anything hot to sell, but she offered us the use of the microwave oven in the large room attached to the store, which turned out to be a part-time day care center, although no children were in evidence. Gratefully, we heated hot water and made ourselves cocoa from our own supplies. Then she offered us the use of her dryer in the back room. Alice wasn't as cold as I was, but I took advantage of the offer and managed to warm up considerably by drying my shirt and jacket. Thinking we would not encounter any cold rain until we were farther east, we had brought only lightweight, semiwaterproof jackets. Mine was leakier than Alice's, but neither of us was very comfortable. We looked forward to switching to our good raingear, which we had arranged to acquire in Wisconsin before we went through the rest of the Great Lakes states and the mountains of the East.

As we were warming up, an elderly customer walked in. She introduced herself as Ida and announced that she had driven seven miles to buy a candy bar. She then asked us the usual questions, but unlike others, she went a step further.

"I don't think it's a good idea to ride in this rain," she fretted. "Are you sure you'll be all right?"

Despite our reassurances, she continued to worry aloud. As we prepared to leave, she pressed a one-dollar bill into each of our hands. "I just want each of you to have this in case of emergency," she said. Knowing it would be rude to refuse it, we thanked her sincerely for her thoughtfulness and departed. I was proud of Alice for accepting Ida's largesse.

"I'll pray for the rain to stop," she called, sticking her head out the door as we rode off. We were pleasantly surprised when the rain stopped about fifteen minutes later. It felt good to shed the ineffective raingear and warm up with some late afternoon sun on our backs. Thank you, Ida.

A few miles later, Alice complained that my chain was squealing and suggested that it needed help. At the intersection of highways 1 and 200 we stopped to fish out our rags and lubricant. Three corners of the intersection were open farmland, but set far back from the fourth corner, where we leaned our bikes along a fence, was an old, ramshackle, faded-blue building with a flat roof. It appeared unoccupied. A shabby sign behind the fence labeled it Busy Acres.

Bent low over our bikes with rags and oil bottles in hand, we were startled when a deep male voice boomed from close behind us.

"A female!" he exclaimed.

"Yup," I answered, bobbing up to face the voice. "Two of 'em!"

We found ourselves chatting with an elderly, heavyset man named Bob, who was lodged in a Rascal, an electric scooter-type conveyance for disabled people. Bob was the owner of Busy Acres, which, he told us, had once been a thriving welding business.

"I was going to give the business to my son," he said, "but he died. And then I got sick."

He talked and talked, and offered up gossip about people who lived in the area, about upcoming roads we would be taking, and even about restaurants in Cooperstown.

"Cooperstown has two restaurants," he explained, "but stay away from the one at the Coachman Inn. It's expensive and not very good. The pizza place is the only decent one."

We were finally able to ease away, but it seemed to me that Bob must have been lonely and that he loved putt-putting out to the corner when bicyclists came by on their way to or from Cooperstown. It had to be rare for anyone to stop there, even though it was on one of Adventure Cycling's main cross-country routes. Apparently it was even rarer for passersby to be women of our age not traveling in a group, so I was pleased that we had been able to brighten a small chunk of Bob's afternoon.

We arrived in Cooperstown and, after checking into the Coachman Inn, showered and went to the coin laundry, where we washed everything. We patronized Bob's preferred restaurant, Pizza Extreme, which was part of a local chain, and reluctantly returned to our dreary motel for the night.

We agreed with Rascal Bob—the Coachman Inn was not our idea of a fine establishment either. Even though he had discussed only the restaurant, his judgment might also have applied to the tiny, dim rooms of the motel. We rated the size of a room by how much furniture had to be moved to accommodate our bikes. Never, never did we leave our bicycles outside overnight. This room required stacking furniture in a corner near the bathroom, which made it hard to maneuver, so we gave the inn our lowest rating so far—a half wheel. But at least the room was dry and reasonably quiet. Besides, by staying there we were able to get an earlier start than if we had camped. Ah, another reason not to camp.

Day 38 — *Wednesday, August 6*
Cooperstown to Fargo
96 miles

At the Coachman Inn cafe for breakfast, two of the sourest waitresses we had ever met provided the slowest and most minimal service imaginable. Despite their lethargy, we were proud of ourselves to be on the road by 8 a.m. for our long ride to Fargo. We hoped, perhaps a bit too optimistically, that it would be the last of our very long days.

Skies were clear and the wind blew from the north. We were heading east and south, so we hoped the wind would not change. Appropriately, our first town was Hope, twenty-five miles away. There, while stocking up on Gatorade at the grocery, we met Shelly, a local cyclist. Blonde and petite and wearing the requisite black bike shorts and colorful jersey for long-distance riding, she looked younger than thirty even though we later reasoned she must have been closer to forty-five. We left Hope with Shelly, who rode a sleek, lightweight Cannondale road bike. She lived in Colgate, the next community away, which consisted of a few houses and a grain elevator. Shelly's husband and father were engineers, in business together building grain elevators. When they had moved to North Dakota, her father and she had both taken up bicycling, so she rode a lot with him. Her only child, a son, went to North Dakota State University in Fargo, where he was studying engineering, following in his dad's and grandfather's footsteps.

We asked Shelly how she coped with living in such a small community. She explained that life there revolved around the Lutheran church, and that was the organization that kept everyone going. We talked more about her life as we rode along three abreast—Alice on one side, I on the other.

"Everyone knows everyone," Shelly said, "and the local joke is that if you accidentally dial the wrong number, you end up talking to the person for half an hour anyway."

"The people in North Dakota are so friendly," I commented. "Everyone waves or talks to us."

"That's because we're so lonely!" said Shelly with a laugh. Our half hour of riding with her before she turned off toward her home passed too quickly.

At Page, the next town, we devoured the best soup and sandwiches imaginable, and the peach pie and chocolate chip and oatmeal cookies were still warm from the oven. It was hard to know which to eat first. After such a filling lunch, we felt sleepy, but with fifty more miles to go we had to push on.

Roads were excellent on the eastern side of North Dakota, with little traffic and several sections of new pavement. Alice's wheel became more wobbly again, so the new pavement eased our worries a bit. A strong tailwind from the northwest enabled us to go twenty miles per hour in stretches. The only problem was the occasional approach of trucks from the other direction. The combination of wind and the type of load on the huge farm trucks resulted in sprays of fine gravel, so stinging that we had to close our eyes for several seconds each time we met one.

In the course of watching for UPS trucks and imagining they were carrying Alice's wheel, we realized that we had seen three particular commercial vehicles almost every day of our trip—UPS, FedEx, and Schwan's ice-cream trucks. It became a game to spot them, and we joked that if we had any money left after the trip, we should invest it in these companies because they seemed to be doing a good business everywhere.

On our last eastward stretch of the day, about three and a half miles west of Argusville, we came upon a farmhouse with a crowd of people in the yard. Squealing children were jumping in an inflated "bouncy house." Others were playing tag. Adults were lounging in lawn chairs and chatting. I heard someone yell, "Want a drink?"

Without hesitating, I headed into the driveway, calling back to Alice, "We're going in. They invited us for a drink!"

"What?" cried Alice. "Are you sure?"

"Yup. Come on."

Alice followed reluctantly because she thought I must have heard wrong. We found ourselves in the midst of a three-generation family reunion. Cam and Marian, their four grown children, and thirteen grandchildren had gathered from as far away as Billings, Montana, and Toronto, Ontario, for the weekend.

They offered us cold drinks, and we took them up on some sparkling lemon water. After learning our route, Marian exclaimed to one grandson, "Mitchell, do you realize these ladies are Grandma's age? Can you imagine them riding their bicycles all the way across the United States?" Mitchell shook his head.

The family was so warm toward us that we almost felt like staying for the rest of the day. Several of the grandchildren, especially cousins Victoria and Mitchell, both ten, asked loads of questions about the bikes and our trip. They gave each of us a mini–New Testament for our travels. About a half hour later, we were on the road again, eager to reach Fargo and rendezvous with our cycling friend Deb from Wisconsin.

Finding our way through Fargo, which seemed to be enjoying rapid growth, was not easy and not unlike our memory of Minot. Railroads and rivers, as well as two interstate highways, interrupted the grid of numbered streets and avenues, making it hard to find our way on streets that were safe for cycling. We finally succeeded and were glad to find Deb at the prearranged motel.

Deb had cycled with us on several week-long trips in previous summers, and she had offered to drive along with us for a few days, carrying some of our gear in her car. After several minutes of reunion joy, we unloaded our panniers, showered, got in her car, and headed for dinner. We arrived at the restaurant just before it closed and indulged in their "bottomless bowl of soup" special.

Day 39 ***Thursday, August 7***
Rest day

Our rest day in Fargo was productive. Alice's wheel had finally arrived, and the mechanics at the local shop installed it without incident. She was not sad to give up her old wheel, even though she was proud of it for having gone so far with a broken flange and two useless spokes. Finished at the bike shop, we found the nearest massage therapist and indulged ourselves for the fourth time in five weeks.

Downtown Fargo was undergoing renewal, and we enjoyed visiting the shops, especially a consignment store where we tried on all sorts of clothes, marveling at how we had each gone down a whole size. We hadn't dropped that many pounds, but we had clearly re-distributed some. If only it could last when the trip ended. We each left with a couple of "new" outfits, one size smaller than usual.

Back at the motel we unloaded our bikes and put the packs in Deb's car. We were looking forward to light bikes for a few days while Deb drove ahead and played golf as we pedaled toward her.

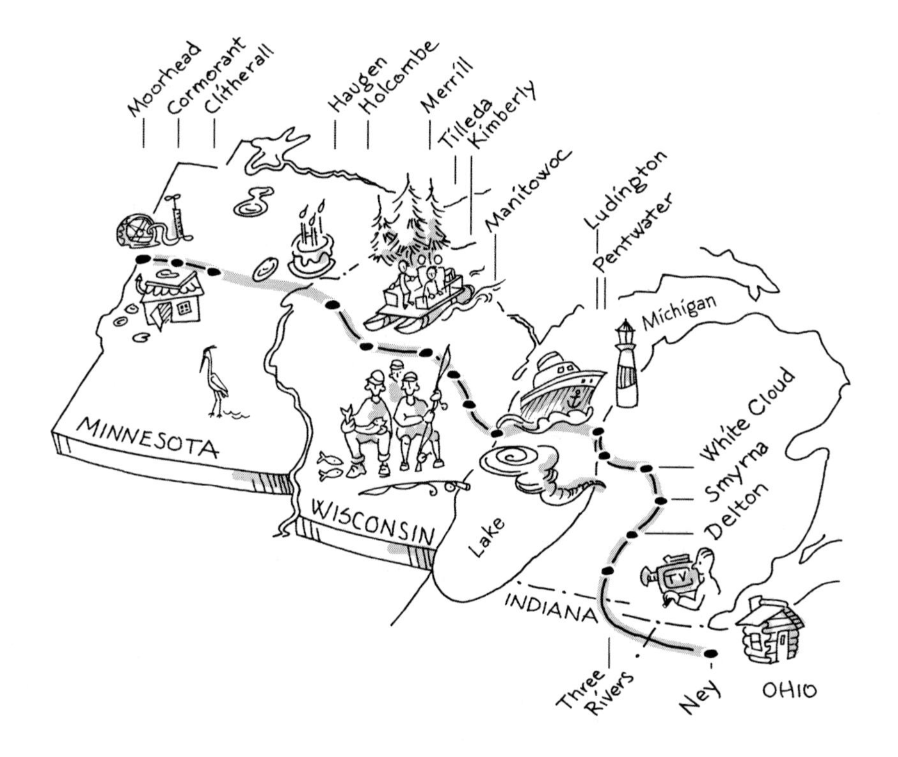

4

Through the Upper Midwest

Minnesota, Wisconsin, Michigan, and Indiana

The scorching, arid West seemed long ago and far away. Because our route called for us to angle across Minnesota, we anticipated seeing some of the 10,000 lakes advertised on the state's license plates. We thought we might even swim in one or two of them, but our self-proclaimed ability to deal with the unexpected would be tested in the next few days.

Day 40 Friday, August 8
Fargo to Cormorant, Minnesota
30 miles

We woke up ready to head over the border into Minnesota, but Deb surprised us. She reluctantly informed us that she needed medical attention. She planned to visit a clinic in Fargo to find relief for a severe case of anemia. So we retrieved our gear from her trunk, repacked our bikes from front to back, arranged to stay in touch via cell phone, and rode off, fully loaded once again. Oh, well. We were used to the way the bikes handled, and although we found a strange sort of comfort in having everything we needed within easy reach, the change of plans was a bit disappointing. We had looked forward to riding lean and mean, but it was more important that Deb get the care she needed.

Winding our way through Fargo and across the Red River to Moorhead was difficult because of fairly heavy traffic and streets badly in need of repair. We stopped at the Welcome to Minnesota sign for our obligatory pictures, then continued until we spotted a sporting goods store. There we decided to look for long pants that might offer some protection in a cold rain.

We had adopted the habit of taking turns staying with the bikes when we couldn't keep them in sight, so first Alice tended them while I shopped, and then it was my turn. While I was inside, Alice reported later, a shaggy-haired drifter wandered by, offered his hand to Alice in greeting, and began questioning her.

"So, where're you headed?" he asked in a gravelly voice.

Alice replied, "To Maine."

"Yeah?" he replied. "Where'd you start?"

"Fargo this morning, but we began in Oregon."

"Oregon Oregon?" he asked.

"Yup."

He seemed impressed as he inspected the loaded bicycles, nodding and shaking his head in alternate motions.

"I had a bike once—when I had a day job," he said. "But I'm not so good at following orders. Don't work no more."

He poured out his troubled work history, every thirty seconds or so reaching out to shake Alice's gloved hand. Even though the glove's padding must have felt funny, he kept on shaking her hand as the conversation continued for almost fifteen minutes. Alice then took her turn in the store, and when she emerged, he watched as she stowed her purchases.

"Well, have a good trip. Be careful out there," he said as we pushed off.

"You too," Alice called back. "Take care."

We remarked to each other again that the men we thought of as way down on their luck always stressed the danger of being "out there" and made sure to caution us to be careful. I wondered what they may have seen in their on-the-road adventures. Many people had expressed concern about our safety on the road, and we knew they were concerned not only about traffic but about human threats as well. As we pedaled on, we discussed again the question of just how much danger was real and how much was perceived as a result of Hollywood suspense thrillers and sensational media reports. I was beginning to think that maybe there was far less danger than most people thought, and Alice agreed. All it would take was one crazed person to do us in, we knew, but the farther we went, the more we believed that the odds were mighty small.

U.S. 10 was one of the worst roads we had traveled. Traffic was exceedingly heavy because a rock concert was about to begin at Detroit Lakes, a popular nearby summer entertainment venue. The pavement was breaking up, the shoulder was littered with broken glass, a strong crosswind hampered our progress, and after about ten miles Alice had her first flat tire of the trip. She switched tubes, pumped up the new one, repacked, and in a half hour we were back on the potholed and debris-strewn asphalt.

The terrain and scenery had changed remarkably, from the sparsely populated northern plains west of Fargo to more closely spaced farms and resorts outside Moorhead. We were clearly no longer in North Dakota. Lakes appeared over every rise, and vacation homes lined the rolling hills. We wondered if people would treat us differently in this more populated area of the country.

Late in the afternoon Deb caught up to us, having been treated at the clinic, and we decided to take a bump from her because we had had such a late start and wanted to stay on schedule. No camping was available anywhere nearby, so we landed at a brand-spanking-new, log cabin–style motel called the Cormorant Inn. We immediately liked Bette, the manager, who cheerfully shared with us that she had stayed up till 4 a.m. getting new extensions and bleaching her thick, wavy hair. She didn't seem any less charming for lack of sleep. She patted her voluminous, blonde coif and arched her perfectly plucked eyebrows.

"What do you think? This is a new look for me. My daughter did it. She's a hairdresser, you know."

I assured Bette that her new "do" was striking.

"Well, I really want to have my own airbrush tanning studio. I'm helping my boyfriend out here with the new motel, but, eventually, I'll have the studio too."

We admired Bette's boyfriend's craftsmanship in the room with its rustic, hand-hewn bunk beds and beautiful tile work everywhere.

Because the dining room wasn't yet functional, we drove to a bar down the road to celebrate Deb's birthday with a big dinner.

Day 41 **Saturday, August 9**
Cormorant to Clitherall
51 miles

Hoping her medical problem was solved, Deb transported our gear, so for the first time we traveled lightly. What a difference! We were flying down the road. We could get used to this incredible lightness of being.

At Edwards we found Ye Olde Schoolhouse Bar and Grill. The driveway was empty, so we were a bit surprised to find it open, but once inside, we met the owner, a retired nurse named Gail. She and her husband had bought the bar about ten years before, and when he died she continued running the place on her own. As we drank our root beers, Gail told us she had been the director of a nursing home in another state.

"Many a night," she said, "I went home and cried because of the physical and mental abuse the patients were subjected to. It was awful. I called the state and we worked hard and brought that place back up to standards. I'm proud of that work," she told us.

Gail had met many bicyclists on this route, and she described the several times she had allowed them to camp in her yard. She remembered one young woman who was so lonely, tired, and dirty that Gail let her shower in her home and then fed her a good meal before the girl crawled into her tent in Gail's yard.

Perhaps it was our perceived vulnerability because of our mode of travel that moved people to approach us. Our pared-down, slow-rolling existence on bicycles allowed us to experience the qualities of generosity, friendliness, and strong work ethic in those, such as Gail, who lived along our path. Many times we remarked that if we had been doing this trip in a car, we would never have been allowed these glimpses into people's lives. We agreed, however corny it sounded, that we felt honored and uplifted to see such spirit.

Our maps did not show the town of Maine, Minnesota, probably because it consisted of only a few houses and a boarded-up general store. But it did have a sign, and we took pictures of ourselves by it, pretending we had reached our final destination. Alice joked about keeping the photo in reserve in case we didn't make it to the East Coast and using it to claim that we did. We found some welcome shade and a plot of cool grass, where we ate our picnic lunch. It was so relaxing—no bugs, just the right temperature. Such simple pleasure. A siesta would have made the stop perfect, but we didn't have the time if we were going to meet Deb at our planned destination.

We rode to the village of Battle Lake, near Clitherall, only to find no rooms and no camping places. Rows of small white tents filled fields on the edge of town. Vendors were selling everything from funnel cakes to crocheted doilies, and people had come from miles around to buy and sell. We met Deb, loaded our bikes onto her bike rack, and spent the next three hours driving around the area in frustration, looking for a place to stay. Was this our punishment for using a car?

A family-style resort, ten miles from the village and on the opposite end of Battle Lake, finally agreed to rent us a two-bedroom cabin for one night. They usually required a minimum three-night stay, but it was late in the day, and travelers were not exactly lining up to stay there, so we suggested that renting a place to us for one night would be preferable to not renting it at all. After I volunteered to change the sheets in the morning, they relented.

The resort was its own village of weary, 1940s-type cabins, used primarily by families for their summer vacation. The floors of our ramshackle cabin tilted to one side, and the whole place smelled musty. The bathroom had none of the amenities that motel rooms have, including soap, and its spongy floor had the distinct feel of rotting wood beneath the worn linoleum. Packs of children ran screeching between cabins down to the lake, but we were so glad to have shelter that we did not complain about anything. We just brought our gear in, did our necessary chores, and, after a lackluster meal at a nearby supper club, the three of us went to bed.

Battle Lake ended our sixth week on the road. Week number seven threatened to begin with storms, so we went to sleep wondering if we'd be lucky enough to dodge them.

Days 42 to 45 Sunday, August 10, to Wednesday, August 13
Rest days

We had stripped our beds of their linens and were about ready to leave our pathetic cabin, looking forward to riding another day without our loads, when Deb emerged from her room with sad news.

"I'm sorry to say this, but I have to drive home to Madison while I can. I'm getting anemic again. I think I need to see my own doctor." One look at her was enough to confirm her self-diagnosis. Not only was she pale, but she had none of her usual energy and enthusiasm.

Without hesitation Alice announced, "I'll go too. I'll keep you company and I can check up on Booth." She had learned on the phone about his visit to the doctor after his trip to Minot. The doctor had examined him and announced on the spot that not only had his wife missed surgery number one, but she would also miss surgery number two. The doctor proceeded right there in her office to repair the herniated incision that had made Booth's trip to Minot so uncomfortable.

Mindful of our commitment to being infinitely flexible, I chirped, "Road trip, girls!" I could get in a few days of cycling around Madison while Deb recovered and Alice ministered to Booth and his ailing body and spirits. Some Madison friends were planning to travel north to ride with us for a few days, so we knew we could hitch a ride back to our route with them. We would miss about three days of riding in Minnesota but would get in most of Wisconsin.

By that point we had realized that we were not the kind of cross-country cyclists who had to pedal every linear inch of the route to feel that we had met our goal. We were stubborn and determined, we decided, but not rigid and competitive—well, not completely. Sure, Deb could have made it home on her own. Sure, I could have continued on my own if Alice went with Deb. Alice could have caught up when she got a ride back to northern Wisconsin with her Madison friends. But we were good friends, after all, and we were in this together, Deb included. All three of us saw this as another part of the adventure. We would make the road trip fun and accomplish several goals at once.

On our drive to Madison we passed through Minnesota's Twin Cities and close to my childhood home in Roseville, so my pals agreed to help me find the house that held many memories for me. After a great deal of circling around the suburb on streets that had not existed almost fifty years earlier, we found the house that I was sure had been mine. My family had moved when I finished third grade, but the house was distinctive and I really wanted to see the inside. Deb and Alice waited in the car while I went to the door and knocked. Eventually a man came to the door.

It took a bit longer than I thought it would to be invited in, but when I told him about the quarter embedded in the concrete under the tile in the front hallway, he realized I wasn't a con woman trying to case the place. The living room was exactly the same as I remembered it, and I relived a few nostalgic moments.

Back in the car, I told Deb and Alice, "It was fun to see the house, but everything looked so much smaller." We all had a good laugh.

Alice was especially glad we had taken the time to do this because she was planning to visit her childhood home when we passed through Michigan. She said it was only fair that I also got to "go home again." What a good friend.

We reached Madison late that night and dropped Alice at her house while I went on with Deb to stay with her. Deb got the medical attention she needed and began to grow stronger. Alice spent several days with Booth and saw him begin to heal. On Wednesday we drove north along with Madison friends Joyce, Shirley, and Terry, who had previously arranged to accompany us for a few days. Joyce would drive the support van and carry our gear. On our way back to our planned cycling route, we stopped at the famous Norske Nook in Osseo, where I sampled lefse for the first time. Restaurants throughout northern Wisconsin catered to their clientele of Scandinavian heritage by including this Nordic version of the tortilla on their menus. I had a hard time convincing my Wisconsin friends that people in Cincinnati wouldn't have any idea what lefse is.

Home that night was a KOA at Rice Lake, the first KOA we had patronized. It was also the site of our first campfire, compliments of Terry. It was a special treat to sit—in portable lounge chairs, no less—around the fire. How luxurious! We almost wished we could strap the chairs to our bikes.

Day 46 ***Thursday, August 14***
Haugen to Holcombe
65 miles

On Thursday morning we broke camp, packed our bikes, and headed to breakfast at Lona's Corner Cafe in Haugen. It was fun biking with friends but by that point the two of us were so used to carrying our own gear and knowing where everything was when we needed it that we decided not to put it in the van. Besides, we were afraid we might get used to the light bikes and then have trouble readjusting to the weight when our friends headed back to Madison in a couple of days.

Alice was tickled to be biking in Wisconsin, where she had lived longer than in Michigan, and I was the beneficiary of both her enthusiasm and the great road system. Wisconsin is famous for its 70,000 miles of paved secondary roads, a legacy of the early-twentieth-century effort to turn gravel into asphalt in order to speed fresh milk from farms to markets. Thanks to Wisconsin's dairy industry we had many options for getting from one place to another.

Traffic was light on most of the back roads we chose, and motorists were invariably considerate, but on our first day of pedaling in Wisconsin we did have an unpleasant incident. We were minding our own business, tooling along single file on a newly repaved road, when a motorcyclist suddenly zoomed up past Shirley, Alice, and Terry with only inches to spare and swerved toward me with a great roar. Adrenalin rushed and heart rates soared in all four of us as he passed, but he appeared and disappeared so fast that no one could react. Instead, we each spent a few moments imagining how close we had come to disaster. If I had wandered to the left at the moment he gunned toward me, his little game would not have been so much fun. That incident and the one in Montana when a truck driver purposely kicked up clouds of dust in our faces were the only times we had had to deal with true jerks. Friendly acts were far more common.

Nerves finally calmed, we continued riding south and east against a moderate headwind—nothing serious, just annoying. Air temperature reached the upper eighties by midday, but the landscape was flat, and we pedaled easily on rested legs. Shirley, who rides like a twenty-something, was celebrating her forty-fifth birthday, so we sang to her several times along the way.

In a climate where roads repeatedly freeze and thaw, summer equals construction and repair season. We came to a significant stretch of road that was torn up in the early stages of preparation for new asphalt. The washboard surface was strewn with large, sharp stones. It looked unrideable with our narrow tires and heavy loads. After a few minutes of discussion among the four of us about how to handle it, Joyce came upon us in the van. Because the van could take only two bikes at a time, Shirley and Terry loaded their bikes first and hopped in. We waited on the side of the hot, dusty road for the van to return.

After about ten seconds, we looked at each other and laughed. "What are we waiting for?" I asked. "We haven't ridden this far to wimp out now. We can ride this stuff."

Alice looked hard at the rocky mess.

We usually agreed on what to do in any given situation—when to eat, where to stay, how to solve some problem or other—and to keep to our policy of going along when one person felt strongly and the other didn't. Before the trip began, friends and family members wondered how we would get along, and sometimes I think they were disappointed not to hear about any huge fights or intense drama regarding our relationship. Some trips, we knew, ended because the companions couldn't stand to be with each other anymore. But that wasn't us.

"Look, Bobbi," Alice had said one day after apparently thinking about this issue. "I like to be in charge and so do you, but neither of us is a control freak." And we agreed that because we considered the other person competent it was easy to let go.

So Alice made up her mind. "OK, let's ride it." Off we went, bumpety-bumpety-bump on the terrible road. It was tough staying upright as we skidded and lurched along, but we felt we had covered too many miles to let a rough road surface stop us for very long. The ride was unpleasant, but it was less than a mile, and by the end of the stretch we realized that both our bike-handling skills and our confidence levels had grown.

Shirley's parents live on Lake Holcombe, a flowage made possible by a dam where the Chippewa and Flambeau rivers join. Jean and Lewie welcomed us warmly and treated us like celebrities. They gave us a long, leisurely ride on their pontoon boat and then a full-scale spaghetti dinner, followed by birthday cake and ice cream and more singing for Shirley.

Alice's cell phone rang. "It's Ted!" she exclaimed. Her son was calling from New Jersey to tell us that a huge power outage was affecting the whole East Coast. Millions of people were stranded on trains, in elevators, and, like Ted, in traffic jams. Power was out for several hours and caused innumerable problems, but in the North Woods of Wisconsin, such problems seemed far away. We hoped the outages wouldn't migrate in our direction, although the only electricity we were interested in was for refrigeration in the stores that sold us Gatorade. A narrow view, we knew, but once we found out that international terrorism wasn't involved in the blackout, we didn't think more about it. Ah, living simply had so many benefits.

Day 47 — ***Friday, August 15***
Holcombe to Merrill
78 miles

Shirley's parents set out a huge breakfast for us, so we felt well supplied for what we knew would be a long day. A last check of our tires revealed several metal shards in the treads just waiting to create punctures. Such shards are a common by-product of ruined truck tires, and bike tires pick them up easily. We tweezed out the tiny pieces, packed up our tools, and pedaled off, thanking our hosts as we waved good-bye. It was 8 a.m.—for us a good early start.

The wind shifted to the southwest as we flew along the rolling terrain. After denying ourselves light bikes the day before, we decided to go ahead and put everything in the van for just one day after all.

Joyce promised to stay close to us, so we figured we would be able to get to our supplies if we needed them. The route followed country roads though the Chequamegon-Nicolet National Forest (pronounced sha-WAH-muh-gun), and we avoided villages completely. Traffic was extremely light. We had food in our packs from a grocery visit in Chetek the day before, so all we had to do was look for shady spots whenever we needed a snack or lunch. We could never have too many picnics.

A highlight of traveling on rural roads everywhere is noting rural residents' creativity—in the color they paint their houses, the way they landscape, or the style they choose for disguising their mailboxes. Whether mailboxes doubled as swans, lighthouses, bicycles, or mythical creatures, they provided endless entertainment. One mailbox that drew our attention that day consisted of a lumberjack poised with his chain saw encircling the metal tube where letters could be deposited. As we stopped for a photograph to add to our collection of such folk art, we realized that was only the beginning of the display. Behind the mailbox was another exhibit, one that gave new meaning to the term "chain saw art." I don't mean bears chopped out of logs by outdoorsy artist-lumberjacks wielding chain saws, such as we had seen numerous times in yards and gardens. No, I mean the chain saws themselves. In one area of about fifty square feet, seven telephone poles thrust skyward, each about eight feet from one another, all in a row, with at least twenty chain saws inserted straight into each of the poles like toothpicks, handles on one side and blades sticking out the other. This unusual sight left me wondering how anyone could have worn out so many chain saws.

Hot and thirsty, we stopped at the P'town Inn. "P'town" is "Perkinstown" on the map, but we learned that no local person calls it that. The P'town Inn wasn't open for business at 10 a.m., but Dick, the proprietor, heard us rustling around on the porch and caught us peeping into the windows for signs of life. He let us in and offered us

Where have all the chain saws gone?

cold sodas. The air temperature was forecast to be ninety-four degrees that day, and the humidity was already making us uncomfortable. We had become used to dry heat, and it was taking a few days to acclimate to the mugginess of the Midwest. As we slurped our root beers, Dick told us proudly about the snowshoe race he started and built into one of the largest in the country. It was hard for me, used to southern Ohio, to imagine how much snow Wisconsin could get, but Dick assured me that they usually had plenty.

By late afternoon we arrived at the vacation cottage of our friends Bill and Dory, a few miles west of Merrill, where we planned to stay overnight. They had given us instructions for opening up, but when Alice started downstairs to turn up the water heater, she saw that the basement was flooded with about three inches of water. Bill was due to arrive a little later, but we were sticky and thirsty, so instead of waiting for him we decided to discuss our options over root beer floats in town. Our Madison friends were heading home, so we booked a motel room in Merrill and left poor Bill to handle his flooded basement. We felt a bit guilty, but by that point our trip had acquired a life of its own and we protected it when we needed to. That meant that we needed a good night's sleep to stay strong and keep going. We hoped Bill would understand.

Day 48 ***Saturday, August 16***
Merrill to Tilleda
68 miles

Back on fully loaded bikes, we left our motel and soon found ourselves in hills—mostly rolling hills, but more work than we had encountered in some time. One hill not far from Merrill was actually a killer. We plodded slowly up the steep monster and decided that we would never again take our gear off the bike for even one day—it was too hard getting used to it again. As we reached the crest of the mini-mountain, we passed two women who had just scaled it on foot. When they turned toward us, Alice called out to them, "Good for you for tackling this hill!"

One replied, "We were thinking the same thing about you!" Then, the other woman called after us the words that no experienced cyclist ever believes: "It's all downhill from here!" Actually, it was downhill for several miles, so we did enjoy a long coast. The wind, however, had shifted during the night and was coming out of the southeast, exactly the direction we were going. Back on flatter terrain, our average speed dropped to ten miles per hour, pretty standard for us with loaded bikes and a hindering breeze.

Alice was glad to be cycling in what had become her home state, and we both loved the route through central Wisconsin—past dairy farms, many working, some decaying. Small cheese factories dotted the landscape, and they also appeared in various states of prosperity. We understood how California with its megafarms and serious mechanization could overtake Wisconsin in production of milk and how it was threatening in cheese production also. But no matter how much cheese California produced, we couldn't imagine Angelinos becoming cheeseheads.

Several times we passed farms growing ginseng, one of Wisconsin's newest export crops. These farms were distinctive with their trellislike structures covered with special netting that allowed light to filter through. They were constructed to simulate the forests in China where ginseng grows in the wild. Now, we had learned, China was purchasing this cultivated crop from Wisconsin. Cheese from California, ginseng from Wisconsin—we were seeing the effects of an increasingly global economy firsthand from the seat of a bicycle. Our education continued.

All day we angled east and south, avoiding construction zones several times by taking town rather than county roads. The strategy worked well. The pavement was amazingly good all along our route, and again traffic was extremely light. By crossing the state on back roads we missed most villages. In fifty miles we reached Mattoon to learn that we were too early for the day's pig roast. A cashier at the grocery store told us that the road we were planning to take south to Bowler was under construction and the pavement had been completely removed. We figured out an alternate route that turned out to be quite pleasant. Once again, a good tip from a local resident.

At Bonnie's Bar and Grill in Bowler we met Bonnie herself, an energetic woman, and her teenage daughter. The restaurant in the bar was busy with customers, and the two women bustled about efficiently, joking with their guests while they took orders. They seemed to take turns cooking the food, serving it, and busing the tables. We saw no evidence of any other help yet we heard no complaining. They both worked hard, putting in long hours each day serving hearty meals. We downed huge burgers, thankful that we didn't have to check our cholesterol anytime soon.

The last leg of the day's route, from Bowler to Tilleda, followed curvy, shaded roads, the first shade we had ridden in since the Pacific Northwest. It was so unusual for trees to be arching over us that we stopped several times to take pictures. Pictures of shade? How boring. Only we would understand.

Several times we crossed the Embarrass River and wondered what kind of events had inspired that name. Later we learned that early French Canadian lumberjacks had labeled it Rivière Embarrase because of the difficulty of guiding logs down its tangled, driftwood-strewn course. At Tilleda we camped at an RV park on the banks of this curiously named waterway.

Half of the campsites in the park consisted of permanent summer "homes," some with decks, storage sheds, and lanterns ringing the small lots. The other half of the campground was saved for travelers. The toilets left much to be desired, but our site was grassy, level, and quiet—all that we needed. Many commercial campgrounds were so full of noisy, vacationing families that we sometimes found it hard to get a good night's sleep. Not so at Tilleda Falls Campground. What's more, we had electricity, so with a plastic bag slipped over our devices to ensure dryness, we were able to plug in all our electronics. It was nice to have technological equipment, but it was not always easy to keep the devices charged.

Our campsite neighbors—Donny, Billy, and Roger—seemed intrigued by our loaded bikes, and after a few questions and answers they invited us to share their campfire and a dinner of venison tenderloin and fresh trout. Although we had already eaten in Bowler, it was impossible to turn down their hospitality. They were there to fish, they told us—dad, son, and nephew—and had more food than they could eat.

"We caught a hundred and fifty fish today," Donny proudly proclaimed.

"Oh?" I questioned. "A hundred and fifty? That's a lot of fish."

"That's pretty impressive," Alice added.

"Well, we threw most of them back."

"Yeah," interjected Billy, "we're the catch-and-release kind of fishermen." He and Donny exchanged glances.

"We have a secret place not far from here that's always good. We've been fishing here for fifteen years," Billy told us. "We get together every year and come here. How long you been ridin' bikes?"

Sensing they wanted to change the subject, we answered their questions and with very little prodding told a few of our favorite road stories. We didn't know the local fish and game rules, so we just enjoyed exchanging notes on each other's lifestyles and shaking our heads about theirs as they must have about ours. Same country, different cultures.

At the risk of offending them, we declined the offer of beer with excuses of being too tired and went back to our site and bed. We drifted off to the sounds of campsite cleanup and crackling campfire, feeling lucky to have met and been entertained by the three avid sportsmen. To us they were part of another world, one that our journey by bicycle allowed us only to glimpse.

We were about to begin our eighth week, which meant that we were more than halfway. It was hard for us to believe that we had been on the road for so long. What had seemed strange and unorthodox in the beginning had now become a routine way of life. One day Alice surprised me by saying, "This is like a job. We get up and go to work and then we eat and go to bed only to get up the next day and do it again."

"I can't believe you said that!" I was puzzled. "This is better than any job. We get to be outside all day, we get to meet interesting people, we get to learn all about the land and the crops. And we see fantastic scenery. How is this like a job?"

"I just meant that it's what we do every day. It doesn't really feel like any job I've ever had, but in the morning I know I have a certain number of miles to ride. We have to find food and a place to stay, and at night we have to do our laundry and get ready for the next day. I guess it's just that, even though we've scaled down drastically, we aren't entirely footloose and fancy free. We still have responsibilities to fulfill in order to make it work."

"I can see that," I said. "It's pretty routine now, like a job would be, but we chose to do this. You still like it, don't you?"

And of course Alice did—she loved it and had fun every single day. We both did. It was just strange to keep on riding bikes day after day after day. We realized that we had ridden through six states and were on our seventh out of fifteen. We still knew that anything could happen to derail the rest of the trip, but we both felt sure that we could ride the whole country—that we were really doing what we had dreamed of for so long. It was a great feeling.

I decided we were far enough east to send the postcard I had promised some bike mechanics at a shop in Walla Walla. They had asked us to send a picture from a "faraway place." I thought

Wisconsin was far enough from Washington to qualify. Alice suggested I send them one from Maine later on, too, proof that the two "old gals" had made it.

We hoped for continued sunny skies, although we knew that much of the country needed rain. We were glad to have missed the power failures of the East, but we figured that other sorts of adventures awaited us. Not knowing who or what was around the curve or over the next hill was a large part of the fun and made us feel sometimes a tiny bit like Lewis and Clark must have felt. Many times we discussed this adventure aspect of our trip and wondered if we had become addicts of the open road, the simple life, and the unknowns around the bend.

Day 49 — Sunday, August 17
Tilleda to Kimberly
74 miles

After eating one of our increasingly rare camp breakfasts—good old instant oatmeal and hot chocolate—we cleaned up, packed, and left before our neighbors even stirred. In twenty miles we were ready for a second breakfast, and on the edge of Shawano (pronounced SHAW-no) we spotted a bare-chested, fit-looking man harvesting squash from his garden. We stopped to ask him where we might find the best restaurant for breakfast. He gave us directions, and, still standing astride our bikes at the side of the road, we answered his questions and asked some of our own. Tom was a forester with the state's Department of Natural Resources, and our conversation turned to fire—about how he fought them out west with a team in past summers and how we rode near and then skipped around them in Montana. Seeing him tending his garden in rural Wisconsin, we would never have guessed that he was an experienced forest fire fighter in the West. We realized how complicated people's lives often are and remarked again at how this trip allowed us to catch such varied snapshots of American ways of life in the most unpredictable settings.

In fact we often noted the different kinds of people we met during our trip. Old and young, employed or homeless, male or female, well-to-do or hard-scrabblers, they expressed interest in our exploits, which was fun for us. We always explained that we were living our dream, and we secretly hoped that they would somehow work on fulfilling their own.

The Home Plate, Tom's recommended restaurant, turned out to be full of Sunday after-church diners. Forgoing a table in the smoking area, we squeezed onto a couple of stools at the counter and chatted with the gentlemen on each side of us. Alice's neighbor was an elderly man eating his main meal, which he did every day after visiting his wife in the nearby nursing home.

He said, "I always take some home for my next day's lunch, since my wife isn't home." As he carefully compartmented his turkey and potatoes and gravy into the Styrofoam container, he continued his story. "Used to have a dairy farm, but with all the development, I couldn't afford to continue farming. Sold it and moved away."

His farm and a lot of others near his now comprised a densely populated suburb of Milwaukee. This was a trend we had noticed in state after state. We didn't need to view census data or study statistics to see that big business and development—and people leaving their farms—were changing the face of the countryside.

The man next to me was a long-haul truck driver who asked us the usual questions and then some. He seemed especially interested in hearing about the draft we felt when trucks like his passed us and how different the road looked from our perspective than from his high up in his cab. It may not be a big deal for him to run over a piece of glass or a stray six-inch bolt or a cooler lid in the road, I explained, but for us, one of those items flying off a vehicle or appearing in our path could mean the end of our trip. Our views of each other as a hazard were mutual, but I did not sense that he was muttering "those damn bikers" under his breath. On the contrary, he seemed genuinely interested in various aspects of cycling even though I got the strong feeling that he would never exchange his motorized wheels for our self-propelled ones.

We welcomed the chance to interact there in the restaurant rather than while trying to hold our two wheels steady behind the last of his eighteen on some narrow road. We showed him our maps and the route we were planning to take out of Shawano. He suggested a better one because of some construction, and we happily took it, pleased that our two worlds could intersect so congenially.

Maybe we were just glad to be in the Midwest, our home territory, but despite our scary incident with the motorcyclist farther north, we loved riding in the green Wisconsin landscape dotted with barns and silos. It was hot—though not as hot as in the West—and always humid. This was less dangerous but more uncomfortable than the arid heat of the West. As we pulled into Shiocton, we discussed the need for some sweet, hard ice cream, maybe black cherry or butter pecan. This was not exactly a novel idea, but rather one that occurred frequently—alternately with the wish for root beer floats and peach pie à la mode. We stopped to ask the first people we saw where we might find our hearts' desire. Linda and Gordy were working in the yard outside their home. They were marathon runners, they told us, and had just begun bicycling and wanted to do more. While we took turns answering Gordy's cycling questions, Linda went inside and brought out cold, bottled lemon water and some snack bars. How thoughtful!

As we were talking with them, a huge truck rumbled by, overflowing with basketball-sized cabbages. When we commented on it, Linda explained that cabbage was a big part of Shiocton's economy. In fact, the largest sauerkraut production facility in the world was just a few miles away. The truck rumbled past before we could capture the sight with our cameras, but I knew I would remember that pale green mountain of giant cabbages. Alice commented on what a scene bouncing and rolling cabbages would create if the latch on the truck's gate broke.

Much to our disappointment, the ice-cream shop Linda and Gordy directed us to was closed. A neatly printed note on the door said the parking lot was to be repaved that day. We saw no evidence of any paving being done—or even planned. Something had gone wrong.

In a snit, we speculated. "Maybe the paving crew just didn't show up," Alice suggested.

"Oh, I bet the ice-cream shop owners wanted a day off to go swimming," I grumped.

"No," Alice countered, "I think the sign makers made a mistake."

Damn it, we wanted ice-cream cones! Dejected, we headed to the convenience store across the street, where we bought a pint of deeply frozen chocolate chip cookie dough ice cream and two flimsy plastic spoons. By the time the ice cream softened up so that the spoons wouldn't break, I realized that it was almost as good as what I had fantasized about. My blood sugar levels restored, I felt less grumpy.

It was funny how snacks became so important that sometimes one or the other of us would admit to hallucinating about grilled cheese sandwiches or cold chocolate milkshakes. These visions would keep us going in the heat or hills as we pedaled lengthy stretches of highway, and if the particular treat we wanted wasn't available when we stopped for it, we would indulge in only a moment of regret before we decided on something else. Fortunately, we were usually so hungry or thirsty we were happy with anything short of dog food.

By midafternoon our handlebar thermometers registered halfway between eighty and ninety degrees, and we were piling up the miles, so we were glad to reach our friend Dennis's parents' home in Kimberly, where we had arranged to stay. Margie and Norbert let us take showers right away and then run a load of laundry. Having a clean bathroom, plentiful hot water, and an automatic washer seemed like heaven after all the places we had stayed that didn't even have hot water or sink stoppers. We realized that the labor-saving appliances of our previous existence had become luxuries. On the one hand, we could see how we took for granted our pre-ride standard of living. On the other hand, we realized now that we could live without those luxuries—at least for three months. Best of all, Margie served us a home-cooked, all-American meal—ham, mashed potatoes, and green beans with french-fried onions on top. A cherry-crumble dessert topped it all off. We went to bed early, satisfied and comfortable in clean jammies.

Day 50 ***Monday, August 18***
Kimberly to Manitowoc
56 miles

After thanking our hosts for their generous hospitality, we left Kimberly and the Fox River Valley and angled south and east on rural roads, continuing to use our own maps until we rejoined the Adventure Cycling route just west of Manitowoc. We could have stayed on completely rural roads the whole day, but to find food and water we dipped into Brillion and then Reedsville. In Brillion we found another one of the best cafes ever. Randy's Diner had homemade chicken dumpling soup, and we had a couple of great sandwiches on thick, homemade bread.

In Reedsville we stopped at the first bar we came to and guzzled the best-ever root beer—Baumeister, brewed locally. We had learned that stopping at small-town taverns was a good idea, whether or not we wanted real beer. With their peeling paint and dusty driveways, the buildings often looked dubious on the outside, but inside we usually found friendly people and some pretty good but greasy food. The Reedsville bar was no exception. In Reedsville the local bikers—motorcyclists, that is—showed a friendly interest in our adventure, offered advice about the route to Manitowoc, told us where to catch the ferry across Lake Michigan, and teased each other about which of them could give up their engines and do it our way. None of them, was the answer.

A few miles outside Manitowoc we encountered a nearly impassable road, one that our bar friends had not mentioned. Before the trip, we had wondered how many times we would have to walk, backtrack, or inconveniently alter our route because of construction, but it wasn't until we reached Wisconsin that we met our first freshly tarred country road. Walking in the grass on the shoulder and pushing our bikes up a steep hill in the oppressive humidity and heat was hard, sweaty work, but we soon realized that our luck hadn't run out: only a hundred yards separated us from the better road we were turning onto.

The Adventure Cycling maps routed us into Manitowoc by the most circuitous and nonscenic route imaginable. As we took turns grumbling about the extra miles, I realized I should have looked more closely at the map and persuaded Alice to go straight into town by a more direct way. We had learned early on that although we could always get where we needed to go, we did best when we combined Alice's map-reading skills with my instinctive sense of direction. We understood later why the maps routed us the way they did into Manitowoc—to take advantage of a paved bike path and the county fairgrounds, where camping is permitted—but when we arrived the annual county fair was underway. Rather than be kept awake until the wee hours by stock car races and midway honky-tonk, we decided to look for one of the cheap motels the Reedsville bikers had spoken of on the north end of town.

I think I can, I think I can . . .

On our way there, we spied a bike shop. We didn't really need anything, but we had found bike shop proprietors to be the best source of detailed local information. They usually could look at things from our perspective and knew what would interest cyclists, whether we knew to ask or not. We would also ask about motels in the area and check on whether anything interesting was on sale in the shop. So we leaned our bikes against a bench outside the window and sauntered in. The man behind the counter looked us over.

"Goin' cross country?" he asked.

The question surprised us because most people just asked where we were going and where we had come from. We realized right away that this guy saw many cross-country bicyclists because he was on the main northern route established by Adventure Cycling. We answered yes.

"Still talking to each other?"

We looked at each other with yet more surprise, and Alice said enthusiastically, "Well, sure."

"Oh, you're having a *good* trip," he said.

He then told us about all the cross-country cyclists who had entered his shop hating each other. He had heard stories about the idiocy of one or the other of those the complainer was traveling with. Almost in unison, we assured him that we were even better friends now than when we started, but I'm not sure he believed us. In fact, some of our own friends—via phone calls and our Web site—had also started asking us how we were getting along, so we discussed this issue as we pedaled toward the motel strip.

One reason we got along so well, we knew, was that our friendship was more important than "winning" any debate we might have. Although sometimes one of us gave in because the other one felt strongly about something, those occasions were rare, and we truly enjoyed each other's company. Before the trip, we had discussed our objectives, and they were essentially the same—to really see the country, experience the various local cultures, try living without a car and a full wardrobe, and talk to people we met along the way. We both considered ourselves problem-solvers, an essential characteristic for a successful shared life experience. In the end, we decided that perhaps the most important of these happy conditions was the fact that we usually wanted to do the same things anyway. Talk about luck!

The Reedsville barflies were right—the motels on the north end of Manitowoc were cheap—not just "inexpensive." We took the first one we came to—a 1950s-style low frame building with about twenty rooms in a row. Our room, without air-conditioning, came equipped with a shower clogged up with wads of hair and an inch or so of standing water. The paper-thin walls transmitted not only shower noises but even snoring sounds from the rooms on both sides of us. Our hand-laundered bike clothes wouldn't dry because of the humidity, and the beds were virtual hammocks, but the motel's location redeemed it—a coffee shop appeared two buildings away and a gorgeous Lake Michigan beach was right across the road. Dinner at a full-service restaurant overlooking the water, a mile up the road, restored our spirits. The path along the lake was well paved and landscaped, and we appreciated our first views of the immense lake as we strolled to and from dinner.

Day 51 Tuesday, August 19
Manitowoc to Ludington, Michigan
10 miles after the ferry

We were looking forward to taking the carferry (yes, the Lake Michigan Carferry Company spells it as one word) across Lake Michigan to Ludington, especially because of the four-hour rest we would get. Having pedaled five days in a row, we declared that it was time for a break. The ferry didn't leave until afternoon, so we spent the morning hanging around downtown Manitowoc—checking e-mail at the public library, visiting the bike shop again, picking up sandwiches to take on the ferry, and just killing time. We didn't get to kill time often, but we had no trouble adjusting to an undemanding schedule.

I was surprised to see how popular—and big—the ferry was. It could take 620 passengers and 180 vehicles, which were mostly cars, but a couple of eighteen-wheelers were boarding also. As instructed, we walked our bikes up the gangway, parked them alongside several Harleys, and tied them down with bungees. Passengers are not allowed to stay with their vehicles, and after a few moments of wondering about the safety of our bikes and belongings, we followed the rules and climbed several flights of stairs to the upper deck. The SS *Badger* was celebrating fifty years of service. It showed its age, even though it tries to entertain and accommodate its passengers with a number of lounges, movie theater, gift shop, playroom for children, and sleeping berths for those who book the overnight crossing.

On her way to a chair on the upper deck, Alice tripped over a low pipe and went sprawling face first across the deck—right in front of a line of people already lounging in their chaises. She feared for her left knee, which still had a sore spot from her spill on the first day of the trip way back in Oregon. I rushed to get a bag of ice, and after a few on-and-off sessions, the pain calmed down.

As Alice was recovering from this fall, the two women sitting next to us struck up a conversation. Susan and Sam—mother and daughter—were on a trip from Baltimore to the Midwest to scout out colleges for Sam, who was interested in art. She didn't like just any kind of art. She wanted to study and create comic book art. She was especially interested in Japanese comics. Susan had done a few solo bike tours because she didn't like riding with other people. That changed, however, when she was bitten on the hip by a pit bull on one bike ride. She doesn't pedal much at all anymore.

We noticed other people nearby listening in on our conversation. Before long, a man approached, leaned toward us, and snapped our picture—no explanation, no questions. We had often felt like small-time celebrities as people fussed over us when they learned about our adventure, but here was the negative side. We got a tiny glimpse of why real celebrities hate the paparazzi. We doubted that the rude man on the *Badger* could get a good price from the *National Enquirer* for a picture of two middle-aged nobodies dressed in geeky bike clothes.

Four hours and a few ice packs after we boarded in Manitowoc, the ferry docked in Ludington. By the time we had worked through the crowds and down the stairs to our bikes, unfastened the bungee cords, disembarked, and stopped to take our pictures by the Welcome to Michigan sign, it was nearly 6 p.m. We had lost an hour by entering the eastern time zone, so we had only enough time to pick up takeout dinner salads before heading to the state park ten miles north of town.

It was close to sundown by the time we passed the entry point into the park. We had heard that Ludington State Park was Michigan's most popular place to camp, so we weren't surprised that the sign said the park was full. Its policy, however, was to allow self-contained bicyclists to camp in an overflow area, or what they called their "fluff" site. This is a common policy in state parks, and we were grateful for it, but the only spot level enough for our tents had a foundation of solid rock under a half inch of sand. Our tent stakes wouldn't penetrate, so we weighted down the outside corners with gallon bottles of water we bummed off a neighboring camper, just as we had done in Washington, and hoped for a night of gentle weather.

Immediately after arriving at our site, another neighbor came over.

"Would you like to join us for dinner tonight? We're having Polish sausage."

We looked at each other, regret in our eyes.

"Gee," I said, "that would be really nice, but we've already got these dinner salads. And we have to get our tents up soon."

Alice added, "Thanks so much, but we'd better not."

Later we discussed how we had lost an opportunity to meet new people and learn about their lives, but we were eager to call it a day.

Day 52 ***Wednesday, August 20***
Rest day

The long ferry ride had made that day a rest day technically, but we liked Ludington State Park so much we decided to stay an extra day. Unfortunately, that required us to move from the overflow site to a regular one, and the particular campground we were in, which was one of several, had no sites available. This meant about two hours of work because of the two-and-a-half-mile ride back and forth to the campground office to complete the paperwork, take down the tents, repack our bikes, pedal to the next campground, unpack, repitch our tents, and rearrange our gear once again. And we thought we'd enjoy a relaxing day. All of this would have been fairly easy if we had had a car, but then if we had had a car we wouldn't have been able to camp there in the first place without making reservations months in advance.

Time out of the saddle in the state park was worth the trouble, and we spent half the day walking the beach—all the way to the Big Sable Point Lighthouse, which was inaccessible by car. There we indulged ourselves in souvenir shirts and a few postcards at the gift shop and met all the volunteer workers. They were mostly retired people who took turns staffing the historic lighthouse, and they expressed interest in all the tourists who went to the trouble to hike there. When they heard our story, John and Janice offered us the use of their Lake Michigan cottage, sixty miles or so down the coast.

"You're welcome to it," Janice said. "Just help yourselves to whatever's in the refrigerator. We won't be there, but feel free to stay as long as you like." We must have looked trustworthy, but we marveled at their generosity toward total strangers. We weren't going to turn down this offer.

We weren't sure whether we were getting more attention because we had made it so far or whether Michiganders were even more hospitable than people farther west. While in Michigan we received three invitations to spend the night in people's homes. One came from yet another neighboring camper in Ludington State Park, one from a friend of mine in Ohio who had a summer home in Michigan, and one from someone in Michigan who had found the link to our Web site. Their invitation came via e-mail, which we had found when we logged on in Manitowoc.

Each time we checked our e-mail, we found messages asking us to rendezvous with one person or another. We learned, however, that it was impossible to plan more than a few hours ahead, so we often had to turn down the friendly invitations. We had not foreseen this development, but we came to realize we couldn't accommodate others' schedules and maintain our own.

When we curled up in our cozy tents that night, the dark starry sky was clear and we both felt rested. We could see Mars, a pronounced red in the southern sky; the Milky Way straight overhead; and myriad constellations twinkling everywhere in the blackness.

A big surprise came at about 4 a.m., when we were wakened by thunder and lightning. It crashed and banged and poured, and we felt lucky our tents didn't collapse as they would have if we had still been on the overflow site where the stakes didn't penetrate the ground. The storm ended by 6 a.m. We went back to sleep and didn't wake up until 7:30. Power was out in the campground and carloads of people were packing up and leaving. We soon rolled up our own slimy tents and followed suit.

Day 53 *Thursday, August 21*
Ludington to Pentwater
27 miles

Tired of rural pedaling, we decided to avoid the Adventure Cycling inland route and go instead through the little towns along the Lake Michigan shore. We would head toward the vacation cottage we had been offered. In about twenty-seven miles we came to Pentwater, the first upscale community of our route thus far. Other places had been wonderful in many ways, largely because of the warm and friendly people we had met there, but most towns as small as Pentwater were in economic decline. With its yacht harbor, art galleries, and boutiques, Pentwater was very much alive on this hot and humid summer day. Although its winter population was a few hundred, in summer up to 10,000 people lived in the town, and the streets bustled with tourists.

We were each enjoying a soft drink and some baklava in a little bakery on the main street when some friendly people expressed concern for us. "Did you know that a tornado warning has been issued for this area?" one man volunteered. "It's in effect till 7 p.m."

His wife chimed in with a less-than-reassuring comment: "Yes, we heard that one touched down south of here."

We looked at each other. We were headed south to John and Janice's place.

Without much debate, we decided to spend the night in Pentwater. I asked a woman coming out of a realtor's office about places to stay.

"Why, I happen to own a B&B myself, right around the corner!" the woman answered. How convenient.

I negotiated a price with her on the spot, and we walked our bikes to the Pentwater Inn, where, with our host's permission, we promptly draped all our wet equipment over the upstairs porch to dry. We hated missing the vacation cottage offered by our new friends from the Ludington lighthouse, but we agreed that we shouldn't ride any farther and risk being caught in a tornado.

We loved the inn and hoped we could return someday. The owner is a quilter, fiber artist, and painter, and Alice, a quilter herself, especially enjoyed the many works of fabric art adorning the walls, not to mention the paintings in various media. Our room was comfortable and attractive with the little touches many B&B owners are so good at. The threat of tornadoes disappeared and we slept peacefully.

Day 54 ***Friday, August 22***
Pentwater to White Cloud
50 miles

Months earlier we had agreed to rendezvous with Alice's brother and sister-in-law, David and Roberta, in the town of White Cloud on this date. To do that we needed to turn inland, so we abandoned our idea of riding down the lake's shoreline. Heading east, we arrived in Hart, where we stopped at the public library to browse the Internet on a big screen and check our e-mail once again.

"Are you the women pedaling across the country?" a librarian wondered as soon as we walked in. We were surprised.

"Well, yes," Alice answered, "but how did you know?"

"Oh, I'm a friend of Janice and John's," she said. "Weren't you supposed to stay at their place last night? The neighbors put out a welcome sign for you and they were so disappointed when you didn't show up."

Unbelievable. The kind offer and then neighbors who were looking out for us. We felt even sorrier that we hadn't made it to the cottage down the coast, but we were glad that we were able to tell the librarian why so that she could tell our would-have-been hosts.

Not knowing anything about White Cloud, we had arranged to meet Alice's family at the post office, wherever that turned out to be. According to plan, David and Roberta were waiting there in their motor home when we arrived at about 6 p.m. They had located a campground—run by the city—so we followed them there, set up our tents, and hopped in their motor home to go find dinner. An all-you-can-eat seafood buffet for $6.99 apiece had the calories and carbs we were craving. Inexplicably, Alice had developed laryngitis during the day, so I did the talking for both of us. This was a deed I didn't have any trouble performing, though it was hard on Alice.

Day 55 — ***Saturday, August 23***
White Cloud to Smyrna
68 miles

The next morning Alice's voice was still nonexistent, but she gobbled up Roberta's scrambled eggs and buckwheat pancakes anyway. They were much better than the eggs and pancakes we had been having in restaurants. The hearty breakfast lasted us all morning. Before pedaling off at about 10 a.m., we offloaded some of our heaviest gear into their motor home—sleeping bags, mattresses, and tents. We planned to meet them at a campground near Smyrna, sixty-eight miles away.

Our route wound through apple orchards and past fields of well-established corn, squash, and watermelons. We were in the fruit belt, which Michigan is rightly proud of, and we searched for a fruit stand, but none appeared, probably because we were mostly off the beaten path. Although the scenery was lovely, the rural roads our maps designated were another story. None of them—not even the occasional state highway—had a shoulder but were narrow with heavy traffic. Too often motorists didn't seem bothered by a double yellow centerline but sped up and passed us on curves and before the crests of hills. Several times oncoming cars had to hit the ditch in order to avoid an accident.

"Alice, those guys in Montana were right. This is truly scary!" I gasped as yet another car passed us on a blind hill.

Alice was too busy hugging the white line to respond. No shoulder meant that only inches separated us from disaster.

We reached the Double R Ranch campground near Smyrna about the same time as Roberta and David, who had dilly-dallied to make up for our slow progress. We were happy to find showers, but their poor condition and the location of our campsite—a mile and a half down a steep gravel hill—made us lament the twenty-six-dollar fee for the night's stay. We decided the *R* stood for "ripoff"—the Ripoff Ranch campground. But Roberta's meal of soft-shell tacos and garden salad and fresh blueberries made up for the difficult ride and the overpriced campsite. Great food and good company were our reward.

At 10 p.m., as we walked to the bathroom, Alice exclaimed—in a whisper—how grateful she was to be off in a fairly remote area of the campground because many people seemed to be at the Double R for late-night revelry. Laughing and chatting groups of friends clustered around campfires, children roared over the camp paths and roads on bicycles (even after dark), music blared from radios, and some people were even watching TV near their fires. All of them seemed to be having a great time, but we simply wanted a good night's sleep.

Back at our quiet campsite, our appetites satiated, and content that we had completed our eighth adventure-filled week, I drifted off, hoping that Alice's voice would return soon. She had been trying to spare it, but for someone as social as Alice, silence did not come easily.

Day 56 *Sunday, August 24*
Smyrna to Delton
68 miles

A late start had meant a late arrival at the Smyrna campground the day before, so we needed to leave early. We decided to forgo breakfast in the camper, and David saved us a long walk by shuttling us up the long, deeply rutted, gravel road, one at a time. We would get something quick to eat, we figured, in the nearest town, Saranac. But we should have realized that nothing would be open on Sunday. All we could find was a small grocery store, so we bought some cheese, bananas, and doughnuts, and were so hungry that we ate them sitting on the sidewalk outside the store, all the time regretting our decision to skip Roberta's breakfast.

Inadequate pickup meals were sometimes necessary on the road. Most of the time we maintained the mindset that the simple life wasn't perfect. That way minor disappointments did not affect our attitudes. We were so grateful to be spending time as we were that nothing dampened our spirits for long.

According to our maps, none of the towns along our route that day had restaurants, so we decided to detour to Hastings, a city of about 8,000 and the seat of Barry County. Countless other communities had disappointed us with their banners stretching over the main street showing that we had missed a summer festival by a week one way or another. In Hastings, however, our timing was right and we found what appeared to be all 8,000 residents celebrating Summerfest. Alice was delighted because she had been searching for just such an event.

We meandered through the white tents of the craft fair, and Alice bought a couple of baby bibs (gifts that fit our weight constraints) for her forthcoming grandson, and we both took some photos. Part of the festival included an auto show with classic and antique cars lined up in double rows along the main street.

A woman with a sunbonnet-clad Yorkshire terrier in a specialized dog-carrier on her chest walked by. I was intrigued and amused at the sight of the small dog being carried like an infant. "May I take your picture?" I asked, which led to a conversation with the woman, Anne, about her love for her dog, Raspberry.

"I take Raspberry everywhere," she explained. "She would be insulted if I left her home." We agreed that we were extremely devoted to our respective hobbies.

On the road again, we saw that the land was changing—hills became more frequent, and farms in that part of Michigan didn't seem as plentiful or as prosperous as farms in Wisconsin.

Alice's brother had alerted WKZO, the CBS affiliate in Kalamazoo, that we would be riding through Alice's nearby hometown of Prairieville. Because Alice's voice was weak, I exchanged cell phone calls with a WKZO newsman who wanted to videotape us and get our story as we entered Prairieville. Meeting, however, was difficult to arrange, partly because we couldn't predict exactly how long it would take us to reach a designated rendezvous point, and partly because Alice's laryngitis was worsening. She could barely even whisper.

We were trying to meet up with David and Roberta before our interview because we had left our tents and sleeping bags with them that morning, and we didn't want to be seen on TV without our full loads. Call us vain, but we hadn't pedaled across seven states fully loaded to be seen with less than what we usually carried. After several calls back and forth to both David and the newsman, we met David, piled on our equipment, and went on our way. We didn't know exactly where we would meet the reporter, but we felt prepared for our media debut.

The news "crew" consisted of the reporter-cameraman Connor, his car, and his equipment. We hooked up about five miles north of

Raspberry riding in style

Prairieville, and he shot us going uphill and down. He set up his camera and tripod in the middle of the road, filmed us, then drove ahead to another spot and repeated the exercise—about five times. He also interviewed each of us alongside the road for the story to be broadcast on the 11 p.m. local news. Poor Alice—her five minutes of fame were marred by her hoarse voice. In order to conserve it, she hadn't spoken much all day, but she could barely finish the interview.

When we arrived in Prairieville, David and Roberta had already landed and arranged for us to camp at the community baseball field. At the same time they were booking our "accommodations," we were on the other end of the small town looking at Alice's childhood home and talking with the current owner, Sherry, who was mowing the front lawn. A recent widow, Sherry mentioned that Alice's father had officiated at her wedding about forty years before. Alice would have enjoyed the visit more if her laryngitis weren't so bothersome. She was not getting better and just wanted to set up camp and go to sleep.

While I was holding up the conversation with Sherry, a woman rode up on her bike with a dog in a carrier on her chest. At first I thought that I was seeing yet another dog lover carrying her pet in a front pack and that I had discovered the latest trend in pet travel, but I then realized it was Anne and Raspberry, whom we had met in Hastings. It turned out that they lived in Delton, three miles away, with Anne's widowed mother, Nellie.

"I'm so glad to see you again," she said as she greeted us. "My son once rode his bike across the country, and I remember him telling me about the people who took him in for the night. I would love it if you would stay overnight with my mother and me. Mother would love to talk to you, and I could be paying back the kindness people showed my son."

How could we turn down such an open-hearted, spontaneous invitation? The fact that we would be able to watch the news and see our interview was another plus. When I told Anne that we were accompanied by Alice's brother and sister-in-law in a motor home, she offered her driveway to Roberta and David. Later, we found out that Anne had a large motor home of her own, which she had driven to Alaska not long before. We had met a fellow explorer.

After conferring with David and Roberta, we canceled the plan to camp in Prairieville and happily accepted Anne's invitation to meet her at her home in Delton in a few hours. In the meantime we explored the rest of Prairieville, where Alice enjoyed showing me Zara's Grocery, the ancient general store where she had bought Popsicles fifty summers earlier. The two-room brick school she had attended was gone and replaced by a ball field, but her father's little white church, where she had pulled on the thick rope to ring the heavy bell on Sunday mornings, still stood next door to the general store. I enjoyed her whispered reminiscences, getting a glimpse of her childhood, which was quite different from my own.

At Anne and Nellie's house we socialized, waiting for the eleven o'clock news to come on. Nellie and her husband had traveled the world in his job for the U.S. Agency for International Development, and with Anne had lived in several countries in Africa and South America. Their home was filled with lovely artwork and mementos of their travels, and we enjoyed hearing their travel stories.

Although it was difficult to stay awake for the news, especially for Alice, we managed and were pleased with the coverage. Retrieving a blank tape from his motor home, David even recorded it for us using Anne and Nellie's equipment.

Day 57 ***Monday, August 25***
Delton to Three Rivers
58 miles

Thanking our hosts, we headed out early to meet David and Roberta at our prearranged spot and enjoyed another great breakfast, compliments of Roberta. Alice was still voiceless, but the route that day promised to be less hilly, requiring less heavy breathing, which we hoped would be helpful to her recovery.

The scenery that day included something new—huge gladiolus farms with many fields of just one color—pink, yellow, white, and orange. As we pedaled by the bright fields, we felt the heat and humidity typical of Michigan summers. Not only was the weather good for gladiolus farming, but it was also apparently good for road construction. Some roads had been newly oiled and pea-graveled, so we had to be especially careful not to spin out on the loose pebbles.

Towns were starting to appear closer together, so we were learning not to stop each time we came to one. Convenience stores also appeared more frequently, but we were unhappy to see that increasing numbers of them had signs reading No Public Rest Rooms. In most cases, as soon as a clerk saw how we were traveling, he or she made an exception and allowed us to use the facilities, especially after we had purchased something. In the little town of Scotts, Michigan, we faced more of a challenge. The dreaded sign appeared in the store where we stopped to buy some juice. When Alice bought her drink and asked the clerk in her raspy whisper whether she might use the restroom, the answer was an uncooperative no.

Without another word Alice walked outside, where she stood beside her bike thinking for about ten seconds. She returned to the store, approached the counter, and plunked down her just-purchased can of V8 juice. Looking the clerk in the eye, with a smile on her face, she whispered hoarsely, "I like V8 juice a lot, and I really wish I could drink this, but I can't. I can't drink a drop until I go to the bathroom."

In silence she waited, her hand poised on the V8.

"OK, come on back," the clerk finally said. When Alice was finished, without trying to speak, she pointed out the restroom to me, and I headed in that direction. The clerk didn't make a peep. We had apparently just broken some kind of barrier. Some establishments needed to monitor their restrooms carefully, of course, but we hated having to fight to satisfy a basic human need.

Both men and women can find the saddle of a bicycle uncomfortable, but women are at a greater anatomical disadvantage when it comes to "roughing it" without a bathroom. At the beginning of our trip we wondered how we might fare, but in a short time we had learned that it was quicker and easier to find a spot somewhere off the road than wait for miles for what was often a substandard public restroom. The West was great—we could see the road for miles in both directions and hardly had to hide. It was where Alice set a new record of eight seconds from shorts down to shorts up. She seldom needed to be that fast in desolate areas, but the skill came in handy on occasion. New England would have forests, but the Midwest was trickier with its more densely populated areas. By the time we reached the Midwest we had lost our citified inhibitions and made do quite well when indoor facilities were not available. Fortunately, more population meant more indoor facilities most of the time.

On the day after the TV coverage, each time we stopped we met people who had seen the eleven o'clock news the previous night. It amused us to be recognized, and it proved to us in a personal way the power of the media. The interviewer had begun the story of our trip saying, "Some people slow down when they retire, but others speed up." Yup. We had gone full speed ahead with our plans for this trip of a lifetime, and here we were.

"Hey, aren't you the two ladies biking from the Pacific Ocean to the Atlantic?" a man asked me at a convenience store in Galesburg.

He asked more questions, listened carefully to each of my answers, thought for a few seconds, and then, with a look of both incredulity and envy, asked one final question: "So, you mean, for three months you are doing just what you want to do?"

Yes, that was about it. And it was great.

When we were lunching under a shade tree in a rural area, a young man saw us from his car window and pulled over. He, too, had seen the story on the news and recognized us. He even knew why only I spoke to him because he remembered the problems Alice was having with her voice. He said he had ridden across the country with a group of people a few years before, so it was fun to compare notes. He lived just down the road, he said, and was thinking of establishing a campground for cyclists, especially because he knew his property was on the Adventure Cycling route. I encouraged him to pursue the idea.

Several times during our trip we met people who had ridden across the country or on other long tours. They wanted to share their stories and hear ours. We commiserated about typical problems and laughed about some of our shared experiences. It occurred to us that we were becoming part of a subculture—one that we were glad to join. We wondered how many people each year rode across the country, supported or unsupported. We know of no way to determine these numbers, and we later learned that even Adventure Cycling cannot make such an estimate.

We arrived at David and Roberta's home near Three Rivers at about 5 p.m. David had called his local bike shop and arranged to have our chains and gears cleaned the next day while we rested, so we loaded them in his motor home and rushed them down to the Kickstand before it closed. Diane, the owner, was clearly passionate about bikes and cycling, and we liked her immediately.

Another great home-cooked meal by Roberta was exactly what we needed. She served up spaghetti and green salad with tasty tomatoes from their garden. For dessert we enjoyed fresh Michigan blueberries and peaches. How could any two cyclists anywhere be so lucky? Roberta and David treated us so well, going beyond mere hospitality at every opportunity.

Day 58 *Tuesday, August 26*
Rest day

Because Alice's laryngitis was developing into a cold, she was especially glad for a day off, and spent much of it sleeping. When we returned to the Kickstand to pick up the bikes late in the afternoon, we found them looking like new with their sparkling clean chains and derailleurs. Diane also creatively repaired a bad fastener on my rear pannier. She clearly took pride in her work. She even surprised us with little gifts—a nylon ditty bag for each of us that she had made herself. Each bag contained items useful for bicycle touring—waterproof matches, fire-starting sticks, a battery-operated fan for hot nights in a tent, and some extra tent stakes, just in case. She was yet another example of the generosity we encountered so many times.

It rained on our day off—another lucky break. For the umpteenth time I wondered if we were using up all our good karma. We certainly would need to do some good deeds to repay all that had been done for us.

Day 59 *Wednesday, August 27*
Three Rivers to Ney, Ohio
96 miles

By the next morning we were ready to tackle the rest of Michigan, head through the northeast tip of Indiana, and make our way into Ohio. Leaving Three Rivers, David cycled with us for seven miles or so—a first bike ride together for brother and sister. He was twelve years older than Alice, so they had grown up rather separately. The past few days had been a bonding experience from Alice's point of view, and she would miss him and Roberta as we ventured forth on our own once again.

In just a few miles we were in the Amish country of northern Indiana. We saw a good number of work horses and buggies and numerous prosperous-looking farms being run without electricity. As we tooled down a quiet road, our reverie was broken by the tune from Alice's cell phone. She saw it was from Booth and stopped to answer.

"Hi, Sweetie," she rasped. "How are you feeling?"

"Well, I'm just fine, but, ah, er, ah, my printer seems to be ill," he answered.

Oh, dear. Alice was pleased she could be more helpful with this condition than with his gall bladder. So she listened, suggested a few clicks, and sure enough, a few minutes later, his printer was performing again.

While Alice was busy on the phone in the middle of Amish country, I found a patch of shade in which to wait. As I rested, I spotted several young Amish girls working in their garden across the road, picturesque in their bonnets and long, prim dresses of muted blue, green, and gray. I had just decided to respect their privacy and forgo a photo when out of the house behind me emerged a clearly non-Amish man and two young children. Finished solving Booth's printer problem, Alice signed off and joined me in the shade.

"I'm a Baptist preacher," he told us, "and these are my children." The little boy, about five, studied us curiously, but the girl, possibly seven, hid her eyes behind her daddy's pants leg.

After a few minutes of conversation, Alice asked, "How do the Amish and non-Amish people get along?"

"Oh, the Amish and the English do just fine as long as everyone minds their own business," he said.

When he learned where we were headed, he informed us that we were on the wrong route and then tried to describe a better one. We often depended on and always appreciated advice about routes from local people, but we were quite sure that the road he thought we should take was out of our way. He continued to insist that the road we were on was the wrong one but didn't explain why he felt so strongly. We didn't argue with him but were taken aback by his stridency. After he had questioned us for some time about our trip, we thought it might be fun to hear from his daughter, who was occasionally peeking out from behind his legs.

Alice leaned over and in her weak voice said, "Do you have any questions for us?"

"No," she said shyly. But then as we chatted more with her father, she emerged. I smiled encouragingly. Finally she spoke.

"Don't your legs ever get tired?" she asked.

We both chuckled and Alice answered, "Yes, but not as much as you might think. We practiced a lot before we started our big trip. Practice makes this all possible, even for people our age. Our muscles grow strong, so we can ride a long way if we keep eating because our food is fuel just like wood is fuel for a fire."

The youngster nodded.

As we turned to our bikes to leave, the minister said, "Do you mind if we pray?" We accepted his overture, pleased that he was taken with our adventure and concerned enough to pray for our safety.

Several hours later, in Lagrange, we ate lunch with a group of antique car buffs who were touring with their Auburns. Our lunch companions had many questions for us and seemed as interested in our hobby as we were in theirs. Their beautiful, spit-and-polished antique cars parked near the Amish buggies made the town square a picturesque study in contrasts.

After lunch as we rode out of town, we saw our Baptist preacher friend at a distance and waved to him.

I asked Alice, "Why do you think he was so determined that we should take that other road to Lagrange?"

"I don't know," Alice mused. "Why do some people just pronounce without having all the facts? He seemed pretty dogmatic to me about our route."

For several miles, we ruminated aloud about what might be behind his behavior. Did his religious persuasion make him dogmatic in other areas? Or did his personality cause him to be more dogmatic in the first place?

At South Milford we stopped for some cold sports drinks, a bathroom, and a county map. Once again, because we were headed to a friend's house that was off the route, we were striking out on our own and not following the Adventure Cycling maps. When we were about to leave the store, I noticed that I had a flat tire—on the rear wheel, of course. So together we unpacked everything and changed it, but that added a half hour to our day, a half hour that would make a difference later on. No glass or anything sharp had gone through the tire. The tube had simply fatigued, having split at a seam, not unlike the flats I had had in Montana. We were determined to figure out which brands of tubes are better than others because, as our experience was teaching us, some were clearly not intended for loaded touring.

Just before reaching Hamilton, we came upon a two-year-old boy sitting on a stubbly front lawn screaming, tears cascading down his dirty face. No adult was in sight, but some other children were playing in a backyard a few houses away. I thought the child was much too close to the busy road and so did Alice, so we stopped.

I approached the toddler and asked him, "Where is your mommy?"

He pointed two houses away, so I picked him up, carried him there, and knocked on the door. He sobbed all the way.

A woman carrying a paper plate filled with hot dogs and potato chips answered the door. She flung a cursory "Thanks" at me and addressed her child angrily: "Donald, did you hurt your toe again?" She pulled Donald into the house and closed the door. As we wheeled away, we wondered whether we should have called Child Protective Services.

Using ordinary highway maps instead of a gazetteer or topographic maps, we had underestimated by about thirty miles the distance from Three Rivers, Michigan, to my friend Jim's home near Ney, Ohio. We had left Three Rivers at 8:15 a.m. and by 9 p.m. had made it to Bryan, Ohio—about eight miles short of our destination. For the last few miles into Bryan we rode with our red taillights and Alice's halogen headlight, but it was too dark to ride eight more miles in unfamiliar territory. We weren't going to be stupid. So we phoned Jim, and he came with his pickup truck to get us. Through the dark summer night we rode in the comfort of the cab to his log cabin home, where he fed us a great meal, and we went to bed in the loft to sleep off our ninety-six miles.

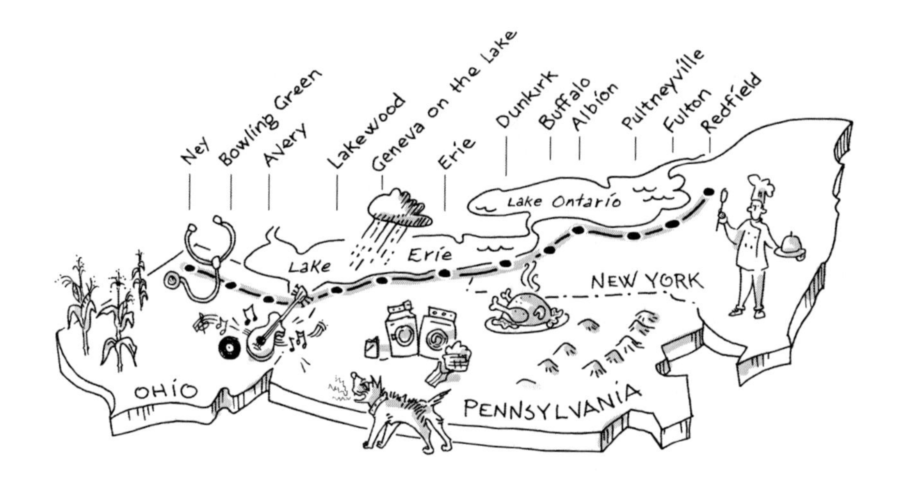

5

Along Lakes Erie and Ontario

Ohio, Pennsylvania, and Western New York

In the Midwest, the end of summer meant allergies, which apparently were the source of Alice's laryngitis. Matters would worsen before they improved, but she kept her legs moving up and down despite her challenged respiratory system. Sleep was good medicine but I missed my conversation partner. We never ran out of things to discuss—from ex-husbands to careers to child-rearing to—of course—food. Jim, our host, proved a helpful substitute for Alice for the time being, but eventually he had to go to work. Alice and I didn't distinguish a weekday from a Saturday or Sunday, but we had to recognize that not everyone our age had retired.

Day 60 ***Thursday, August 28***
Rest day

Alice's voice was actually improving a wee bit, but when she awoke in the loft of the log cabin, she faced a new problem—her eyes were glued shut. Conjunctivitis, probably. A phone call to Jim, who was already at work at his law office in Defiance twelve miles away, got us the directions to his doctor's office in town. We grabbed a quick bite from Jim's kitchen, and after Alice managed to get her eyes open, we pedaled to Defiance, following Jim's route.

The nurses and a doctor at the clinic examined Alice, asked questions about the bike trip, and prescribed some ointment. They told her that she was passing through the "allergy alley" that northern Indiana and Ohio were famous for. No wonder Alice was having so much trouble. She had had only slight fall allergies before, but on the bike she was breathing harder than in her normal life.

While Alice was attending to her medical needs, I was visiting a bike shop. The people there diagnosed and solved a rubbing problem I had with the tire that I had changed the day before. All our business finished, we met and rode back to Jim's house, where he and his officemates Dawn, Millie, and Tiffany, who had been following our journey via our Web site, arrived with a filling lunch of specialty cheeses, crackers, and huge bagel sandwiches. Jim had arranged for a journalist from the Defiance newspaper to interview us, so I told stories while a photographer took pictures. Alice spent the rest of the afternoon in slumber while I did laundry and planned the route for the next few days. Our spreadsheet itinerary had been useful, but we were deviating from it once again.

When Jim came home from work, he made another fabulous meal—grilled salmon with three different salads. We felt absolutely pampered. I made sure to tell his wife, Ann, when she called from North Carolina, that she had trained him well, but Ann took no credit. Jim was just that kind of guy.

Day 61 ***Friday, August 29***
Ney to Bowling Green
62 miles

Jim had drawn a detailed map to get us back to the route I had planned as Alice was sleeping the previous afternoon, but when we woke it was raining. We waited for the thunder and lightning to stop, which it did most conveniently, so we were on the road by about 9:30. Once again we were lucky—we had slept indoors, not out, and we wouldn't have to strike camp and pack wet, dirty tents.

It drizzled off and on for most of the morning and some of the afternoon, but it wasn't cold and it didn't really bother us. In fact, as we rode we concocted a list of reasons that light rain was actually good: (1) it meant it was not so hot anymore; (2) it gave us the excuse to get a motel; (3) rainwater was a good moisturizer for mature faces; (4) it helped lower pollen counts and flying allergens; (5) it generated sympathy from those who saw us riding in it; and (6) it felt so good when it stopped. Constantly rotating pedals seemed to encourage thoughts about almost anything just to keep our minds occupied.

We hit Napoleon in time for lunch with the local office crowd at a restaurant in one of the restored downtown buildings. Afterward, on the way out of town, we thought that we had pedaled into an Andy Warhol painting as we passed a gigantic red and white can of tomato soup. It turned out that we were at the gate of the world's largest Campbell Soup factory. It was another of those unpredictable, unimaginable moments—a fun discovery on what could have been a humdrum day.

"I just love not knowing what's up the road ahead," said Alice.

"Yeah, me too. I wonder what our next surprise will be."

We were becoming giddy. Should we have been so amused by a giant tomato soup can? Who needs drugs or alcohol to have fun? Pedaling through the countryside for days on end did it for us.

The picturesque town of Grand Rapids sits on the Miami and Erie Canal, which parallels the Maumee River. Once a major commercial corridor, the river and canal now draw tourists. It was time for another break, so we happily spent an hour and a half wandering in and out of Victorian-era buildings restored as gift shops. We were happy just to window-shop because we couldn't carry anything, and we didn't want to have to find a post office to mail our purchases home. Too complicated.

"Look, Alice," I said. "Living simply is saving us money!"

Alice laughed when I brought up this idea. She pointed out, though, that we had invented numerous reasons not to camp and so we were spending more on accommodations than we had budgeted. We weren't living as austerely as some who make the transcontinental crossing, but who said that "simple" equaled "camping-only"?

In only fourteen more miles we reached Bowling Green. Without a second thought, we checked in at the Best Western, showered, and splurged yet further on a cab to take us to dinner at a highly recommended restaurant on Main Street. Returning by cab to our motel, we laughingly reminded ourselves that we were not purists or

Spartans. Why would we walk or pedal to and from dinner when we could take a cab? We hadn't seen a city big enough for cab service in weeks.

Day 62 ***Saturday, August 30***
Bowling Green to Avery
65 miles

At the end of our ninth week, we left Bowling Green for Avery. All day we rode alongside and between fields of corn and soybeans. Soybeans on one side of the road, corn on the other, corn on both sides, or soybeans on both sides. Except for a few sheep, the only variation in scenery was the change from corn to soybeans and back again. Alice, her voice having improved with medication, chanted behind me, "Soybeans and corn, corn and soybeans, soybeans and soybeans, corn and corn . . ." I wondered if the trip was getting to Alice, but was reassured when she giggled—and stopped chanting.

At Pemberville we stopped for our usual second breakfast, where our waitress told us, "Oh, I want to travel so bad, but I could never get away from here. I need the work and they need me."

We realized once again that we were extremely fortunate to be able to travel for three months. It was sad that she could not get away. She looked as if she needed a break.

Fremont was a larger town—large enough to have a bike shop—so we stopped there to look for Chamois Butt'r, the product I applied to the inside of my shorts to prevent chafing. I was worried because I was almost out of it and it was a true necessity. They didn't have that particular brand but sold me a substitute. Farther on we passed a wedding taking place in a park gazebo. The bride in white and the guests in their colorful summer finery made an attractive tableau as we rolled along.

Avery was our goal, but we didn't realize it was only ten miles from Sandusky, where thrill-seekers flock to the roller coasters of Cedar Point Amusement Park on the shore of Lake Erie. That meant the lowest price for a room was one hundred dollars—and that at a Motel 6. Because we were trying to avoid the outside air in order to alleviate Alice's allergies, we gulped and paid the price. With the help of three different prescriptions, Alice was managing her symptoms, but air-conditioned sleep was also an important part of the therapy.

At a gas station, I approached the sheriff when I saw him at the gas pump. We had learned that local law enforcement could be an excellent source of all kinds of information and we were looking for a good dinner. On his recommendation we tried the Homestead Inn, a restaurant in a refurbished Victorian house about a mile from the motel. It was dark by the time we finished and we were about to call a taxi to return to the motel, but Trudy, our server, said she would like to drive us because she didn't have any more tables to wait that evening. We were touched as we always were when people offered to go out of their way to help us.

Day 63 ***Sunday, August 31***
Avery to Lakewood
53 miles

Regretting the new dent in our already wrecked budget, we were glad to escape Motel 6 and head north to Lake Erie's shore. As we pedaled in that direction, we were still stewing about the overpriced room. As if the cost of the night there wasn't bad enough, it offered no continental breakfast, the towels were thin and scratchy, and there wasn't even a box of Kleenex in the room. Who ever heard of a motel room without Kleenex? We decided that facial tissue—whatever the brand—was essential. We didn't know that we would shortly be experiencing accommodations that lacked more than just Kleenex.

As we came into the town of Huron, we stopped to ask some people on the street where we should go for breakfast. They pointed us to Berardi's, which we figured must be good because we had to wait about fifteen minutes to get a table. It had been a long time since we had seen items other than eggs and pancakes on a menu. Wow. I particularly enjoyed my feta and spinach omelet while Alice savored her broccoli quiche. We enjoyed eating yuppie food again. So much for the simple life.

After breakfast we headed east on U.S. 6, which parallels I-90. The maps suggested that it was a low-traffic route, but at the beginning of the Labor Day weekend everyone seemed to be on their way to one event or another. The broken pavement was narrow, and we worked hard to dodge holes, ruts, bumps, and debris of all sorts. Traffic was heavy, and at one intersection an elderly driver turned right onto a side street three feet in front of me. Seeing what was happening, Alice yelled just as I quickly turned right, following alongside the car to avoid hitting it broadside. I called out to the woman—"Hey!"—but got no response, and we guessed that the driver never even knew what she had done. We understood firsthand why right-hand turns in front of bicyclists are the most common type of motor vehicle–bicycle accident.

A bit farther down this unpleasant route, a teenage girl swerved recklessly around us in a Mustang convertible. One of her girlfriends yelled out to us, "Get on the sidewalk, Bitch!" as the driver gunned the engine.

My patience at an end with the traffic, poor road, and almost being hit, I replied with a loud and heartfelt, "Go to hell!" This was real—my life was on the line. I briefly continued a one-sided conversation, mumbling about laws that prohibit adult cyclists on sidewalks. Most motorists don't know all the reasons for cyclists riding in roadways, and cyclists don't have a way to educate them on the fly. We didn't know how to solve this communication problem, but we knew we needed a break from the traffic soon.

West of Vermilion we stopped at a small county park for that much-needed rest and to catch our first good view of Lake Erie. On one end of the park was a mobile home court. The home closest to the park had a beautiful, well-cared-for flower garden with a little white archway at the entrance. Welcome to the Garden, a sign said. So we entered. Strolling on fragrant pathways set among the brilliant red, purple, and white petunias, we read a plaque explaining that this was a garden that the man who lived there had built as a memorial to his beloved wife. A neighbor saw us, came over to greet us, and introduced himself as Dave. He explained that the town had given the grieving widower an unused boat landing in exchange for cultivating this colorful garden. Dave asked us to sign the guest book, which was kept carefully protected in a white wooden enclosure near a six-foot lighthouse in the middle of the garden.

Then, with a twinkle in his eye, Dave asked, "Wanna see a ten-foot-tall tomato plant?"

Of course we did. He took us straight to his prize specimen. Neither of us had ever seen a tomato vine that tall. Growing alongside his garage, it stretched up onto the roof right through the crevice between the gutter and the shingles. Alice took a picture of him proudly standing by his supersize plant. From his other plants he gave us a yellow pepper and two beautiful tomatoes. We enjoyed them at our picnic lunch that day along with our peanut butter and cracker sandwiches.

We were approaching Cleveland. The pavement became more and more broken, and traffic increased. On an especially savage bump in a one-lane construction zone, one of Alice's rear panniers bounced completely off her back rack right onto the roadway beside her. With nowhere to go between all the brightly colored cones, and a six-inch drop-off to the sandy shoulder, she had no choice but to stop in the middle of the lane. Traffic behind her came to a sudden halt and then waited while she hopped off her bike, retrieved the pannier, repositioned it, and jumped back on. Not only had she become trimmer in her nine weeks of pedaling, but she could move pretty quickly too when the situation demanded it. At least no one yelled four- or five-letter words.

Homes along the lakeshore in Vermilion are a mixture of styles and levels of sophistication. Mansions are interspersed with tiny 1950s-style cabins, and mobile homes appear next to grand estates. Zoning must have been a concept that came along after these properties were developed. After stopping to walk through the little Vermilion downtown area, we proceeded on through Lorain, Sheffield Lake, and Avon Lake. At Bay Village we came upon a Renaissance fair where participants were dressed in period costume. I snuck into the fair without paying admission in order to buy us both some lemonade. The stand was three feet from the rope fence, so my crime consisted of stepping over the rope, taking three steps, and leaning on the counter to order the cool drinks that had been the subject of some of our fantasies on many hot days out west.

By the time we reached the elite suburb of Lakewood, where we had reserved a room, it was 6 p.m. We expected the motel to be a dive at the price of sixty-two dollars but we were pleasantly surprised. We were in an upscale community, surrounded by elegant homes and fancy condominiums, and the place was comfortable and reasonably priced, if not downright cheap. It made Avery's Motel 6 look even worse. We understood about markets and supply and demand, but the difference between the two establishments was striking. The contrast became even sharper when Joseph, the front desk clerk, was unusually welcoming. He was remarkably friendly and began asking us questions as we maneuvered our fully loaded bikes through the lobby. He chatted with us at length and for some reason, which neither of us understood, took special pleasure in telling us about how he had worked for Shirley MacLaine when he lived in Hollywood. As we passed through the lobby later, he introduced us to a friend of his. We were in the biggest city so far, and had found someone who defied the stereotype of unfriendly big city inhabitants. He was a reminder not to fall into the trap of generalizing.

We ate at an Italian restaurant a short walk from our lodgings and went to sleep wondering what it would be like to pedal through downtown Cleveland on Labor Day. An air show was scheduled on the waterfront, so we were dreading more heavy traffic.

Day 64 *Monday, September 1*
Lakewood to Geneva on the Lake
63 miles

And what a Labor Day it was. It began in the rain, poured all day, and ended in the rain. We made sure we put everything in plastic bags—double-bags, in fact, as we had done in North Dakota. Getting through Cleveland, however, was much easier than we had anticipated. Because of the weather, no air show took place on the lakefront, no picnics, no community events. Translation: no traffic. It just rained and rained, sometimes straight down, sometimes blowing sideways in sheets. It was enough to have to avoid potholes, whose depths were disguised by standing water, and other obstacles in the road without having to worry about cars and trucks passing us and knocking us off the road with their powerful spray. No problem. Everyone but us stayed home.

I especially wanted to tour the Rock and Roll Hall of Fame, and our route took us directly past it, so we stopped. Alice had no particular interest in rock-and-roll history, but she indulged me and came along, while I promised I would make it up to her somewhere down the road. We would normally have been concerned about leaving our bikes unattended, but it was raining so hard that no one would be tempted to fool around outside any more than necessary. We usually locked the bikes when we left them out of our sight, and we did at this spot, too, but that served only as a mild deterrent because our bags and their contents couldn't be secured, and the thin cables could easily be cut.

With its valuable artifacts like Little Richard's appliquéd jacket, Fats Domino's suits, and innumerable guitars once strummed by rock-and-roll greats, the museum exercised tight security measures. A guard tried to keep Alice from entering wearing her CamelBak, the specialized backpack that held her drinking water supply. When she showed him that it was just her water supply and that she went everywhere with it, he relented, shaking his head. We doubted that he had seen one before, especially on someone visiting the Rock and Roll Hall of Fame. She could have left it with the bike, of course, but she was used to taking it everywhere with her so she could swig water frequently.

The hour and a half we spent in the museum was hardly enough time to absorb much but just enough to check it off the list of Cleveland sights not to be missed. We left the museum still damp and a bit chilled.

Rain continued to fall as we pedaled through the rest of Cleveland on the series of streets and off-road paved paths along the lake that our maps outlined. East of Cleveland we passed through Euclid. We stopped as little as possible, knowing we would be cold when we did. The Last Chance Cafe in Willowick looked inviting, and we were getting hungry for lunch, so we decided to take its name literally. Right away we figured it was a good pick because the menu featured a "bottemless" cup of soup. Even though someone couldn't spell, he or she did know how to make good chicken noodle soup for cold bicyclists on a nasty day. As word nerds, we were always on the lookout for misspellings, but as long as the food was tasty, we didn't complain. Adding to our satisfaction was the hot chocolate that actually stayed hot in thermal mugs. All the warm liquids fortified us and emboldened us to get back on our bikes despite the well-justified belief that we would be soaked and cold again soon. The rain did not let up and the thermometer hovered in the midsixties.

After Willowick came Eastlake, Lakeline, and Mentor. At Mentor we moved away from Lake Erie for a few miles, then meandered through Painesville and on to Madison. At Madison, while stopped again to warm up, we met several Harley riders who were on their way home from the one-hundredth-anniversary celebration of Harley Motors in Milwaukee. They were drenched to the skin in their leathers and were shivering with cold.

"You guys are probably warmer than we are. At least you get to pedal," one rider pointed out.

"But you get there faster," I replied, "and your leathers are a lot better looking than our Lycra." They grinned, tossed their empty cups in the trash, and sped off with a roar.

At Unionville, when we stopped at a convenience store to get water, well-intentioned advice turned ugly. After asking about our destination, an older gentleman asserted, "Oh, you gals are on the wrong road. You want U.S. 20. Let me show you on the map."

As he reached out for our map, a woman standing nearby cut in, "Oh, no, they ain't. All they have to do is turn here. They're just fine." She was practically yelling.

"Nope," rejoined the man sternly, "you're wrong. They need to get to 20 or they'll be ridin' all night."

"I am not wrong," she answered, her voice rising. "You don't know what you're talking about! You're goin' to take them way out of their way." She looked daggers at him.

We had no idea what was really going on between these two, but the tension was palpable, and the argument seemed headed toward violence. Without waiting for either of them to win, we mounted our bikes and rode away on the road we had originally chosen.

Geneva on the Lake is an old-fashioned, honky-tonk resort town with numerous mom-and-pop motels. The first two we inquired at would not allow us to use their clothes dryer, which we desperately needed in order to recover from the day and have dry clothes for the next day. At the third place the owners quoted a high price but said we could use both the washer and the dryer. Ordinarily we would have shunned such a run-down-looking motel at any price, but that night we would have paid almost anything for a dryer. Even if we had to wash our clothes by hand, they would never air-dry overnight. So after hoisting our dripping bikes up a couple of steps into the room, we ordered in pizza, took hot showers, and located a few dry things to wear while the all-important laundry machines went to work. After dinner we collected some rags and old newspapers from the motel owners, spread out the newspapers under our bikes, and cleaned them. What a gritty, greasy mess. That task finally accomplished, we oiled our chains, cleaned up, folded and packed our dry clothes, and went to bed.

Just before turning in, Alice exclaimed, "What's this on my pillow?" She had found a lovely piece of foil-wrapped chocolate. It didn't take her long to figure out that it wasn't the motel's turn-down crew who had placed it there.

"Bobbi! Did you do this? What a treat!" A new tradition had begun right there in Geneva on the Lake, New York. From that point on, occasional chocolate treats appeared on our pillows.

Day 65 **Tuesday, September 2**
Geneva on the Lake to Erie
53 miles

We were glad to leave that motel, which was worth the expenditure only because of the dryer and the shelter from the rain. It was a true pit. The carpet was old and stained, so soiled that we avoided stepping on it with bare feet. The bathroom door was falling off its hinges, which meant that to open or close it we had to lift it up off the floor. The couple in the next room, with their mangy, barking dog tied to a stake in the muddy pit outside their door, appeared to be permanent residents. They left their TV on all night. We knew this because the walls were hardly thicker than the faded wallpaper separating us. Not only could we hear every sound they made, but we almost felt we could see them. Lovemaking sounds were one thing, but these were something else altogether. We kept the bathroom fan on to drown them out, but a glaring light stayed on with it. Our room had no Kleenex, no phone, and no comfort. Our rating: no spokes up at all—rather, a flat tire and bent wheel. By morning we almost wished we had camped in the rain. Almost.

Dry but overcast skies appeared in the morning, and the scenery and terrain were changing again as we left town. The landscape became more rolling, and along the shore of Lake Erie little communities popped up frequently. Between them were nurseries, vineyards, and peach orchards—no room in this part of the country for forests or wilderness.

We suspected more rain was on the way, and we needed warmer, more breathable clothing. Our goal was to find the Eastern Mountain Sports store at the Millcreek Mall in Erie and go shopping. Some more of Alice's family, from Pittsburgh, were going to meet us in Erie, so we devised a route to the mall, a good rendezvous point. We knew that Pennsylvania was hilly, but we didn't expect all the hills our route covered that day. We soon discovered how underused our hill-climbing muscles had been in recent days.

The mall turned out not to have the EMS store that had been there when Alice drove through several years before, but a Fairfield Inn was situated on the edge of the parking lot. It had a clean, well-appointed room for the same price as the pit we had stayed in the previous night, so we signed in, showered, and connected with Alice's family via cell phone. Our fathers used to talk about having gone from horse-drawn vehicles to spaceships, but we remember party lines and Lily Tomlin operators. We had been in many areas without cell service, but in the East, cell towers—as well as cars and people and potholes—proliferated.

We enjoyed spending a few hours with three generations of Alice's relatives—her nieces Tracy and Leigh and their preschool-aged children, as well as Tracy's parents, David and Roberta, who had driven over from Michigan. Henri and Cloe, unable to come because they were in school, sent Alice a gift—a visor embellished with their photos and a heartfelt message that read: "Your great, Aunt Alice!" Alice's family treated us to dinner and then delivered us to our hotel before they made the two-hour trip back to Pittsburgh. We were both touched by all their attentiveness.

Day 66 — *Wednesday, September 3*
Erie to Dunkirk, New York
53 miles

We used a city map of Erie to find our way from the Fairfield Inn back to our regular route—about ten miles. Traffic was heavy and roads were narrow in Erie, but most motorists gave us wide passage. The streets were not really suitable for cycling but we managed. Once back on our prescribed route, it became a "grape" day. That is, we were in grape country—a land of large Concord grapes grown almost exclusively for Welch's grape juice cooperatives. It really was a perfect day for cycling—partly cloudy, about seventy degrees with a slight tailwind. Our route kept us close to Lake Erie, traversed myriad vineyards, and became fairly hilly.

The last town on our route in Pennsylvania was North East, where we came upon the Freeport Restaurant. We had planned to eat a picnic lunch again, but because we were both so hungry we quickly discarded the idea of looking for a grocery store, opting instead for the restaurant in North East.

Alice said, "Can you imagine the confusion when people say they live in North East, Pennsylvania, when they actually live in western Pennsylvania? Sure, I know it's in the northeastern corner of the little panhandle, but it's still on the western side of the state."

"Alice, you overthink these things sometimes," I chided.

"I know, but it's one of those times when not being able to see the capital letters and the commas could make all the difference."

Spoken like a true editor. She may have retired, but some things would never change.

After only a few more miles, we crossed into New York. The sign welcoming us to our twelfth state was right next to a golf course parking lot, so we prevailed upon a golfer to take our photo. For the first time we were in a photo together on a state line.

At Barcelona we saw our first Lake Erie lighthouse and stopped for a brief rest at the picturesque harbor. A few miles down the road we saw a sign advertising the Vinewood Acres Sugar Shack and offering "free syrup tastings." We didn't really need another rest stop, but we were intrigued enough by the sign to ride down the long, gravel driveway winding through a field of seven-foot-tall corn to see what this Sugar Shack was all about. Once there, we tasted every conceivable kind of syrup—blueberry, peach, persimmon, and about ten others—on ice cream provided in little paper nut cups. Luckily for all of us, Gail, the owner, had a mail-order business, so we bought several souvenirs and arranged to have them shipped home. In fact, we managed to buy more items there than we had anywhere else—Christmas stocking stuffers, various kinds of syrup for hostess gifts, and a couple of baskets made by local Amish people. While Gail packed up our purchases, we chatted.

This Gail, like nurse Gail whom we had met in Edwards, Minnesota, was also a woman of conviction and action. About ten years earlier, soon after her husband died and left her with a farm to run, she had become persona non grata in her community. A cardboard

Sugar Shack Gail, queen of syrups

recycling company wanted to locate in this fertile area of farms and vineyards, and everyone was excited about the possibility of sorely needed jobs. When Gail did some research she found out that the company would be running toxic wastes through orchards and dumping them into Lake Erie. She and twenty-five other stalwarts struggled for several years amassing evidence, hiring a lawyer, and spending money and time they didn't have. They became the spoilers, the "damn conservationists," and were ostracized by their neighbors—even threatened—because they were hindering the establishment of the factory. No one wanted to believe the source of good jobs was a polluter. When Gail's little cadre came up with hard evidence, they were able to stop the factory and, in fact, also upset the company's plans for locating a factory in Ohio. Still, no one seemed grateful for her activism.

She said, "I became a very bitter person. Everyone hated me. I guess I just lost faith in people and myself. I was angry, and it came out in the way I'd talk to people sometimes. One day, a friend who had fought the paper plant with me, a New York State–licensed engineer and born-again Christian, came out to the house. He looked me right in the eyes and he told me, 'Gail, you used to be a nice person. You used to laugh and smile, but now you're just a mean and nasty old lady. You need to do something positive. Right now.'

"Oh, I was so mad at him, I kicked him right out of the house. Then I went and looked in a mirror and by golly, the meanest, nastiest old lady looked back. I called him up and got his wife and said, 'Bring him back over here,' and they both came out to the house. I didn't have anything to serve them with coffee except plain vanilla ice cream, so I went down to the basement and saw a bottle of my strawberry syrup. I remember to this day it was highlighted on the shelf like a word in a sentence. To make a long story short, he told me I should sell syrups—fruit and maple.

"After two months of his harassing me, I cleaned up this shack, sterilized two cases of Welch's grape juice bottles, stuck awful computer labels over the word 'Welch's' and filled them. I did it as a joke just to shut him up.

"I painted an old sheet of plywood white and wrote Fruit Syrups—Six Flavors—Free Tasting. Oh, it looked awful, but I went down to the end of the driveway and put it up. I was halfway back to the house when my first customer drove up. He was from New Zealand and on a trip around the world. He wanted to taste syrup. Then he asked what it was, so I told him. He bought two bottles. A week later some people from John Deere came out and wanted to learn about grapes. That was my first grape tour. Now, ten years later I have three big binders bulging with mail from all over the world from people who've come to my pancake breakfasts, maple syrup tours, and tastings. And I started it all as a joke."

We wished we could have stayed longer because we found Gail to be one of the most upbeat people we had met. Her spirit and enthusiasm were uplifting, and her hard work to make a success of her life inspired us.

Eighteen miles more and we were in Dunkirk, where we signed in at a large Ramada Inn on the lakeshore. After Labor Day, prices had dropped, so we paid only sixty-two dollars—a bargain. Rain was again threatening, so we decided that we would not take a chance on camping because we wanted dry clothing the next day, having planned to store our bikes in Buffalo and fly to our respective homes for a short break. We were looking forward to seeing our families, but we didn't want to return to find the things left in our bags all mildewed. Any excuse for getting a motel rather than a campsite, we decided, was a good excuse, and this was one of our most creative excuses yet.

Day 67 ***Thursday, September 4***
Dunkirk to Buffalo
53 miles

Somehow we again overslept. The clock said 8:30 when we woke, so we packed up quickly and wheeled down through the lobby. Yay, sun! Our first order of business was to find breakfast—at Aunt Millie's Kitchen in Silver Creek, nine miles east. It had been recommended to us by Gail at the Sugar Shack. When Aunt Millie's didn't appear as soon as we thought it should, we stopped to ask directions from a woman walking her dog. She gave us clear, detailed instructions, unusual because people often garbled their directions.

When Alice said, "Wow! You sure give precise directions," the young lady smiled and said, "Aunt Millie is my aunt."

That explained it.

Aunt Millie's turned out to be one of the better breakfast places.

As we parked the bikes, I quickly wrapped my little black skirt around my shorts so I could feel as though I looked a little more "normal" when we entered. I hadn't had many opportunities to do this, and Alice teased me when I did while admitting that she wished she had one.

"Oh, there you go again," she whined, "looking like a million bucks while I'm all greasy and stinky. I want one of those things."

I knew she wasn't really serious, though, because she wouldn't have wanted to carry the additional several ounces. Now if I would carry it for her, maybe that would be different. But I didn't offer, and she wasn't about to buy one anytime soon.

Besides having her usual eggs and potatoes, Alice indulged in a caramel pecan roll that ranked right up there with the one at the Wild West Diner in Culbertson, Montana. Some things we wouldn't forget. The other thing we wouldn't forget about Aunt Millie's was the response I got when I asked, as I usually did, for the non-smoking section.

"You're in New York now, Honey," the server informed me with a frown. "Everything's nonsmoking." We learned that New York had recently banned smoking in all restaurants and bars, and it was obvious that some people weren't happy about it.

After breakfast and back on our bikes, we had gone about fifty yards when we discovered that Alice had a flat tire—on the back wheel, of course. The culprit was a teensy piece of strong wire that had gone all the way through the tire and tube, probably another truck tire shard. It was only her second flat, so we couldn't complain much. Her little pump worked well with its footrest and a T-shaped handle so that she could easily pump her tires to 110 pounds. No matter what, it always took us about a half hour to change a flat, including the unloading and reloading of our packs. Some people can pop out a wheel without unloading their gear, but we never could manage to do that no matter how skilled we became at the actual tire change.

Back on our way to the lakeshore on a little road paralleling Highway 5, we passed through the Cattaraugus Indian Reservation where several smoke shops sold discount cigarettes. These outlets seemed to be the only source of people's livelihood in the area, which we thought was pretty sad. After we passed the reservation, we came upon Evangola State Park, where we wished we could have camped because it looked so appealing. From that point on, the properties along the lake became private land, and grand estates lined the shore. We had traveled along Lake Erie for several days and were coming to appreciate how immense it was: 159 miles long and about 53 feet deep on average. Five hundred shipwrecks had been found in the immediate area.

When we finally came to a little public beach, we stopped. I had been yearning to dip into Lake Erie, and here was my chance, so I splashed around while Alice rested on a bench writing postcards. Not long after our little break on the beach we came into the Greater Buffalo area. First came Hamburg, then Blasdell, then Lackawanna, and before we knew it we were inside Buffalo's city limits. We had called a Buffalo bike shop for advice on the best route through the city to Kenmore, where we were planning to store our bikes for the upcoming weekend, but some bridge construction and a detour intervened, so we tried to work our way around them on our own. As we navigated between the tall buildings through the busy downtown streets of Buffalo in late afternoon, Alice announced that she needed to find a restroom.

"Oh, Alice, you'll never find one around here. You'll just have to wait."

Just as I said that, we turned a corner and found ourselves facing a row of about twenty bright blue portable toilets across the street from a large park where a big event was about to take place. We enjoyed a good laugh at my expense. It turned out they were for a Thursday night concert that would draw thousands in the next couple of hours.

Right place at the right time

Stopped at a traffic light on our way out of the downtown, we met a young man on a bike, dressed in his business clothes, pant legs secured with clips to keep chain grease off his cuffs. He introduced himself as Mark and asked where we were headed.

"I can take you to Kenmore," he offered. "It's near where I live." We eagerly accepted. He led us through Buffalo, explaining the architecture and history of the grand old buildings we passed. He took us on quiet, winding streets with light traffic during rush hour. Some of the route consisted of bike paths and overpasses that we never would have found on our own, reminding us of our experience with Walter in Portland, Oregon. On one of the pedestrian and bicyclist overpasses, we met Michael and Mitch, two middle schoolers who were in-line skating. They had lots of questions, which we tried to answer. Ever the teacher, I asked why they were out skating on a school night.

"Don't you have homework?" I asked.

Grinning, one boy replied, "It's only the second day of school, and teachers aren't allowed to give homework the first week."

Not allowed? I wondered how that could be true, but I gave them the benefit of the doubt and just smiled.

After Mark left us we found our way easily to Diana and Norb's house. Although Alice knew Diana's brother in Wisconsin, we had never met this couple, but we were struck by their warm hospitality. We had arranged just to park our bikes in their basement, but Diana invited us to dinner, which consisted of turkey and all the trimmings—an early Thanksgiving served on a lovely table set with china, crystal, and silver. After the feast we unloaded our bikes, bumped them down the stairs into the basement, and picked out items we needed to take home, dirty laundry included. We then called a taxi, thanked our delightful hosts sincerely, and headed for our hotel near the airport so we could fly out the next day.

Days 68 to 70 *Friday, September 5, to Sunday, September 7* *Rest days*

Before we left Buffalo to fly to our homes for the weekend, we compared flight schedules and realized that we were on the same flight from Detroit back to Buffalo. "The miracle of it is," I said to Alice, "we're glad." We both laughed, remembering the bike shop owner in Manitowoc who had told us about all the feuding cyclists he had seen.

We realized that we had not tired of each other in any way and in fact were better friends than ever. We usually agreed on the necessary course of action when faced with a dilemma. We never argued—we discussed. Alice was still always ready first in the morning, but she did not announce it and just waited patiently for me to catch up. On the bikes, I still liked to lead and the distance widened between us on serious uphills, but Alice often outcoasted me on the down slopes. And even though I took longer to pack in the morning, Alice was slower at meals, so we had fallen into a comfortable pattern of give-and-take. We each saw every day as a new adventure, and we thought of our compatibility as a great gift that helped make our trip such a good one.

At home in Madison for the weekend, Alice accompanied Booth to the first University of Wisconsin–Madison football game of the season, which, she was proud to report, the UW won, 48–31. In Cincinnati, I joined Bob and my family and caught up on the lives of our children and grandchildren. I had a long talk with my daughter, who was adjusting to her new life, but she let me know that she was anxious for me to come home permanently. We loved being at home to visit our families, and we assured them that our big adventure would really end one day.

Our flights connected on time, and we arrived back in Buffalo at 10 p.m. Sunday. We took the shuttle to the University Inn and went to bed, eager to see what the final stage of the trip held for us.

Day 71 **Monday, September 8**
Buffalo to Albion
53 miles

We had picked the University Inn because it was the only hotel away from the airport district that offered free shuttle service. We needed the transportation, but we wanted to be as close to Kenmore as possible. We liked it for other reasons, however: the price was more reasonable than the big chain hotels, and its continental breakfast was the best of the entire trip. A beautiful buffet was spread over a large table covered with white tablecloths at one end of a gracious dining room. Fruit, breads, cereals, waffles, and even hard-boiled eggs were attractively arranged on the table. It wasn't the usual high-sugar, high-carb filler with no protein. Sure, we needed carbohydrates, but we needed a nutritious balance, and we fueled up enthusiastically for the day. The University Inn earned a five-spokes-up rating for sure. We agreed that we'd stay there even if we weren't on a bike trip.

Inexplicably, the cab company we called sent a small limo to pick us up at the University Inn. We joked about being visiting celebrities, but dressed in our colorful Lycra cycling outfits, we felt out of place climbing into a limousine. The limo delivered us at 7:30 a.m. to Diana and Norb's house, where we began loading our bikes with the cold-weather gear we had brought from home. Diana was preparing for her day of teaching school, but she pointed out the brownies and pumpkin bread she had made for us to take along, and Norb took photos of our preparations. We can still see them both, standing in their driveway, waving us off as we left their neighborhood. They had made all this effort for complete strangers, known only to a family member far away.

On our way out of Buffalo, we stopped to watch a firefighter's funeral procession. The hook-and-ladder trucks were positioned so that their tall ladders arched over the roadway. The deceased's fellow firefighters in full dress uniform lined both sides of the street in somber tribute as the cortege passed under the ladders. It was a ceremony neither of us had seen before. Usually not one for ceremonies, I saw firsthand that this form of respect and honor was important in such a dangerous career.

After stopping at a local bike shop, getting local road information, and purchasing new chain lube and some neoprene toe covers for Alice's bike sandals, we found our way through the northern suburbs of Buffalo to Lockport. There we stopped for lunch at a diner before making our way to the Canalway Trail along the Erie Canal. We were disappointed when we saw that the trail was unpaved, and in less than a mile we decided to go back to the roads. It would have been great to get away from traffic for eighty miles, but a surface of limestone screenings was just not suitable. We were surprised that Adventure Cycling recommended the unpaved surface for long-distance riding. Such trails are great for families or recreational riders, but with our heavy loads and skinny tires, riding it would have required a great deal more concentration and effort and also would have slowed us down. At least we got to see the famous waterway. I sang a couple of verses of the Erie Canal song I had learned in elementary school before we left the trail.

So we stayed south of the canal, following highways 31 and 31E. Hampered by a nagging headwind again, we slowly wound our way through several old canal towns—Gasport, Middleport, and Medina. We examined our tires at one rest stop and found a piece of metal protruding from Alice's front tire so slightly that neither of us could extract it. So we decided just to keep on pedaling, figuring that if it went flat, we would work on it then. It held all day, so it must have not been very deep. Lucky for us.

We had been looking forward to camping again, but we were tired from battling the headwind, so rather than hunt for the campground, we stopped at a motel when we reached Albion. Thinking that the season was over, and mindful of our blasted budgets, I didn't want to pay full price, so I negotiated a lower price than the one advertised. We felt justified in not forging ahead.

Day 72 — *Tuesday, September 9*
Albion to Pultneyville
63 miles

Once again, a stiff wind came out of the east, supplying more evidence to dash the prevailing westerlies theory. Even though Alice's handlebar thermometer registered a comfortable seventy degrees, the headwinds were wearing on us for the second day in a row. At breakfast I struck up a conversation with four officers from the

Orleans County Sheriff's Office. They advised us to avoid Highway 104 and instead head north and pick up the Lake Ontario State Parkway, the notorious "road to nowhere." It had been planned as an expressway from Buffalo to Syracuse, they explained, but the state had run out of money and never finished it. They promised us that the road had no traffic and we would like riding on it. On his way out of the parking lot, Officer Aaron gave us two maps from his glove compartment, one a county map and the other a laminated guide for the whole state.

Orchard Road, running north to Lake Ontario, was appropriately named. Apple and peach orchards lined the road, and produce stands proliferated. In front of one old frame house, a large wooden crate was filled with apples. A sign said "Take One," so we did. At another orchard we bought Ginger Gold apples, a variety neither of us had ever tried before, and they were crisp and tart—perfect to carry with us and munch whenever we needed a snack. It was my new favorite apple.

The headwind on the empty "road to nowhere" was vicious—the strongest we had encountered so far—but we plodded on in the bright sunshine, occasionally glimpsing the sparkling waters of Lake Ontario on our left. Looking for a picnic lunch destination on the map, we spotted a community named Manitou Beach about a mile off the route on a road that ended at the lake. I figured we would find the beach and take a break from the wind. When we reached the community, however, we could find no public beach. The waterfront seemed to be completely privately owned, dominated by expensive homes entirely fenced off from the rest of the world. Instead of relaxing on a beach, we parked our bikes against the wrought-iron fence of one mansion and stretched out on the narrow border of a perfectly manicured green lawn that stuck out beyond the fence. While the family's friendly St. Bernard and black Lab reached their noses toward us from inside the fence, we spread out our bandannas and dined once again on our crackers and cheese but with the addition of Ginger Golds. The sun felt pleasantly warm and Alice took a brief siesta while I relaxed against the fence.

We reached Rochester and learned that the drawbridge at the mouth of Irondequoit Bay was not usable. In summer it was open for boat traffic and closed to cars, and our maps had warned us of this possibility, but the Orleans County officers had told us that it would be open for vehicular traffic. Unfortunately for us, they were wrong. As we rolled into a convenience store to ask directions, we spotted an ambulance parked in front. Who better to ask directions from than an ambulance driver? So I walked over to the driver's side and, seeing he was not involved in an emergency, explained our dilemma. I told him of our backup plan to ride south and use another bridge to cross the bay.

"What would be our best route?" I wondered.

He looked hard at me and said, "Throw your bikes in the back." He didn't explain and he didn't say, "I'd be happy to offer you a ride" or even "Would you like a ride?"

"Alice," I called, grinning in anticipation, "we're getting a ride in an ambulance!"

"Really? Great!"

If I had really thought about it, I might have wondered why we would be allowed to ride in an ambulance, but I was so glad to avoid the rush hour congestion and what I knew would be two or three extra hours of high-traffic riding that I was glad to jump in.

The driver's name was Jim, and he was our first road angel on what would be a two-angel day. He had just finished work for the day and had an hour to spare before picking up his son for soccer practice. When Jim opened the back door, we learned that the "ambulance" was really his work truck. He had recently bought it but hadn't gotten around to repainting it. The tool- and equipment-filled back barely had room for both bikes, but he hefted them in single-handedly,

Our own personal rescue squad

packs and all. I rode in the cramped back with the bikes and a jumble of equipment while Alice climbed into the cab with Jim. He drove south to the base of the bay, around the bottom of it, and back up to the shore of the lake—ten or fifteen miles. He was interested in our trip and posed a different question than others had before him: "Where in the country have you seen the most beautiful scenery?"

It was a hard one to answer. Alice told him about our route through the Columbia River Gorge, across Idaho along the Lochsa and Clearwater rivers, over the mountains of Montana, and past the sunflower fields of North Dakota. The Great Lakes states, too, had their own sort of beauty, so we had to admit it was impossible to choose one favorite.

As we drove he told us, "I hate to drive my truck across that bridge at this time of day. No way was I going to let you ride bikes across—even if you were allowed, which I doubt." As we drove past the Highway 104 bridge and saw the multiple lanes of rush hour traffic moving at high speed, we realized how lucky we were to have met Jim. I classified him as a higher-order road angel for helping us past this dangerous obstacle.

Jim dropped us off at a safe place, unloaded the bikes, and headed to soccer practice. We remounted and made our way toward Sodus Point, following the shore of Lake Ontario. Toward the end of the afternoon we stopped at a convenience store about fifteen miles west of Pultneyville to buy supper to eat at the campground where we planned to spend the night. In line to buy drinks and sandwiches, we heard a woman ask, "Where are you biking?"

Alice replied, "Tonight we are going to camp near Sodus Point, but we started in Oregon and are going to Maine."

Immediately the young woman, whose name was Wendy, became excited and said, "My nephew hiked the entire Appalachian Trail and many people helped him along the way. I would love it if you could stay the night with my son and me. We live about nine miles east of here."

We took Wendy up on her offer and spent a delightful evening with her and Steven, a charming, bright third-grader who showed us his coin collection and various school projects he was working on. We ate our convenience-store sandwiches while they had their supper, and for dessert she served us all chocolate ice-cream sundaes.

At bedtime, Wendy said, "You're welcome to use my bedroom. I can bunk with Steven."

"Oh, no," said Alice. We have great air mattresses. We'll be just fine if we can sleep on your living room floor."

So that became our campsite. Wendy achieved road angel status when she told us that the campground we had planned to stay in was closed after Labor Day. Our good fortune had not run out. In fact, this day had been one of the luckiest of the whole trip.

Day 73 *Wednesday, September 10*
Pultneyville to Fulton
55 miles

We thanked Wendy and Steven, said our good-byes as they prepared to leave for work and school, and were on the road by 8:10. Four miles east was the Pultneyville Pickle, a coffee shop and deli situated in the middle of a fork in the road—a 1940s converted corner gas station. The stop was worth every minute we spent there. We met the clerks and one of the co-owners, Jim, who made us sub sandwiches for our lunch with fresh homemade bread and turkey roasted right there. The fresh pastries were so delectable that we wanted to take a dozen or two with us. Only the lack of carrying space restrained us. Outside we met a cyclist who told us he rode forty miles daily in the area. He shared information about the road ahead, including the news that the hills would be increasing.

He was right about that. Without doubt, we were approaching the Adirondacks. Nothing was flat, but at least the headwind was finally gone. The air temperature was in the midseventies—quite comfortable. We enjoyed many rest stops that day, feeling the relief from both the recent headwinds and the terrible heat of the West. At one quaint country store, we both indulged in gifts to be shipped home—especially toys for my grandchildren and Alice's grandson-to-be.

One of our stops was at a collection of extraordinary wood sculptures. They were not the usual crude, roughly hewn tree-trunk sculptures, but fine, smooth, carefully detailed works carved in maple. We took pictures of the pieces in the yard—graceful dolphins, a mariner with lantern held aloft, and a fisherman and his wife. We saw someone working on the house, which was set back from the road, and he turned out to be Paul, the artist. He had bought the house the previous year, he told us, and was rehabbing it to be his home and studio. He invited us in to show us some of his other works—intricate, hand-carved walking sticks of all sorts, a bust of Elvis, and a larger-than-life wolf staring down at us from a "rocky" ledge. The rocks, ledge, and wolf were all carved from a single block of maple.

Paul showed us a photograph of his sculpture of a life-sized Robert E. Lee and said, "I sold that to a guy in Georgia for $40,000." It was a fine sculpture, but I wondered if that price was accurate. It seemed like a lot of money.

We fell in love with his wolf sculpture, but neither of us could afford even the smallest example of his work, so we chatted some more and took additional pictures—with his permission. Our photos would have to suffice.

We pedaled on, passing more orchards of ripened apples. By 6 p.m. we made it to the North Bay Campground just west of Fulton.

Before our trip I had made friends through an e-mail group with Joy, a woman who lived in the area. Joy had enthusiastically followed our Web site and left messages in our guest book. She was so excited about our trip that she and her husband drove to our campground, picked us up, and took us out for a lovely dinner at an upscale restaurant on the Oswego River. Joy said she would e-mail the rest of the women in the e-mail group to let them know we had made it to New York. I appreciated meeting this friend whom I had known only in cyberspace and whose face I could now match with the name on my e-mails.

Day 74 ***Thursday, September 11***
Fulton to Redfield
50 miles

We awoke to dew-drenched tents and soaking wet bikes. Everything left outside was wet. Even our sleeping bags and clothes inside the tents were damp. The arid West was long gone. Now we remembered why we preferred camping in the West.

On our way out of the campground at 7:30, we stopped at the office to pay but learned that we didn't have to because we had camped on a site that was vacated only the day before by a seasonal renter. We were happy for the free night, especially considering how awful the bathrooms had been. Just as we were pedaling away, we noticed that Alice's rear tire was flat, the victim of an ordinary metal staple. Our tires were often impervious to such things, but the staple had hit at just the wrong angle and had penetrated both tire and tube. A half hour later we were back on the road and looking for breakfast.

The breakfast spot recommended to us was the Top of the Hill Diner in Volney, four miles uphill from our campsite. A banana and energy bar sustained us for the climb, and we were there before we knew it. Everybody in the small cafe—patrons and waitresses alike—was friendly and welcoming. It was the closest thing to Alice's Restaurant of movie and music fame we had seen yet. Our blonde, middle-aged waitress took great pleasure in scaring one of her regulars with a fake mouse on his plate. The whole place dissolved in stitches over her successful practical joke, which apparently was revenge for some prank of his the previous week, and we joined in the fun. We consumed the fluffiest buckwheat pancakes ever, along with our usual eggs.

Our route from Volney took us north, back toward the Lake Ontario shore, orchards bordering the roads once again. Along the Great Lakes in Wisconsin, Michigan, Ohio, and New York we had seen many orchards of apples, pears, peaches, and cherries. It would not have been hard to pick samples right off the trees as we pedaled by, but we restrained ourselves. Instead we once indulged in a little fun at an orchard where the pickers must have been taking a break. Someone had deserted a tractor with its apple wagon, and we couldn't ignore the picture possibilities. Taking turns, we each

Always wear a helmet when harvesting apples

climbed into the driver's seat and pretended we had new jobs. A waste of time, sure, but our way of life allowed for such detours.

Once again we altered our route, staying on Highway 3 rather than taking the back roads. The new route took us through Mexico, New York. We just missed Texas, New York, but eventually made it to Port Ontario for our last glimpse of the easternmost Great Lake. Then it was on to Pulaski. There we found a Laundromat, and Alice tended the wash and visited the post office while I went to get sandwiches.

Alice's rear derailleur had been refusing to shift into its lowest gear—the "granny"—on steep hills, so we needed to get that fixed before we met the Adirondacks. Our maps showed a bike shop in Pulaski, but we learned it was no longer in business. Out of necessity we decided to attack the mechanical problem ourselves. When none of our adjustments to the various set screws seemed to make any difference in how the chain moved across the freewheel, we applied our most serious problem-solving skills. In a stroke of brilliance, for one who is mechanically challenged, I deduced that we had not reseated the rear wheel properly after changing the flat tire, so when we adjusted that, her shifting was smooth once again. Alice was relieved that she would have use of the full range of gears on the mountains that were fast approaching.

Our last errand in Pulaski was to find ice cream. For that necessity we headed to a shop recommended by a local bicyclist whom we had met out in the country. Taylor Marie's was everything the cyclist said it was and more, and we spooned up the best hard ice cream we had tasted in several weeks—pecan turtle for Alice and coffee toffee for me. We liked Pulaski.

While enjoying our cones, one well-dressed patron asked about our trip. After a few minutes of chatting, she said, "Aren't you afraid for your personal safety?"

It was the second time that day we had been asked this question, both times by women. It hadn't come up much since Montana, but we thought that being in the more populated East might mean that people were more concerned with security issues in general and women's safety in particular. We honestly assured our questioners that except for a few traffic hassles we had not felt seriously threatened at any time while with our bikes. We're not sure if they believed us.

Should we have been concerned about climbing in a nonambulance with Jim? Should we have not trusted Wendy, who asked us to stay in her home? Perhaps some people thought so, but we felt that we were reasonably good judges of character and did not make poor decisions. Besides, we had each other as a check. If one of us hesitated, we wouldn't do whatever the other was pondering. We agreed that too many people miss out on great learning and growing experiences because of fear of what "could" happen. Some risks were worth taking.

From Pulaski we once again rode eastward across rolling terrain through Richland, Orwell, and some wetland areas in between. We made it to Redfield, where we had a reservation at the only shelter available for miles around—the Crossroads Inn, out in the country a mile beyond town. Once again I negotiated a lower price than advertised, even though only one room was left. The one room turned out to be an entire cabin, a charming, meticulously clean, 1950s-style little place. The other patrons at the inn, which spread across a number of acres, were fishermen who had arrived for the opening of salmon season. We all ended up eating dinner at the only restaurant within several miles. It looked ramshackle, as did the rest of the small town. The food was slow to arrive, and both presentation and flavor were bland.

We had forgotten our lights, and with no moon to show us the way, we rode ever so cautiously back to our cabin through the pitch-black Adirondack night. Safely back, Alice went to organize her gear and then was off to bed. I stretched my muscles and then drifted off to sleep, musing about what challenges the next day would present as we began scaling the mountains of the East.

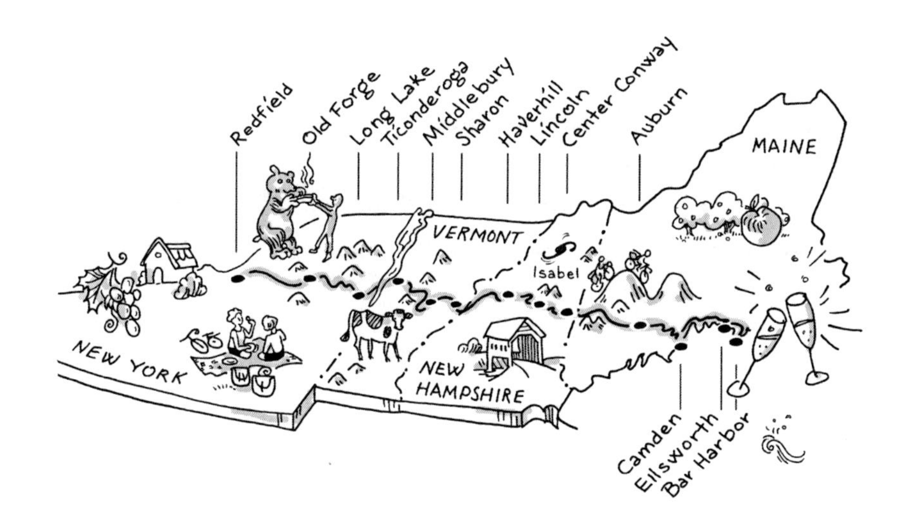

6

Over the Adirondacks and across New England

Eastern New York, Vermont, New Hampshire, and Maine

It was mid-September, the days were growing shorter, and even without seeing a calendar, we felt the end of our trip approaching. Along with everyone else, we found ourselves stopping behind school buses. We came upon football practices with coaches shouting, whistles blowing, and young boys running plays in the warm, late afternoon sun. It was back-to-school time in America.

Day 75 ***Friday, September 12***
Redfield to Old Forge
60 miles

Reluctantly, we left our trim and cozy cabin outside Redfield and immediately encountered hills. On the way to Osceola and then West Leyden, we experienced one of the optical illusions common in mountains—the appearance of going downhill when we were actually going up. Our legs knew we were climbing even if our eyes didn't comprehend. The illusion toyed with our psyches even though we had experienced it countless times before on other trips.

Many of the hills that day were extremely steep, and both of us walked one monster. It was the first time I had walked a hill, but when I saw it rising up in front of me like the steepest incline of a major roller coaster, I quickly dismounted. I didn't want to get partway up, stall, be locked into my pedals, and fall over.

At a Radio Shack in Boonville, where we stopped so that Alice could buy a new cell phone battery, we gained a mascot. A tiny, stuffed brown and white puppy—Little Nipper, son of the original Nipper, the RCA dog—was a gift from Cheryl and Ben, the friendly clerks. They also treated us to some new plastic bags to replace ours that were worn. What was trash in our complicated, at-home lives became treasure—they were essential for keeping our gear dry. Nipper took the place of honor on the top of my load, admiring the early autumn Adirondack foliage from his perch.

The terrain east of Boonville was not as rugged as it had been in the morning but was still challenging. We pedaled steadily, gaining some elevation on the busy state highway leading to Old Forge. It had a wide shoulder, but heavy traffic was speeding its way north along with us to the Adirondacks for the weekend.

After a great deal of comparison shopping up and down Main Street in Old Forge, we finally chose a motel. Maybe our room didn't have a whole kitchen, but the refrigerator was a bonus, and we felt it offset in some way the exorbitant cost of the room. Tourist season wasn't quite over in Old Forge, and we had to pay top dollar.

For dinner we downed huge portions of salad, pasta, and meatballs. We decided to take back our leftovers for breakfast or even a picnic lunch the next day. Walking back to our motel, doggy bags in hand, we stopped at the pharmacy for a few incidentals. The clerk gave us a long look and asked, "Are you walking far with that food?"

It seemed a strange question, but when we showed our surprise, she said, "Bears around here go for people who carry food, so we don't carry food outside much. My mother was taking a pan of lasagna over to the neighbors when a bear blocked her way. She had to put the lasagna down and back away. The bear got a great meal."

That story was hard to believe, but the clerk was serious, and we became a bit nervous. We walked briskly to our next stop, the grocery store, only to encounter an excited checkout clerk. "Did you hear about the bear?" she asked.

We looked at each other and said in unison, "What bear?"

"Just an hour ago, a kid on a bike crashed into a bear on Main Street!" she informed us. This had happened while we were eating dinner. Now we really were nervous. We practically ran back to our motel and safely stowed our food.

Bear stories proliferated. We didn't see one of the beasts, but if we had, it wouldn't have been unusual. They were reported to frequent Adirondack villages even in the middle of the day. In one nearby village a bear had to be shot because it went through the screen door into someone's kitchen and made a huge mess rampaging around when it couldn't find its way out. Bears ransacked garbage cans each night, and some people wouldn't even let their children weed the family garden because these animals would wander through in the middle of the day. At least they weren't grizzlies. They were black bears, but still they could be dangerous.

Day 76 ***Saturday, September 13***
Old Forge to Long Lake
50 miles

With dark rain clouds threatening and thoughts of marauding bears not far from our minds, we rolled through Adirondack Park—up and over endless hills, down and around lakes, through dark forests, and past "camps," which is what easterners call their summer homes. We were constantly entertained by the names that families had assigned their vacation hideaways—names like Loon-a-tik Lodge, Seventh Haven, or Whit's End.

At the town of Inlet we stopped for a couple of hours because we found a bike shop where we could get our drive trains cleaned. The chains and derailleur mechanisms were pretty dirty and we could get them only so clean on our own. We wrote a few postcards and relaxed in a coffee shop while the owner of Pedals and Petals (bike repair and flower shop all in one) worked on our bikes. Alice was offended for a second time when the owner admired her Deore XTR rear derailleur, noting that it was "probably worth more than the whole rest of the bike." She tried to forgive him because he wasn't old enough to realize that her Holdsworth Mistral was actually a collector's item—and a darned good bike even though, on its fifth paint job since 1982, it looked a wreck. Her bike fit her perfectly and had taken her thousands of miles. She loved it like an old friend and didn't appreciate the disrespect for her faithful Black Beauty.

"He was probably born after they stopped making my bike," she later grumbled. "What would he know?"

Leaving Inlet we followed a chain of lakes, which included Raquette Lake, Blue Mountain Lake, and Long Lake. In the town of Blue Mountain Lake a huge Adirondack furniture show was taking place with some pieces displayed alongside the road, but we were running late and didn't have time to stop to admire the artisans' handiwork. With eleven miles still to go to Long Lake, we rolled on, rain threatening. The surprise of the day was the steep, two-mile climb up from the shore of Blue Mountain Lake. I rode it without stopping, while Alice rested once partway up the grade. As we cruised along after we reached the top, several motorists passed us and cheered.

"You rock!" they shouted out their window. We had no trouble agreeing.

The Shamrock Motel in Long Lake was a step back in time—to the 1950s at least. The motel was clean, comfortable, and quiet, and the view of Long Lake was striking. Adirondack chairs dotted the expansive lawn fronting the lake. The scene reminded me of my youthful summers on my beloved Crescent Lake in Maine. Our room had no phone, but a pay phone was available at the end of the parking lot by the highway, and a coin laundry was conveniently located in another building on the premises.

We tried the Blarney Stone for dinner, but when Alice asked that we be moved to a table that was not directly under the air conditioner fan, our waitress did not cooperate. She didn't seem to care whether we stayed or left, so we left and walked down the hill to the Adirondack Hotel, where the prices were lower, the atmosphere less pretentious, and the waitstaff more accommodating. We made sure we cleaned our plates so that on the long, dark walk up the hill to our cozy motel we didn't have to worry about bears hungry for leftovers.

Day 77 ***Sunday, September 14***
Rest day

The first day of our next-to-last week was a rest day. We left our bikes parked in our room at the Shamrock Motel, walked back and forth a half mile or so into the town of Long Lake for meals, and spent the rest of the day relaxing. Breakfast at the Long Lake Diner and lunch back at the Adirondack Hotel filled us up so well that we decided to sit in the chairs by the lake and use some of our own provisions for supper. The sunset over Long Lake turned both sky and water several shades of vivid pink. We enjoyed this sleepy little retreat and agreed it would be a good place to vacation someday.

Because it was the first day of bear-hunting season, we heard the pop of distant gunshots. According to the locals, the sound of rifle shots would send the bears back into the woods, and we were glad. When Alice went out in the inky black darkness at 10 p.m. to use the pay phone on the edge of the parking lot, a hunter was getting out of his truck, rifle in hand. He carelessly pointed the gun at Alice's legs.

"What are you doing?" she asked him. "Would you please point that gun away from me!"

He turned it away, and speaking in a deep, gravelly voice, announced, "It sure is scary out in those woods." And then, with pride, he added, "I just got me a bear," and ambled off to his room.

Alice phoned Booth.

"Booth, dear, I can't talk long because our room doesn't have a phone, we don't have cell service, and I'm at a pay phone out in the motel parking lot. That wouldn't be so bad, but this scary guy in the room next door just told me he shot a bear. Now I'm more afraid of the hunters than I am of the bears."

As we were preparing to leave the next morning, we saw the Shamrock's owners engaged in conversation with a Department of Environmental Conservation officer. It seemed that our gruff hunter had shot both a mother bear and her cub, an illegal act, and the motel owners and their neighbors were upset. Alice contributed her story about him carelessly pointing his gun at her, and the officer noted it. The motel owners thought the hunter was on his way back to New Jersey, so the police said they would try to nab him. Later we wondered if he escaped with his illegal kill, but as with all the other people we met on our trip, we caught only a snippet of the story. We would never know what happened.

Day 78 ***Monday, September 15***
Long Lake to Ticonderoga
63 miles

Before we pedaled away from Long Lake we followed through on a big decision we had made the day before. We would ship our camping gear home to decrease our load and save ourselves on the steep hills and mountains of New England. People always asked how we managed the Rockies, but the roads in the East were built before those in the West and had steeper grades. The word "hill" does not truly portray how steep or long New England's hills can be. Having ridden in Maine before, we thought we knew what we would be up against, but we had a few more things to learn about New England terrain, such as the disconcerting fact that if a hill had its own name, it was a monster. And many of those hills had names. Also, because it was after Labor Day, many commercial campgrounds were closed, and it was becoming difficult to find camping places. We collected a couple of empty boxes at a gift shop, bought a roll of tape, and stuffed tents, sleeping bags, and other camping necessities into the boxes. The next morning we were at the door of the post office before it opened. We sacrificed some flexibility by relinquishing the gear, but we were tired of camping anyway. The decision could break our budget, but we would worry about that later.

Fortified by another breakfast at the Long Lake Diner, we mounted our lighter bikes and began riding toward Ticonderoga and the New York–Vermont border. Riding through deep forests for the next sixteen miles, we arrived in Newcomb, where we found a general store with a deli. As we pulled into the parking lot, the owner was setting down a paper plate full of leftovers for a wolf that she fed regularly. She was proud that the wolf trusted her enough to come to the diner, and she cheerfully informed us that a bear had ventured into their campground the night before. Hmmm. Maybe it didn't know it was hunting season.

We bought sandwiches to go so that we could eat them somewhere in the next twenty-two miles, which was part of a stretch we knew would have no services. The day's route continued through Adirondack Park, past lakes, over hills, and through thick woods of conifers, maples, and birches. We were too early for full fall colors, but we saw evidence of some trees changing with flashes of red and yellow interspersed with the dominant greens. We got just a hint of how beautiful this area would be a few weeks later. For thirty-eight miles we saw no sign of civilization except for the store and the few houses of tiny Newcomb.

In North Hudson we turned south, following alongside I-87 for a few miles before heading east once again. On the sixteen-mile segment west of Ticonderoga, the road became narrow and busy with truck traffic—delivery trucks, construction trucks, semis, every kind of truck imaginable. One truck passed us from behind against the double-yellow line on a tight curve, and we feared that if a car had been coming toward us, we would have witnessed a head-on tragedy. When two trucks came from behind on the next curve, we steered into the gravel and stopped even though we didn't have much space on the winding, shoulderless road. It was only the second time in 3,000 miles we were forced off the road because drivers were unwilling to slow down and wait to pass.

At Ticonderoga, we found the Super 8 already full at 4 p.m., so we tried the nearby Green Acres Motel. It was one of the dingiest, most disgusting places we had seen, but we took the only room left because we feared that we wouldn't find anything open farther down the road. Without our camping gear, we were a bit insecure about finding shelter, but who would have thought we would have trouble on a Monday night two weeks after Labor Day. That would teach us—we would make reservations from that point on. Our room at Green Acres was green all right—dark green—and also dirty, dank, and depressing.

Day 79 Tuesday, September 16
Ticonderoga to Middlebury, Vermont
28 miles

The Ticonderoga Ferry to Vermont ran across Lake Champlain every seven minutes. We skipped Fort Ticonderoga, an important site in the French and Indian War, because we had been there in the past and were eager to get to Middlebury to look around, find a bike shop, and pick up a few groceries.

As we rolled our bikes off the ferry on the Vermont side, I asked a gentleman standing by the road if he would take our picture by the Welcome to Vermont sign. He seemed happy to cooperate and asked us the usual questions when he saw our loads. He was the coach driver for a group of tourists who were out taking a boat ride on Lake Champlain. When Alice asked him if he knew whether the building nearby had a restroom, he said that it was closed but that we could use the restroom on the coach.

Ahoy! Vermont, here we come!

"The other folks won't mind," he said. "They're out on the boat."

So we climbed the steps and trotted to the back of the bus. While we were there we pretended for a few minutes that we were seeing the hills of New England from the soft seat of a bus. Oh, it would have been so easy, but we truly preferred our means of transportation. The bus driver won our complete approval when, in the course of our friendly discussion, he volunteered that "women are smarter than men and really control things." Such a wise man.

A mile or so up the road, I saw a sign pointing to Norton's Gallery. I had been there once with friends and wanted to show it to Alice.

"C'mon, Alice. Let's take a detour. You'll love this place."

"No," Alice whined, "it's uphill."

"But that means we get to come down on the way back. And the view up there is phenomenal."

"Oh, all right, I'm coming. I guess a mile won't kill me."

She agreed that it was worth the effort because the view of Lake Champlain Valley on a sunny, clear day from the gallery's red barn was stunning, and the whimsical, carved animals inhabiting the yard were a sight she would not have wanted to miss.

Also in the yard sat Wooden Ben and his equally wooden wife, Amanda May, two larger-than-life figures sculpted and painted by artist Norton Latourelle. Ben and Amanda May had been "married" several weeks before, and their human family had hosted a big wedding celebration. Quirky humor was evident everywhere at Norton's Gallery, combined with sophisticated talent. In the gift shop I found a cardinal and a chickadee to represent Ohio and Maine, my favorite states, and Alice bought a beautiful brown thrush, Vermont's state bird. After enjoying our conversation with the Latourelles and the brief downhill back to the route, we spent the rest of the day pedaling uphill as we tackled the foothills of the Green Mountains. We were glad we had jettisoned the camping gear—those hills were steep!

I wondered aloud, "Why would anyone want to live in so many hills?"

Alice answered, "Most people don't spend whole days masochistically riding bicycles up and down them. They just enjoy looking out their windows at them or driving over them."

"I guess you're right. But I'm a bit tired of the up and down—well, mostly the up right now."

Of course another answer for why people want to live in the hills is that one scene after another is breathtakingly beautiful. On this September day, pastoral vistas spread before us as we climbed the hills and then looked down at productive valleys in every direction. Black-and-white cows dotted green pastures, and I thought of the artwork on Ben and Jerry's ice-cream cartons. Ice cream was never far from my mind, but here was a new example of life imitating art.

Hillsides patchworked with golden grains and turning leaves lay beneath a dazzling clear-blue sky. We began seeing the characteristic big house attached to a smaller one, which in turn was joined to a shed and then a barn. Some New Englanders called it "big-house-little-house-back-house-barn" construction. Even the stand-alone gray or white barns were quaint and distinctively New England, and we stopped often for photos on the brilliant Kodak day.

When we arrived in the picturesque college town of Middlebury, set in the hills above the Middlebury River, we first visited two bike shops. I bought a new supply of Chamois Butt'r, and we learned about the best lunch places. We picked Mister Up's, which offered an extensive salad bar, where we purchased lunches to go. The bill: five dollars each. We sat under a tree in the shade and wolfed down the best food we had had in a long time—seafood salad, artichoke salad, assorted greens, and hearty whole-grain bread.

We continued on to the library, where we were allowed a half hour on the Internet. Outside the library, we saw a couple about our age readying their own bikes for a ride. We asked if they knew how to get to the Greystone Motel and whether it was uphill or down. We would go there no matter the direction of the incline, but we wanted to know what we were facing. They gave us directions, said it was a flat route, and then began asking us questions. Before we knew it, Julia and Doug had invited us to dinner and to spend the night at their home. We had already made reservations at the motel and it was too late to cancel them without forfeiting our money, so we reluctantly declined the overnight offer but happily accepted the dinner invitation.

After we showered at our motel, Doug drove us in his black Jeep to their lovely home in the hills above Middlebury. They had retired in June from long-time teaching careers in Florida. They loved Vermont, where they had had their summer home for several years, and they also loved music, art, and travel. Doug grilled chicken and lamb, and Julia added pasta with pesto sauce and homemade focaccia bread with herbs from their garden. Homemade chocolate cake with Ben and Jerry's coffee ice cream topped it all off.

During dinner, Alice happened to mention her husband back home in Wisconsin. Our hosts looked momentarily puzzled and then Doug said, "So you're not a couple?" We laughed and Alice said, "We've wondered if people thought we were. We don't mind if they think so, and it hasn't seemed to affect the way we are treated, so really, it's not an issue as far as we're concerned."

They seemed to understand, and went on to tell us they had retired to Vermont partly because of its political culture, including the state's support of civil unions. Even though it was hard to tear ourselves away from our charming hosts, it soon became time to get some sleep, so we asked Doug to return us to the Greystone Motel and he graciously obliged.

Day 80 — *Wednesday, September 17*
Middlebury to Sharon
53 miles

We backtracked a mile for breakfast at Rosie's at the suggestion of the motel's owner. We usually avoided backtracking, but we were warned that we would find nothing for breakfast in the direction we would be going.

Middlebury's elevation was approximately 400 feet, and by the time we reached the top of Middlebury Gap, we were at 2,000 feet. It was close to a ten-mile climb, but we were feeling strong. Besides, since we had shipped our camping gear home, our bikes each weighed about ten pounds less. That helped. Before reaching the summit we stopped to take photos of the Bread Loaf School of English with its prim campus of antique, ocher-colored frame buildings overlooking quiet, rolling meadows. This institution, begun in the 1920s, is part of Middlebury College, and it offers graduate courses in literature, creative writing, the teaching of writing, and theater arts. We were captivated by its serenity in the off-season, and I couldn't help but think back to the invitation I had received many years ago to attend Bread Loaf. I wished I had.

From the crest we left our route for a mile or so in order to check out Texas Falls. At a roadside park there, we ate another of our picnic lunches. We never seemed to tire of the peanut butter and crackers menu. Besides, everything tasted good when we had just climbed a mountain.

In the town of Rochester we stopped at the Rochester Cafe to answer the siren song of hot fudge sundaes. Set in a historic two-story building, the old-fashioned soda fountain boasted high ceilings and antique ceramic tile floors that had been walked on by ice-cream lovers for at least a hundred years. Following tradition, we indulged ourselves.

For the rest of the day we pedaled past one pleasant autumn scene after another on Vermont's quiet roads—beautiful barns, historic homes, white-steepled churches, and one-room schools, all set against green undulating hills and valleys. The towns of Stockbridge, Bethel, Royalton, and South Royalton were just a few miles apart. Each one had a quintessential Vermont country store, and some also had gas stations or post offices.

South Royalton was home to the Vermont Law School, a small, private institution for about 500 students that emphasizes environmental law. It seemed odd for such a small town in a rural area to be populated primarily by smartly dressed young adults moving briskly along the sidewalks. On the way out of South Royalton we met Martha, a local bike rider, and she accompanied us all the way to Sharon. She was a kindergarten teacher at the Sharon Academy and was out for a late-afternoon bike ride.

In Sharon we had the choice of two establishments. We chose the less expensive of the two and stayed at the Half-Acre Motel, only two doors from Martha's home. She told us to let her know if things didn't work out there and she would help us. I wondered later whether she might have known what a poor excuse for a motel it was. The antique metal kitchenette with its aluminum pans and rusted burner rims and drip bowls allowed us to boil water, but that convenience hardly made up for the room's other deficiencies. The mattresses sagged, much of the floor was covered with ancient shag carpeting of indeterminate color, and no phone or cable television was available. The TV brought in only one channel, which was a problem because we were desperate for news of Hurricane Isabel, rumored to be approaching from off New England's coast. We wanted to know when Isabel was scheduled to hit land so that we could avoid riding into the storm. The substandard TV offered no useful information. We would have to wait.

According to the motel's owner, the nearby restaurant had burned down recently under mysterious circumstances, so we had little choice for dinner—sandwiches, or sandwiches—from the deli in the general store, a short walk away. So we returned with sandwiches to our ramshackle room.

Day 81 Thursday, September 18
Sharon to Haverhill, New Hampshire
38 miles

Despite the too-soft beds, after eight hours of deep sleep we felt ready to ascend the next mountain, which lay immediately beyond our door. A glance outside revealed dark clouds hanging so low that the roofs of nearby buildings were obscured. What little we could see of the mountain looked foreboding under its cape of dense gray. We stalled our departure by riding a bit off the route to Dixie's for breakfast. A couple of friendly truck drivers at Dixie's told us they had seen us the day before and wondered where we were headed. While we answered their questions, they shook their heads continually. Their incredulity amused us. We were a bit surprised to realize that motorists could possibly follow our route for a bit one day and wonder where we were going and then see us again the next. We were so engrossed in seeing the world from the seats of our bikes that we didn't think much about what drivers thought when they saw us. The conversation with the curious truck drivers widened our perspective.

The climb out of Sharon was a serious one, about four miles long, the first two miles steepest. We worked hard to ascend and were relieved to see the clouds and fog disappear as we rode. The long descent was rewarding, as usual, but we braked some because the surface was not totally smooth and we didn't want to risk a blowout. Neither of us let our speedometers register much over forty miles per hour, but Alice overtook me on the downhill as usual.

The next climb was another challenge up to the picturesque town of Thetford Hill, where we ate our lunch on the village green. The weather cleared and the air warmed to a perfect, sunny seventy degrees. The heat of Montana seemed a lifetime ago in Vermont, where red leaves of autumn were becoming more plentiful.

A few miles beyond Thetford Hill we crossed our first covered bridge, stopping, of course, to take photos. A few miles later, we realized what a small state Vermont is as we crossed the Connecticut River into New Hampshire. Because we were on such a rural road, we never came to a Welcome to New Hampshire sign. Oh, well.

As we started down River Road, another bicyclist caught up to us. Joy was on her way home from her job as a librarian at Dartmouth College. We learned that she too was a young grandma. A strong rider on a light bike, she kindly waited for us at the tops of hills as we slogged up with our loads. We enjoyed talking with her about bike trips and got a report on the upcoming hills on our route. We were impressed with her ability to ride so happily in this extremely hilly area. Joy stayed with us all the way to Orford, where we stopped to have our photo taken together. We said our good-byes and went into the country store to find sandwiches for dinner. We were planning to stay at a B&B in Haverhill and knew there was no restaurant near it.

At the stately Gibson House Gallery B&B in Haverhill overlooking the Connecticut River Valley we were surprised to see a For Sale sign on the front lawn. Keita, our host, told us that she was unable to handle all the maintenance demands of the three-story frame colonial and was trying to sell the historic home. She had clearly spent a fortune remodeling the rooms and decorating them to perfection. We all agreed that part of the problem may have been that the New Hampshire side of the river was less traveled than the Vermont side and that tourism appeared to flourish more in Vermont than on the eastern side of the Connecticut River. Keita, an artist of considerable skill, had hung her own exquisite oil paintings throughout the three floors of her home, and we wished that we could have bought even one.

Because we were her only guests, Keita led us on a tour, explaining that we could choose whichever room we wanted. All the rooms were huge and to say they were decorated distinctively would be an understatement. Over the bed in the dark India-themed room, a beautifully rendered, hand-painted Bengal tiger and jungle scene was lit by a bright, eerily realistic full moon. The realism occurred, we discovered, because the moon canvas was stretched over an actual hole in the wall, through which light filtered. Other walls were covered in a heavily flocked burgundy fabric, giving the room an exotic feel. Each bedchamber was as unusual as the next, yet they all were consistent with the historical feel of the house, and every detail imparted a spacious, luxurious, comfortable ambience. We chose a room decorated in shades of white and gold. It was large, light, and airy, and seemed more appropriate for sophisticated tourists wearing designer clothes than for two grubby cyclists in spandex. No matter—in no time we were bathing and primping, taking advantage of a variety of Caswell-Massey toiletries set out on the vanity in the lavish bathroom.

Our simple life on the road was filled with contrasts. We experienced sun and rain, swift descents and grueling climbs, too-full bellies and deep hunger, remote country touring and traffic-filled city riding, starlit camping, and filthy motels interspersed with a few luxurious B&Bs. The swing of the pendulum was part of the appeal for us. Willingness to deal with change and various levels of discomfort made it possible to ride without a support van across this vast land, enjoying the challenges that came from such an adventure.

We had not expected it, but Keita served us a gourmet supper of fresh mushroom soup and homemade whole-grain bread, which we ate on a second floor porch overlooking the placid Connecticut River. It had taken us fewer than three full days to cross Vermont, and we had to remind ourselves that we were already in New Hampshire, looking back across the river to the rolling green landscape of Vermont. After stowing our deli sandwiches in Keita's refrigerator for the next day's lunch, we went to bed satisfied but still wondering what effects Hurricane Isabel would bring.

Day 82 — *Friday, September 19*
Haverhill to Lincoln
15 miles

Breakfast the next morning began at 8:30, so we packed up our bikes first and made sure we were in the dining room right on time for Keita's banana pancakes drizzled with pure maple syrup. The local weather forecast was for Isabel to bring wind and rain—but not until afternoon, so we decided to make a run for it to Lincoln, a mere twenty-six miles away. Unfortunately, almost all the miles were uphill. To reach Lincoln at the base of the Kancamagus Highway, New Hampshire's famous scenic route across the White Mountains, we had to climb two mountains before descending into the town.

In two hours we had made it about halfway when suddenly the sky blackened and strong wind and rain began. The rain was not coming down from directly above us, but the wind was so strong it drove the rain sideways at us, apparently from miles away. I had learned the day before that a shuttle service operated out of Lincoln for hikers and backpackers, so when gusts rose to about forty miles per hour and sizeable branches began crashing to the forest floor and blowing onto the roadway, we didn't have to debate whether to seek shelter and call for a ride. We spotted a Quonset hut that served as an automotive garage, one of two buildings in the town of Benton, New Hampshire, the other being a historic one-room schoolhouse. We pulled in and I asked the mechanic if we could use his phone because we had no cell service in the hilly, wooded terrain. He was friendly and accommodating and let us hang out until the van came for us about an hour later.

As we rode in the van up and over the last big hump to 2,000 feet, we saw that not only were we avoiding the nasty effects of Hurricane Isabel by taking a ride, but we also missed slopping through three miles of mud on a section of highway where the pavement had just been removed in preparation for new asphalt. In one shuttle ride we avoided both bad weather and a nonexistent road. Isabel had caught us at just the right place.

The thirteen-mile bump brought us into Lincoln. There we found a snug Comfort Inn with all the amenities, a great place to wait for Isabel to weaken before crossing our last mountain pass on the way to Maine for the final leg of our journey.

Between meals we got massages from the local therapist, our first since Fargo. When we went into a map store to look for details about our next day's ride, the proprietor said, "Oh, you're going to crank the Kanc, eh?" This was localspeak for pedaling the Kancamagus Highway, which ran through a pass in the White Mountain National Forest. We liked this colorful description, so we adopted it to answer people's questions about where we were going next. One person looked at us soberly and said, "Oh, that's really hard. After the approach, which is a bit of a climb, it's quite a grade for three miles. Are you sure you want do that?"

Yes, we were sure, but we were glad for the day to rest up for it.

Day 83 — *Saturday, September 20*
Lincoln to Center Conway
52 miles

We awoke to crisp blue skies and the obvious disappearance of Hurricane Isabel for our crank over the Kanc, our last serious mountain pass. In the parking lot of our motel, after our complimentary continental breakfast, Alice reminded me that we should check our tires since we had forgotten to do that in our rush to relax on the previous day.

I was shocked to discover a three-inch gash in my rear tire. The tire was still fully inflated, but any bump at all could spell disaster. Our tires were good quality, but with this gash no tire would be able to withstand a bump at high speed when descending a mountain.

We looked around town for a bike shop, hoping to avoid the work ourselves, but nothing was open early on a Sunday. So grudgingly, and with Alice's help, I unloaded all the gear and changed the tire, using the folded spare I had been carrying for twelve weeks.

Finally on the road by 10:20, we started up the pass. It was twelve miles to the top, and to our surprise, the climb seemed downright easy. The air was dry and skies were sunny. Patches of red maples appeared periodically amidst the green foliage as we gained altitude.

Elevation at the top of the pass was 2,855 feet, making it the highest highway pass in the East. Even though the road never leveled out, only the last three miles had a 7 percent grade. We had a good head of steam before reaching the steeper part of the pull, and it was one of those times when we both felt great. We were in the best cycling shape of our lives and this ascent was our payoff. We cruised up the highway, celebrating the glorious day.

We found a sunny patch of grass at the scenic overlook and spread out our picnic lunch where the vista showcased ridge after ridge of changing colors—from shades of green to autumn patches of reds and yellows. A short stone wall separating the grassy area from the sidewalk provided our backrest for a panoramic view of the White Mountains. We were both feeling rather proud of ourselves for finding the once-dreaded Kanc an easy ascent. Other tourists stopped at the same spot and before we could start our lunch, we found ourselves giving a little presentation to a group of about fifteen who gathered around us. Once again, without asking, a man snapped a picture of Alice as she was talking. We felt as though we were holding a spontaneous press conference.

Two couples from England explained that they were touring New England for several weeks, so we all shared our enthusiasm for traveling. Alice was overjoyed when one of the men, Allen, recognized her bike and exclaimed about its quality in his beautiful British accent: "Ah, a Holdsworth! A fine machine!" he raved.

"Oh, wow! You know my bike!" she answered gleefully. She explained that he was the first person in the whole United States to recognize the brand and appreciate its quality. We chatted with their party for quite a while, and Allen and his wife invited Alice to stay with them when she next visited England.

After the twelve-mile ascent came a downhill coast of twenty-two miles. We sat up and breathed in the reward—no pedaling or braking needed as we followed alongside the rock-strewn river cascading down the mountain. As we descended, the temperature rose, so after a few miles we pulled over to shed a layer of clothing. As we were stowing our jackets and turning our maps to the new segment, a carload of people pulled over beside us. They had been in our audience at the top of the mountain and wanted to make sure everything was all right. We assured them that all was well.

Near the bottom of the mountain pass, a man was selling apples from his truck next to a crudely scrawled sign that read "Macouns." Remembering the delicious Ginger Gold apples of New York, I wanted to see what a Macoun was, so I pulled over and Alice followed. He explained, "A Macoun is a cross between a McIntosh and a Jersey Black. Here, take one, and have some free cider too."

The cider was cold, tart, and satisfying, a perfect complement to the superb autumn day. The apples were tasty, but Ginger Gold remained my favorite new variety. We thanked him and rode off.

Because we had made such good time, we detoured a few miles to North Conway and visited the huge Eastern Mountain Sports store. We didn't need anything there or in any other shop and we didn't want more to carry, so we just window-shopped. The town was filled with a procession of tourists tramping from one store to another, laden with shopping bags. Coffee shops and high-end clothing retailers mingled with T-shirt and hardware stores. North Conway was both a traditional, upscale New England village and a base camp for weekend mountaineers from Boston and New York. We found a trendy cafe, where we bought fancy sandwiches for dinner and added a huge piece of chocolate amaretto cake for dessert. Even though our handlebar bags could barely hold all the food, we managed to pack it all in. We were determined to celebrate having blasted—not just cranked—the Kanc on one of our best biking days ever. A few miles later we checked in at the Saco River Motor Lodge and feasted in epicurean style.

Day 84 *Sunday, September 21*
Center Conway to Auburn, Maine
59 miles

We found breakfast at a most unlikely spot—the House of Pizza in Fryeburg, just across the Maine border. Alice's huge Greek omelet and my stack of blueberry pancakes disappeared quickly.

I thought about all the calories on my plate. "I'm sure going to miss my pancake breakfasts."

Alice responded, "Yeah, we have only a few more days for these eating frenzies. How will we ever get back to normal? I just love to eat!"

I was glad to be back in another one of my "home" states—actually my favorite—but I had misgivings about the terrain, which would turn out to be well founded. The day's route took us over more hills than we imagined could exist on any one day's route anywhere. In fact we climbed for more total miles on our first day in Maine than we had the day before on the Kancamagus Highway. The difference was that they were not all in one hill and they were anything but gradual. Instead, we rode up some exceedingly steep grades, then down, then up again, then down—all day long. And unlike Vermont and New Hampshire with their grand vistas of mountains and valleys, Maine's winding roads were lined with pines. No more grand vistas, just hill after hill after tree-lined hill.

Our route from Fryeburg took us over the "Sweden Hills," a local sobriquet we learned too late. The hills were so steep they reminded me of some of the climbs we labored up—and flew down—in the Gaspé Peninsula of Quebec, where we had pedaled a few summers before. Those grades, like these, were terrifying to look at and excruciating to ride. We walked up the last of the killers, and at the top, with vistas of White Mountain scenery, found a remote apple orchard

Maine's never-ending mini-mountains

where a man with a Jamaican accent was tending the weathered roadside stand. The scene evoked John Irving's *Cider House Rules*, and I wondered whether this setting might have inspired him.

The apples looked tasty, but we couldn't carry a bushel, and the man said the orchard owner wouldn't allow him to sell smaller amounts. We were disappointed but we didn't press the issue. While we were preparing to leave, an older woman who had just completed her purchase attempted to carry a crate of apples to her car, and on her way the crate broke. She and the apples tumbled down together, and apples went rolling everywhere. All three of us rushed to her aid, trying not to slip over the still-rolling apples.

"Oh, ma'am, I was going to help you with that!" exclaimed the concerned orchard man.

Her knee was bloody, and she looked frightened, but with his help she got to her feet and leaned against the table. As the man tried to console her, we realized that because he had been talking to us, she hadn't waited for him to help her. Apparently customers were not supposed to take the crates, whose slatted sides easily came loose, but instead were to have the apples transferred to paper bags. But she hadn't known the drill. Alice offered first-aid supplies from her handlebar bag. The man and I picked up the apples and loaded them into bags, and then we helped her to her car with her purchases.

As we were again preparing to leave, the man in charge walked toward us, flashed a huge smile, and silently held out both hands, each with two freshly picked McIntoshes. We were well supplied with apples once again, pleased by his change of heart.

At South Paris we visited John, owner of the hardware store, who had recently married my widowed stepmother, Caroline. When I spoke to Caroline on the phone and told her of our planned route to Auburn, she gasped.

"You don't want to ride there!" she said. "It's way too hilly—and very narrow." She paused. "And it's too dangerous."

She then did some quick research while John talked to folks in the store, and when she called back she suggested an alternate route, which John and the others endorsed. So we pedaled toward Auburn through Hebron and West Minot, wondering all the time how it could be less hilly than the alternatives. We hoped never to find out.

We journeyed on, pushing up more hills, wondering whether the road would ever flatten. Traffic was heavy in that rural area, and we realized that we were in the more densely populated East and that it was the time of the afternoon when school let out. From that point on, we noticed how heavy traffic became after 3:30 p.m. each day on the narrow, winding roads. Dusk was upon us as we neared Auburn, and not knowing which part of town our motel was in, we stopped to ask directions of a man puttering in his front yard. He gave us detailed instructions for the best route away from heavy traffic, and we thought we followed them closely. Somehow, we overshot the motel by about three miles and had to backtrack down a busy highway. By the time we pulled into the motel's driveway it was dark.

Day 85 — Monday, September 22
Auburn to Camden
74 miles

It was the first day of autumn—the day when the sun rises exactly in the east and sets exactly in the west. We could not verify this fact, however, because we rode all day with dark, threatening clouds hanging so low we thought we could reach up and touch them. The Weather Channel had predicted storms for the whole next week, so we were prepared to be drenched.

Maine was the hilliest state of the fifteen we had been through. No one climb was as high as Kancamagus Pass, but if we were to total them, the net gain would probably exceed the elevation of several such passes. We had sworn we would never ride loaded bikes for as many as seventy-four miles in hilly terrain again, but we discovered that we had the choice of either staying overnight at the twenty-five-mile mark in Gardiner or going seventy-four miles to Camden. We wanted to reach the coast, so we decided to go for it. At no time did we pedal on flat pavement—in one segment of sixteen miles we counted twenty-two uphills. Going up took a long time, but going down was faster, so it seemed as if we went uphill all day long. It probably was a good thing that we didn't count the hills for the entire day. That would have been too demoralizing.

We didn't try to take what was billed as the most scenic route that day for several reasons: (1) the scenic route would have been longer, and we were eager just to get to the coast; (2) the weather was ugly so we wouldn't get many good views anyway; (3) main roads were likely to be less hilly than rural ones; and (4) main roads tended to have better shoulders. Both rural roads and main highways seemed to have speeding car and truck traffic, so we figured we might as well ride where there was a shoulder. So we made our way from Highway 126 to Highway 17 and took it most of the way to Camden.

The last five miles of the route—as we neared the coast—were largely obscured by blowing waves of fog. I began to feel as though our adventure had been cyclical rather than linear and that we were starting all over. We had left the Oregon coast in a cool, misty drizzle, and we were approaching the Maine coast in similar bone-chilling dampness. It seemed somehow fitting.

As soon as we reached U.S. 1 at Camden, we turned north, knowing we were coming into tourist territory where motels would be plentiful. The sign for the Cedar Crest Motel was barely visible through the fog, but I was so eager to get safely off the road that without consulting Alice, I pulled into the driveway. It was the first establishment we came to and the price was right, so we signed in. Unable to dampen my elation, I told the manager, Elizabeth, that we had pedaled for twelve and a half weeks to get there. She seemed almost as excited as we were. Within five minutes of checking into our room, she came to our door with a bottle of champagne and two glasses. Short of a parade, a brass band, and keys to the city of Camden, we couldn't have asked for a more wonderful welcome to the East Coast.

Because we still had to reach Bar Harbor, abstemious Alice wanted to save the champagne until we were completely finished cycling, and she even offered to carry it, not a small feat. So instead of imbibing, we high-fived each other and cheered at having reached the coast.

Unfortunately, Adventure Cycling ends its northern cross-country cycling route not at Camden but at Bar Harbor, and we had a rental car waiting for us there, so we were committed to one more day of excruciating hills and bad roads. I started thinking about the next day's ride and fumed, "Alice, I see no reason why we have to ride to Bar Harbor. We know that people modify this route and ride Portland to Portland. We've made it from coast to coast. That should be enough. Do we have to ride to Bar Harbor just because we told everyone we would?" I was suffering a low-blood-sugar-induced meltdown, and a repeat of hills like this day's was just too much to contemplate.

Alice wisely countered, "Let's talk about it later—after dinner." And she called Don's Taxi Service for a ride to Cappy's, the local chowder house.

Cappy's lived up to its reputation, and we enjoyed our celebratory dinners of crab-stuffed salmon and haddock. Dinner and dessert repaired my nutritional and mental imbalance, and I conceded that I didn't want to "cheat" at this point, but I did need to eat more while plugging up Maine's hills in order to avoid low blood sugar.

Day 86 ***Tuesday, September 23***
Camden to Ellsworth
57 miles

The weather improved but that was all. Our earlier theory about main roads having good shoulders did not hold up. We chose to stay on U.S. 1 and not take the Adventure Cycling route, but U.S. 1 was

The other ocean—finally!

dreadful, even though the fog had lifted. It was narrow, without a shoulder, pocked with deep potholes, crumbling on the edges, and heavy with truck traffic that often violated both the no-passing zones and the speed limit. Riding conditions were abominable. By the time we stopped in Lincolnville, about five miles north of Camden, we both truly feared for our lives. There we dipped our wheels in the Atlantic Ocean, had the coast-to-coast cycling ritual memorialized on camera by some genial tourists from Michigan, and went to the post office to find out whether someone there could advise us on how to catch a bus or hire a ride to Bar Harbor. We had decided to consider the ride from Camden to Ellsworth our "victory lap," but there was no sense losing our lives after riding 3,600 miles.

No ride was available, but the postmaster sympathized with us because he often had trouble delivering mail on that route without being sideswiped or rear-ended. He then shared the good news that the road gained a shoulder in only one more mile. So off we went. The road improved, as he had said, and so did our spirits. Once the paved shoulder appeared, we actually enjoyed riding along the coast beside or even far above the sparkling blue waters. We concluded that Maine has no flat spots and understood why some natives applied the term "flatlanders" to those who moved there or visited from other states.

In Northport, we stopped at Northport Landing, an art gallery where Joy, the owner, and Charles, one of her customers, fussed over us. Charles wanted us to stop at the Belfast newspaper office so that they could interview us, but we needed to keep going in order to reach Ellsworth by dark, and so we forfeited another fifteen minutes of fame. We each bought several souvenirs at the gallery and left them there, arranging to pick them up on our way back when we had a rental car.

At Belfast we discovered an old bridge across the Passagassawakeag River (called "the Passy" by some of the locals), which allowed only pedestrians and cyclists. We felt relieved to be off the big bridge with the heavy car and truck traffic. Searsport, a sleepy little coastal town, was next, where we indulged in fried clams at a roadside shack. We could not leave the Maine coast without sampling those crunchy bits of seafood.

The last town before Ellsworth was Bucksport, with its huge bridge under construction. News reports said that it was perennially under construction, but its condition worked to our advantage. The line of cars was long, but we were allowed to pedal to the front of the line—as we had in Portland, Oregon, under Walter's guidance. We rode across at the head of the next group of cars, and the oncoming traffic was held back until we were off the bridge.

After countless more hills we reached Ellsworth, the closest town to Bar Harbor. With only one day to go, we were waxing nostalgic already, knowing we would miss being on our bikes and with each other even if we wouldn't miss climbing hills. Acadia National Park beckoned and we were looking forward to exploring it the next day—mostly by car.

Day 87 *Wednesday, September 24*
Ellsworth to Bar Harbor
19 miles

With only a few miles to go, we slept in and enjoyed a leisurely breakfast. We had spent the last three months traveling slowly and living simply, and we wondered if we could learn to rush again amid all the complications of the "real" world. Maybe we wouldn't bother.

Several hills stood between Ellsworth and Mount Desert Island (pronounced de-ZERT, as in the verb meaning "to abandon"), and we found many photo opportunities, so we spent the entire morning getting there. Although it was time to end our three-month odyssey, we dallied on our last riding day. The traveling life had gotten under our skins and we were both a bit sad to see our dream ride come to its inevitable end. We knew, though, that we would always have the memories to share, not just with family and friends, but with each other.

Bar Harbor Airport appeared soon after we crossed the causeway onto the island, so we pulled in, parked Big Bertha and Black Beauty together one last time, and walked inside to the rental car desk. Our two-wheeled adventure was over—it was time for four wheels and an engine. With some regret I took the keys from the agent.

We explored Acadia National Park in the rental car, climbing Cadillac Mountain the easy way. Standing on the wind-whipped summit, we exclaimed over the striking views of the coastline that had been our destination. Too cold to stay long, we descended, this time together and at the same pace. As evening fell, we took our well-traveled bottle of champagne to 2 Cats, a cafe located on a dark street in an antiquated wood-frame house. We had planned to dine on lobster when we reached Bar Harbor, but 2 Cats had nothing so unimaginative on its menu. Alice ordered seafood jambalaya and I chose the beer-baked chicken. Both, though tasty, seemed unusual for a New England coastal cuisine. Even our desserts—fudge and cookie sundaes with hints of cardamom—surprised us. But the strangeness of our feast was somehow appropriate. After all, we had just enjoyed the most unconventional summer of our lives.

Reflections

Stopping for tea and popovers on the broad expanse of lawn at Jordan Pond in Acadia National Park is a long-established visitor tradition, so we joined those who braved the cool mountain air in early autumn. Rows of chairs and tables lined the slope so that people could chat and sip tea as they watched the light change on the waters of the pond set in front of the North Bubble and South Bubble mountains. So peaceful.

As we relaxed and reminisced about some of our adventures, shivering because once again we had failed to bring our jackets, a couple sitting nearby overheard us and asked some of the questions we had heard so often. It was not unlike numerous other occasions in the previous three months. Everyone seemed to wonder who we were to do such a crazy thing, and they appeared to enjoy hearing our stories as much as we loved telling them.

Not only did the Jordan Pond couple encourage us to write a book, as others had along the way, but they suggested that we do what adventurers often fail to do in such accounts—explain how the trip affected each of us afterward. We liked their idea. Even though we both wrote the story in my voice, as explained in the preface, we believed that Alice should share her reflections in her own voice. Thus we begin our final chapter with her personal afterthoughts about our adventure, followed by my own.

Alice

It was fabulous to fulfill my long-time dream—to pedal such a great distance, play outdoors for a whole summer, live so simply, talk and listen to people along the way. I loved every single day. When I later heard a presidential candidate concede an election, saying, "I will never be the same," I had an inkling of what he meant.

Visiting communities and subcultures different from my own—even for a short time—has led to understanding, and that process has strengthened a value that I hold dear—being able to adjust to and appreciate differences. Some call it a belief in pluralism, some call it diversity, and just about any term we assign to it results in charges of political correctness by one group or another. Maybe it's enough to say that I love to learn and that because of my bicycling adventures and the exposure to so many different and marvelous people and places, I feel safer, more secure, and more optimistic about our country than I ever have before.

Physically, despite my fall allergies, it was not as difficult as I had anticipated—a pleasant discovery. Some friends, even those who knew of my past bicycle touring, wondered whether my body would hold out—heart, lungs, joints. I wondered, too, because I had never attempted such a demanding trip. Anything could happen, I knew, but our bodies became virtual machines. When we gave them the necessary calories and nutrients (and occasional doctoring), they performed well. Any exercise physiologist would say there really is no mystery in that. My muscle tone increased, my not-so-young heart and lungs became stronger, and I felt good, even when I was tired or fighting infection.

Our trip was harder in some ways than in others. For example, certain emotional hurdles were difficult for me to overcome. I like to think I am good at compartmentalizing, but pedaling across the country required true, single-minded focus. I thought of my husband and grown children frequently, missed them desperately, and wished that they could have shared my pleasures. I will be eternally grateful for their support and sacrifices so that I could selfishly pursue my dream for three months, but I don't think they can possibly imagine how tortured I was when my husband was ill or how sad I was that I missed seeing my daughter at the height of her first pregnancy. Little Ethan dutifully waited until my trip was over to enter the world, and I was able to hold him right away, but Booth had two surgeries without me at his side. He had assured me that if it were open-heart surgery he would have wanted me there (and I would have found a way), but only after he had recovered did he admit that he wished I had been there. I was ridden with guilt, but at the same time my own stubborn pursuit of my goal surprised me, and I didn't particularly like what I saw.

Reaching the destination that Bobbi and I had chosen—and within a day of our original plan—was a satisfying accomplishment. I concluded that it was more fun than I could have imagined to live as we did, travel under our own power and appreciate beautiful scenery, consume great quantities of food, and encounter such a wide range of personalities and subcultures.

As the trip ended, I realized that I would have to adjust to more conventional living. When we parted in Maine, Bobbi headed home to Bob, and Booth flew to Portland to meet me. We rented a cottage on a spit of land surrounded on three sides by salty tidewater and spent a glorious week there. Grateful for his healing, we had a good time exploring some of the Maine coast together, relaxing, and renewing our love.

One night he and I had dinner at Cappy's Chowder House on Camden's Main Street, the same place Bobbi and I had patronized the night we reached the coast in heavy fog. The tables were close together, and when Bobbi and I had eaten there, someone overheard our discussion and began asking us questions, as usual. Before we knew it, everyone in our section of the restaurant had joined in and was helping us celebrate having pedaled 3,600 miles. We learned where each of the other tourists was from, and pretty soon it was like a big party. When Booth and I stopped by for dinner, however, we dined more conventionally. We ordered our meals, ate quietly, and never learned about the people an arm's length away. We didn't listen in on their conversation, and they didn't pay any attention to ours. I loved being there with Booth, and it was a relief to be traveling in style and comfort rather than under stress as it had been in the fog, but perhaps I had liked being a bit of a celebrity more than I was willing to admit.

Another notable transition took place the morning after we arrived home in Wisconsin. As I was getting ready for church on Sunday morning, I opened my closet and gasped. I saw white shoes, red pumps, black slings, navy heels—which ones would I wear? Every morning for three months I had put on the same pair of biking sandals. No choice. No matter. And then it hit me: I really loved the lifestyle that loaded bike touring required. I didn't need multiple pairs of shoes or scarves or skirts or anything else. Why did I have closets full of things at home? Why did I have so many choices?

I even had several watches, not one of which I had needed while cycling. On our bike trip we learned almost never to hurry. We pedaled for much of the day on most days; we ate and slept when we were hungry and tired. At ten or twelve miles per hour, we couldn't be in a hurry. What did we need a watch for, anyway?

This realization—that I didn't need so many things—led to a simple resolution: to buy less, use less, "need" less of what I see around me. I don't want to help the nation's economy by going shopping—I just don't need the stuff.

Bobbi

After the trip, people asked me if it had been a life-changing experience. No, I had no blinded-by-the-light epiphanies. My changes crept in subtly—they are those of perspective. The trip has caused a shift in the way I perceive myself and others.

Whether these changes are mostly from the trip or because I have retired from a challenging occupation and now have more discretionary time is something I wonder about. Do I hurry less now because I made the vow while on the trip or just because I have more time? Did I purge my wardrobe when I got home because I liked not having to make clothing choices on the road or because I need fewer clothes as a retiree? Do I appreciate the lovely hillside of trees outside my window because my eyes and heart became more attuned to such scenery on the trip or because I now have the time to appreciate the beauty of where I live? It's hard to say; perhaps it's a bit of both trip and life change, but I believe that it's mostly the trip because it afforded me the experience of living with little, slowing down, and really seeing my surroundings.

To my friends and acquaintances, the trip seemed a huge undertaking, an adventure, and a fantasy that they won't get to realize. That may lend it romance and perhaps some mystery that compels them to tell others about it. But I wonder why it has remained so important to me. I'm not one to live in the past; I have always enjoyed the present moment and thinking about the possibilities of the future. I expected the journey to be physically difficult, immensely educational, a whole lot of fun, exciting, and something I'd be glad I had done. But after it was over, I didn't expect it to hang around in such a prominent part of my psyche. Why have I thought of this trip at least once a day for several years afterward?

Partly because it encompassed three of the happiest months of my life. The proposition of getting ourselves from point A to point B by nightfall, while not being easy much of the time, was a single-minded endeavor. We had one essential goal each day, and all our actions went to attaining it. We had no distractions other than those that were endemic to the journey: weather, need for water and food, people we met, terrain we traversed, and mechanical or physical issues. Actually, these were not truly distractions; they were simply aspects of the trip. Our deadlines were self-imposed, our objectives our own. It was demanding, but in a pure way that allowed for concentration and focused effort. It wasn't easy, but it was simple.

This trip allowed me to see how scattered and stressed I'd become back home. I learned a big lesson in how to live more simply. I try to maintain that focus in my daily life now. When I attempt to do too much, something warns me that I am not living the way I want to and I immediately try to simplify. Sometimes I feel a little guilty. Most people have to work and raise families and shop for groceries and pay the bills and make doctor and dentist appointments and rush from one to the other, squeezing activities into unforgiving time slots that only seem to contract the more they have to do. Because I'm retired, not only do I get to recognize when I am attempting too much, but I can do something about it. The bike trip gave me the time to practice being unhurried, and I was surprised to learn that I liked the slower pace. After a lifetime of rushing to fit everything in, I now eschew a full schedule, and I enjoy this quieter life much more than I thought I would.

How else is my perspective different? I have a lot more respect and appreciation for the people of this country. These are the people who have moved back to small or dying towns in Montana or the Great Plains after having lived elsewhere because they like the people and quality of life even though their standard of living isn't quite what it could be. They are the women of the Tumbleweed Cafe in Berthold, North Dakota, who picked up the pieces of their lives and started a business that they take great pride in. They are the poorly dressed, unkempt men who approached us to tell us to be careful on the road because people were "bad drivers" or "some people are mean." They are the countless good, solid citizens of this country who do not make the headlines that skew our view of this nation's people. These people work hard, raise their families the best way they know how, pay their taxes, love the land, and have pride in their country. They make me proud to live in the same country and I feel honored and enriched to have met them. They populate all parts of this land, quietly living life the way they think it should be lived. That gives me hope for our future. I don't really care about their politics anymore. I respect them for the decisions they have made and the lives they lead. Before, I had simply hoped that such people existed out there; now I know they are real, and I see the strength of this country in them.

I now realize that the central experience of the trip was not the distance we rode. The true center of the experience was the journey itself, the day-by-day adventure of discovering our country and the people who are its living, beating heart.

Lance Armstrong is right—it's not about the bike. I think it is about what the bike allows us to experience: the pedaling, fog, heat, and hills; the physical strength and exhaustion; the emotional exhilaration; the indelible deep blue of the sky and the magnificence of the land. And of course, it's about the people, with their curiosity, kindness, and generosity, who abide in the forefront of my memory.

If you want to get to know yourself and the country you live in, ride across it on a bike. It may not turn you 180 degrees and set you on a new life path, but it will expand and alter your perceptions, help you to shift gears. At the end of the journey you will not be the same person. If you are lucky and have a good trip, as we did, you will learn to be grateful for the beneficence you receive, and you will never take it for granted again.

Oh—one more thing. Did I have fun? You bet. I'd do it all over again in a heartbeat.

Appendix A

Frequently Asked Questions

Loaded bicycle touring generates questions, and scores of people seemed curious about our adventure and way of life. We were peppered with inquiries before, during, and after our trip—from noncyclists and cyclists alike. Listed below are the questions that arose regularly, along with our answers.

Getting Ready

What kind of bikes did you ride?

Alice rode her twenty-one-year-old Holdsworth Mistral, an English touring frame made with Reynolds 531 tubing and equipped with a hodgepodge of Campagnolo and Shimano S-105 parts. I had a Softride Solo, an up-to-date, high-tech frame with mostly Shimano Ultegra components. Our wheels were Mavic Sun rims with thirty-six spokes each, and we both had a Deore XTR rear derailleur, which gave us extremely low gearing, perfect for hauling loads up any kind of grade.

How did you decide which route to take across the country?

We are both members of Adventure Cycling, an organization based in Missoula, Montana, that creates specialized maps for bicycle touring. The organization has mapped three transcontinental routes for bicyclists: a northern route with several variations; a middle route, first established in 1976 to celebrate the U.S. bicentennial; and a southern route from California to Florida. We chose a northern route for three reasons: (1) we were traveling in summer and wanted to avoid the worst of the hot weather; (2) we could cross the western mountains at the lowest possible elevations; and (3) we wanted to ride in each of our home states, Wisconsin and Ohio.

The Lewis and Clark Trail mapped by Adventure Cycling had been developed in conjunction with the Corps of Discovery's bicentennial. It followed the Columbia River Gorge, which avoided scaling the Washington and Oregon Cascades, so we planned to combine the Lewis and Clark Trail with the Northern Tier and the North Lakes routes. In Wisconsin, we would make up our own route because it was Alice's home state and she knew the roads quite well.

Our discussions with each other about the route took place over a two-year period via e-mail and phone. About six months before our departure, we spent a winter weekend together finalizing our tentative itinerary in a spreadsheet.

How did you train for the trip?

Alice rode to work and around town every day, about fifteen miles, something she had done year-round for years. On weekends during biking season, she would do one or two rides of twenty-five to sixty miles each. I rode in winter when the weather allowed and participated in spinning classes twice a week, weight lifting, and other aerobic activity on the days I didn't spin. Starting in April, I rode three to four times a week, from twenty-five to forty miles each time. On Sundays I rode sixty to seventy miles. Starting in early May, I loaded the bike lightly on the long rides. More than twenty years' experience of riding for fitness and touring provided us with an invaluable base of miles that factored into our fitness levels.

How long did you plan to be gone?

We thought that twelve to thirteen weeks would give us enough time to ride at a pace that would allow us to enjoy the scenery, talk to people, and absorb the local culture wherever we were. We planned to have a rest day at least once a week, and we allowed several multiple-day stints for rendezvous with the men in our lives.

What supplies did you carry?

We added and subtracted items occasionally, but for our main supply lists, see appendix B.

How much did the trip cost?

We budgeted $5,000 apiece, which included airline tickets for our partners and ourselves. The trip could have been done for less, but we planned to eat most meals in restaurants so that we would not have to carry much food or cooking gear.

We also planned to camp most nights, but our "rule" was that we did not camp in the rain. As the trip progressed, the rule morphed into "We don't camp if it rains, threatens rain, or even smells like rain, or if we are in grizzly bear, black bear, rattlesnake, or mosquito territory." This was a slight exaggeration, but we overspent our budget because we camped less than we had anticipated.

How did you get your bikes to Oregon?

We each paid our local bike shop to disassemble and ship our bikes. UPS delivered them ahead of time to Hauer's Cyclery in Astoria, a shop we had found via the Internet. For a small charge they reassembled the bikes and had them ready when we arrived.

The Route

How far did you ride?

We averaged fifty-five miles per day. (On rest days we pedaled miles that we did not record.) Twice we logged ninety-six miles in a day—once in North Dakota and once in Ohio. Our total mileage was about 3,600 miles.

How long did it take you?

We were away from home for ninety days, and we rode our bikes on sixty-four of the ninety days. The amount of time we spent on the road each day varied widely, depending on the terrain, weather, our level of organization, and the extent to which we allowed ourselves to be sidetracked. The number of miles from one point to another had little to do with how long it took to cover that distance.

Where did you stay at night?

We camped in both commercial and government campgrounds, and we stayed in motels, an occasional B&B, and only rarely with friends or family. We never camped in "unofficial" spots because we never needed to. We contemplated it a few times, and we knew we could have found spots that were away from the road where no one would have noticed us, but we were more concerned that we had a place to store our food away from animals. Treeless areas made this a challenging proposition.

How did you know which roads to take when you deviated from your planned route?

We used county maps and state highway maps, although state maps are not a particularly good source because they don't include many secondary roads. State gazetteers provide excellent maps, but we didn't use them because the pages are big and bulky, even when folded. We often gathered information from local residents and law enforcement officers as well as bike store owners and employees. Local residents sometimes couldn't answer questions about towns twenty-five miles away because they had "never been there." Bike shop employees, on the other hand, were often the best sources of information because they were used to seeing roads from the saddle of a bicycle.

What was it like to cross the mountains?

By following the Lewis and Clark route, we avoided the Cascades. Both passes we took over the Rocky Mountains (Lolo Pass and Rogers Pass) were long, gradual ascents, increasing in grade for the last three to four miles. The climbs were not especially easy with loaded bikes, but we didn't have to walk on either Lolo or Rogers. On long ascents Alice occasionally stopped to eat a small snack to keep her energy up; I rode on, preferring to get it over with.

Mountain roads in the East—over the Adirondacks, the Green Mountains, and the White Mountains—were sometimes more challenging than those in the West. The roads in the East were built longer ago and have fewer switchbacks, making them steeper than the roads in the West.

The foothills east of Rogers Pass in Montana as well as the hills of Maine were harder for us than any mountain pass. Maine doesn't know the concept of flatness.

Did you ever cheat?

Our original plan was to ride 4,000 miles. Several times we thought it prudent to ferry ourselves somewhere by motor vehicle, twice for what would have been a two- or three-day bike ride. We logged approximately 3,600 miles on our bikes between coasts, which we think qualifies as having ridden across the country.

Motivation

Were you raising funds for a charity?

No. We probably could have raised funds for any number of good causes, and we also might have secured commercial sponsors for the amount of advertising we did for a number of companies: MoJo bars, our favorite energy food made by Clif; Combos, the best post-ride junk food; Specialized for the Armadillo tires we love; Gatorade, the indispensable, ubiquitous electrolyte replacer; and Big Agnes, the most comfortable air mattress ever made.

We found, however, that phoning home and writing for the Web site to keep people informed of our progress were about all the extracurricular activities we could handle. We were tired most evenings, and eating supper, doing our laundry, studying maps, and checking the next day's route prevented us from much else once we had stopped for the night. We sometimes even had to forgo meeting friends and relatives, and we accepted offers of accommodations only rarely because each social engagement left us less time to perform our daily chores and still get enough sleep. The added responsibility of fund-raising would probably have been too much for us. Maybe next time.

So why did you want to ride across the country?

The short answer: for fun! The longer answer can be found in the pages of our book.

Did you ever regret going on the trip?

Both of us had expected days when we would be less than enthusiastic or even ready to give up. Even though Alice hated being away from her husband when he underwent gall bladder surgery and also had a tough bout with allergies, and even though I missed being with my daughter during her family crisis, the answer is no.

We were living our dream and were able to overcome the obstacles that faced us, even though they were different from the ones we had anticipated. We always looked forward to getting on our bikes to see what was up the road ahead. Even when riding was challenging, the inspiring people and ever-changing scenery buoyed our spirits. We knew we were fortunate to be able to fulfill a big dream; how could we have any serious regrets? Our families, dealing without us as they faced their own difficulties, knew how important this ride was to us, and they gamely tolerated our long absences between rendezvous. Both our men were incredibly good sports as they provided emotional and/or technical support on numerous occasions.

Technology

What technological equipment did you carry? Why?

Both of us carried cell phones, even though they were useless much of the time in the West because of lack of cell towers on our back-roads route. We called home most nights either from our cells or from pay phones with our AT&T calling cards.

We had discussed carrying walkie-talkies with a three- or five-mile range, but decided against it because of the unnecessary weight. As it turned out, we rode closely together and didn't need them.

We both had small PCs. They were loaded with Microsoft Word and Excel, and were capable of connecting with the Internet when we were in range of a wireless network. Alice's could accept pictures from her SD camera card. We e-mailed our journal entries to our Webmaster for posting on our site.

A GPS system was unnecessary. We were staying on roads, and we never got lost. Our detailed maps were sufficient.

We both had small digital cameras. Alice's camera was so small it fit into an Altoids tin, something that amused onlookers when she pulled it out; mine was a bit larger, but small enough to fit into its own little pack worn on my waist for easy retrieval. We each took more than 600 pictures.

What was your most important piece of technological equipment?

When we had service, our cell phones were marvelous. Using the cell phones was more convenient than trying to find pay phones, which are vanishing, undoubtedly because of cell phone proliferation. We were also enamored of the small PCs for enabling us to have a Web site and type our journal entries rather than write them longhand.

Daily Activities

What did you do when it rained?

As long as there was no lightning, we just rode in the rain when we had to. We were lucky we didn't get caught in many heavy storms. On the day we rode through Cleveland it rained all day and was a bit cold, but we wore moisture-wicking clothing and just kept riding, although we stopped more often for hot soup or hot chocolate. We experienced only one full day of rain and three partial days on days that we biked. Storms passed through during the night several times but were gone by morning.

What did you do when you got a flat tire?

This question was asked most often by men—older men who appeared to be non-cyclists. They didn't realize that anyone who undertakes long bicycle trips or has ridden for more than a few years, whether male or female, probably has learned how to change flats. Changing a flat isn't terrifically hard, but it is a bit inconvenient when it's a rear tire—which it usually is because most of the load is on the rear wheel—because all the panniers have to be off-loaded and then reloaded. Some people can change a rear tire with all the gear still on, but we didn't even try. We had very few flats, thanks largely to the quality of our tires. They lived up to their reputation as being appropriate for loaded touring.

How did you maintain the bikes?

We inspected our tires carefully for gashes or embedded debris almost every morning, and we often extracted pieces of glass or metal shards that had lodged there but had not yet punctured the tube. We pumped our tires to 110 psi almost every morning, lubed the chains about twice a week, and had our drive trains cleaned every two or three weeks. See appendix B for the list of tools we carried.

Safety and Security Issues

You were two women traveling alone. Were you ever scared?

No human being ever threatened us personally, although a couple of incidents unnerved us when we were not on our bikes. We were aware that not everyone likes bicyclists and that we could encounter mean, unbalanced, or dangerous people along the way, but we came to believe that the odds were slight. Before the trip began I suggested to Alice that I acquire a firearm and take a refresher course in gun-handling, but Alice was adamantly opposed to the idea and I gladly gave it up. We did each carry a small canister of pepper spray.

Traffic was another story. Winding roads, logging trucks, semitrailers, and aggressive drivers threatened occasionally, and on several occasions we had to bail off the road when there was no shoulder to ride on and something huge was about to pass and couldn't move over. Once, Alice was actually blown off the road by a construction truck as it barreled past her. Our helmet-mounted rearview mirrors were indispensable.

What other concerns did you have?

I was concerned that several days of rain in a row would wear me down. I hate to ride in the rain. Alice's worries changed with the area of the country we were in: grizzly bears and rattlesnakes in the West, tornadoes and lightning storms in the Midwest, and black bears in the East. I enjoyed teasing Alice about the odds of seeing any bears, but readily acquiesced to staying inside instead of camping in bear country.

Some concerns fell into the "physical" category. My carpal tunnel syndrome, exacerbated in my left arm, which had been broken on a mountain biking trek, was my main concern. I didn't know if my wrists would last for the entire trip even if I loaded up on ibuprofen. After my fall in Washington, I grew increasingly worried about another part of my body as I became so miserable in my saddle that I feared I might not be able to ride. I called this my "princess and the pea" syndrome. Alice, on the other hand, worried whether the heart arrhythmia that was treated before the trip would recur. After her fall on the first day of the trip, she also worried about her injured knee, and she continued to worry after reinjuring it when she tripped over a pipe on the deck of the Lake Michigan ferry. We didn't think to worry about another hazard—loose items flying off vehicles. Being hit by an airborne cooler lid could have ended our trip at any time. See appendix C for items we were lucky to have dodged.

Friendship

This was a long, arduous trip and you were together 24/7. Are you still friends?

We get a kick out of this question—not that it isn't a valid one. Many riders who attempt a long-distance trip part ways before the trip is over or don't talk to each other for years afterward. Neither of us had any serious concerns about the other before the trip, and we are now better friends than ever. We had been together on several week-long trips in previous years and thought we liked and respected each other enough to be together for three months. Our hunch was right. Although we are both very different personalities, we seemed to complement each other, and, as Alice noted, "We both like to be in charge, but neither of us is a control freak." Usually, we wanted to do the same things anyway, and when we didn't, we were flexible enough to go along with the other one with no residual grumbling. It may seem too good to be true, but there it is. We know that we are fortunate to regard each other now more as sisters than as friends. In fact, we each feel the need to call the other if more than two weeks go by without speaking.

Did anything annoy you about each other?

OK, here's the lowdown. The only thing about Alice that annoyed me was the fact that Alice's bike rolled downhill faster than mine. Alice would skim down the hills, sometimes crying "Wheeeeeee!" in her enthusiasm, and I would have to actually pedal to keep up. What a bummer! But it was a minor thing and I didn't tell Alice until the trip was almost over.

Alice later admitted that the only thing about me that bothered her was the little wraparound black skirt I put on over my bike shorts when I wanted to look respectable. Alice didn't have one and said she always felt as if she looked grungy by comparison.

Reflections

Did you ever doubt that you would make it?

We were both confident but to different degrees. We knew we had prepared as well as two people our age could, but we also knew that some things were outside our control. We planned carefully in those areas in which we did have control and tried to be prudent as issues arose. Despite my concern about my wrists before the trip began, I was outspokenly confident of success. Alice was optimistic but was unwilling to assume that we would succeed. We both knew that anything could happen, but we were equally confident in our ability to solve problems.

What would you do differently if you had it to do over?

Two things: First, we would begin in late May or early June (as opposed to late June). Starting two weeks earlier than we did would have given us the time to be in the East closer to the Labor Day end of the season. As it was, more and more campgrounds had closed as September progressed.

Second, we would ride from Portland to Portland, omitting the busy highways between Astoria and Portland, Oregon, and between Portland, Maine, and Bar Harbor.

How are you going to top this trip?

We don't feel any need to do "bigger" things. Different trips, yes, but we don't want to compete with ourselves.

Would you do it again?

Alice's answer: I was thrilled to fulfill a longtime dream, but I can savor this ride for a while. I'm not interested in replicating it.

Bobbi's answer: Yes, but not this exact route. It was a marvelous experience that could never be duplicated, but I would like to try another transcontinental ride when circumstances allow. We are planning another long ride—across the country from south to north.

Appendix B

Equipment

Alice's bicycle is custom-built from a set of components acquired over a period of more than twenty years. Her Holdsworth Mistral frame was assembled in Great Britain in 1982—a touring model with geometry consisting of gentle angles for comfortable long-distance riding. The tubing is Reynolds 531, a steel alloy. Wheels are thirty-six-spoke Mavic Sun rims on Campagnolo hubs, outfitted with Specialized Armadillo tires (700x25c). Front and rear brakes are Shimano S-105; Campagnolo shifters are mounted on the down tube. Front derailleur is Shimano S-105, rear derailleur is Shimano Deore XTR, a long-cage shifter that can accommodate a wide range of gears on a long chainstay. Three front chainrings have thirty, forty-two, and fifty-two teeth; rear freewheel has six rings ranging evenly from fourteen to thirty-four teeth. Crank arms are Shimano S-105, and pedals are Shimano SPD M535. Blackburn Lowrider racks are mounted on the front fork to hold front panniers; the rear rack is Blackburn. She indicates brand names below for products she was especially pleased with.

Mounted on Alice's Bike

Cateye wireless cyclometer
Topeak Road Morph pump
Cannondale handlebar bag
map in map window
REI front panniers
Cannondale rear panniers
water bottle
pepper spray

On Alice

helmet
glasses, clip-on sunglasses
Look rearview mirror mounted on glasses
CamelBak (70 oz.) water bag
cell phone
Shimano cycling sandals with cleats
bike gloves
bike shorts
sports bra
bike shirt
Performance bright yellow vest

In Handlebar Bag

money clip and coin purse
Sacajawea dollar coins
health insurance card
ID, credit card, ATM card
digital camera
book
padlock key
whistle
Leatherman Micra mini-tool
lip balm
sunscreen
compass, thermometer
highlighter pen
map
pens (3)
postage stamps
spoon, fork
Goop hand cleaner
vitamins
duct tape (wrapped around pencil)
snacks

In Front Panniers

small PC
charger cords for electronics
small spiral notebook
LED headlamp
lightweight coil cable
padlock
White Lightning chain lubricant, rag
chain link remover tool
clipless pedal replacement screws
pliers
Topeak multitool
spare brake and gear cables
spare front and rear spokes
freewheel remover
plastic tire levers
tubes (2), patch kit
spare folding tire
S hooks, nuts, bolts, washers
twist ties, paper clips
MSR PocketRocket stove
small pot with lid
butane fuel canisters (2)
rubber sink stopper
energy drink powder concentrate
dry bag with emergency food
map set

In Rear Panniers

plastic sandwich bags (20)
garbage bags (2)
bungee cords (2)
compression straps (4)
underwear (1 set)
sports bra and bathing shorts

MSR Packtowl
lightweight walking sandals
bike shorts (2 pr.)
bike shirts, short-sleeved (2)
leg warmers
Capilene long underwear
rain jacket
T-shirt for off bike
zip-off pants for off bike
visor/sun hat for off bike
socks (1 pr.)
hat
fleece hoodie
clothespins (2)
safety pins (5)
toiletries: toothbrush, toothpaste, floss, all-purpose soap, brush, comb, disposable razor
first-aid supplies: moleskin, povidone-iodine swabs, Neosporin cream, hydrocortisone cream, Benadryl tablets, Band-Aids, ibuprofen, bee sting kit

On Rear Rack

North Face down sleeping bag
small down pillow
MSR Zoid tent (with rain fly, poles, stakes, ground cloth)
Big Agnes air mattress
blinky taillight

•

Bobbi's bike is a medium-sized Softride Solo, sometimes called a beam bike because the rider sits on a carbon-fiber beam suspended from the front of the bicycle. No down tube connects the seat to the bicycle, resulting in less road shock to the rider. The bicycle is equipped with a Softride shock-absorbing stem to alleviate carpal tunnel syndrome. The wheels are thirty-six-spoke Mavic Sun Open Pro. Front and rear brakes are Shimano Ultegra; the shifters are Shimano Ultegra STI with a triple crank in front and a Shimano Deore XTR rear derailleur, a long cage shifter. The three front chainrings have thirty, forty-two, and fifty-two teeth; the rear cassette has nine rings ranging from twelve to thirty-two teeth each. The crank arms are Shimano and the pedals are Look. The front is equipped with Blackburn Lowrider racks; the back has a Blackburn Expedition rack modified to fit the unique frame.

On Bobbi

helmet
hydration pack
gloves
sunglasses
visibility vest
cell phone in holder
lip sunscreen
eyedrops
camera

In Handlebar Bag

pepper spray
sunscreen
money
credit/debit cards
phone card
driver's license
AAA card
health insurance/dental cards
map case with maps (2)
stamps, magnifier
pen, marker
knife with carabiner
microrecorder
Goop hand cleaner

In Front Panniers

personal hygiene bag: soap, deodorant, toothpaste, floss, brush, shampoo, contact lens solution, scrunchie, tweezers, disposable razors (3), Dr. Bronner's soap
contact lenses
vitamins
eating utensils

Sierra cup
tea, Splenda
glasses and sunglasses
wrist braces (2)
p.j.'s, flashlight, earplugs
Luna bars
bear bag rope and carabiner
extra shoe clips
batteries
electronics bag: PDA in hard case, keyboard, chargers for phone, camera
MSR Packtowls (2)
first-aid kit
water filter
pillow
journal
space blanket
extra bike gloves
clothesline, clips
workout bands

In Rear Panniers

bike clothes: shorts (3 pr.), sleeveless shirts (2), short-sleeved shirt, long-sleeved shirt, bandanna headbands (3), bike socks (4 pr.), sports bras (3)
camp clothes: Capilene T-shirt, running shorts (2 pr.), hiking shorts, underwear, bathing suit top
camp clothes for cold: fleece shirt, zip-off pants/shorts, long-sleeved shirt, short-sleeved shirt, tights
large bandanna
book
folding tire
tubes
dry bag for food
freeze-dried meals
shower flip-flops
mosquito repellent
lens cleaning cloth
extra plastic bags

Petzl headlight
silk sleep sack
Chamois Butt'r (2)
gloves, full-fingered
arm and leg warmers
hiking socks (2 pr.)

On Rear Rack

Kryptonite cable lock
maps
business cards
Luna bars, snacks
sunscreen and body lotion
wrap skirt
rain jacket
bungees (3)
hiking sandals
mesh bag
plastic mug (outside)
sleeping bag
Big Agnes air mattress
MSR Zoid tent

In Under-Bar Bag

Allen wrenches
tire levers
spare tube
cleat covers
spoke wrench

Appendix C

Roadside Finds

Pedaling at ten to twelve miles per hour most days, we noticed the following items that didn't belong near a highway, much less in the middle of the road where some of them actually were. Most finds generated intense speculation about their owners and their origins. We felt lucky not to have been hit by any of them as they flew off a speeding vehicle.

bungee cords, all only half
bolts of all sizes, small to jumbo
hats, most with seed company or farm implement labels
cowboy hat in Pennsylvania
shoes, mostly one shoe of a pair, occasionally an entire pair
assorted clothing items: shirts, thong undies, men's briefs, handkerchiefs, shorts, jeans, belts, bandannas
vacuum cleaner, full size with attachments
chaise longue
double bed mattress (2)
cooler lids (7)
dartboard
empty barrel
telephone, cord and all
too much litter: soda cans, beer bottles, fast-food bags and wrappers, plastic gallon jugs
roadkill: a pica (?), a fox, multiple deer, cats, raccoons, skunks, snakes, and creatures beyond recognition